Handbook for
European Union Election Observation

Election Teams
Directorate General External Relations
http://ec.europa.eu/external_relations/human_rights/eu_election_ass_observ/
Directorate General EuropeAid
http://ec.europa.eu/europeaid/where/worldwide/electoral-support/index_en.htm

Manuscript finished in February 2008

Graphic Design: Fröjdlund Grafisk Form AB, Sweden
Cover photos: Kerstin Dokter, Richard Chambers, Claudia Aranda, David Ward

Printed by Elanders Sverige AB

ISBN 978-91-633-1480-3

Table of contents

Preface

There have been significant advances in the field of international election observation since the European Union deployed its first mission in 1993. Over this relatively short period of time, EU election observation has developed from a short-term, *ad hoc*, operation into a long-term process with a rigorous and systematic methodology endorsed by the Council of Ministers, the European Parliament, and the European Commission. Today, European Union Election Observation Missions (EU EOMs) comprehensively assess all aspects of an election process against international standards.

Election observation is a vital component of European Union activities to promote democracy, human rights and the rule of law worldwide. Election observation can strengthen democratic institutions, build public confidence in electoral processes and help deter fraud, intimidation and violence. Election observation also serves to reinforce other key European Union foreign policy objectives, notably peace-making and peace-building. With these objectives in mind, the European Union has become a leading force in international election observation, deploying 60 EU EOMs to 41 countries between 2000 and October 2007.

This second edition of the Handbook for EU Election Observation has been thoroughly revised to take into account advances in the European Union's methodology for observing and assessing an election process. It highlights that the European Union approach is based on international human rights standards, in particular the Universal Declaration of Human Rights and the International Covenant on Civil and Political Rights. The handbook also underlines that EU EOMs adhere to the *Declaration of Principles for International Election Observation*, a landmark document commemorated at the United Nations in 2005. The handbook explains the criteria used in deciding whether to observe an election, the steps taken to establish an EOM, and how a mission functions.

This handbook is a vital tool for EU EOMs and should be used as a reference to ensure that observation is conducted consistently and to the highest possible standard. I warmly encourage other observer groups, both domestic and international, to make use of this valuable handbook, as well as others who wish to know more about the work of the European Union in the field of election observation. I also offer my deepest thanks and appreciation to all observers who take part in EU EOMs, as well as national staff and others who provide support.

Benita Ferrero-Waldner
Commissioner for External Relations and Neighbourhood Policy
Brussels, 1 November 2007

Photo: Ana Raül Afonso

Introduction

Purpose of the Handbook

This second edition of the *Handbook for European Union Election Observation* provides a comprehensive overview of international election observation by the European Union (EU), including the rationale for its methodology, the basis for its assessment of an election process and a description of how EU Election Observation Missions (EU EOMs) are planned, deployed and implemented.

It is designed primarily for use by European Union (EU) election observers, both new and experienced. In addition, it is hoped that the handbook can contribute to the existing knowledge of work about election observation and its role in the field of human rights and democratisation. In this regard, the handbook may also be used by representatives of host governments, civil society activists, especially domestic observers, election administrators, politicians, and other international bodies involved in election observation.

The second edition updates the previous handbook, published in 2002, and reflects the extensive work and experience of the EU in election observation since the adoption of the European Commission Communication on EU Election Assistance and Observation in 2000,[1] and its subsequent endorsement by the Council of Ministers and the European Parliament. The EU is committed to ensuring that its election observation activities are undertaken using a professional, consistent and credible methodology that is based on long-term and comprehensive observation of an electoral process in accordance with international standards for genuine and democratic elections. Importantly, the second edition draws on the *Declaration of Principles for International Election Observation,*[2] commemorated at the United Nations in October 2005, which has been endorsed by the European Commission and the European Parliament. The *Declaration of Principles* and its accompanying *Code of Conduct for International Election Observers* reflects and reinforces the observation methodology used by the EU.

Structure of the Handbook

The handbook is divided into eight sections.

Section One is an introduction to the *rationale for the EU's observation of elections* in partner countries as part of its commitment to democracy, the rule of law and human rights. It outlines the role of different EU institutions in relation to election observation, the provision of technical assistance on elections and the EU's relations with other international election observer organisations. The section includes the code of conduct for EU Election Observers.

Section Two provides an overview of the framework for *international standards for elections* that stem from fundamental freedoms and political rights contained in universal and regional instruments. The section describes how an EU EOM uses these standards, which are legally or politically binding upon a country being observed, as the basis for its assessment of an electoral process. It also offers an overview of the UN human rights system.

Section Three details the consistent *EU EOM methodology* used when undertaking a comprehensive and long-term observation of an election process. The section also illustrates how EU election observation methodology ensures that an EU EOM provides an independent and impartial assessment, and works in a transparent and cooperative manner with election stakeholders and the state authorities of the host country.

Section Four comprehensively covers the *areas of assessment* of an electoral process that will be observed by an EU EOM. These are: the political context; the legal framework (including the electoral system); the election administration; the registration of voters; the registration of parties/candidates; the election campaign; the media environment; complaints and appeals; human rights issues, including those relating to discrimination; the role of civil society; voting and counting on election day; tabulation and publication of results, and the post-election environment. For each area of assessment, the handbook identifies indicators for a genuine and democratic electoral process, including the relevant international standards and best practice.

Section Five explains the steps the European Commission takes to *establish an EU EOM*. It outlines the methods used to decide whether to observe an electoral process, including the deployment of an exploratory mission and the minimum conditions that the EU considers necessary for effective and credible election observation. The section gives an overview of the stages for planning, preparing and deploying an EU EOM, including agreement of Memorandums of Understanding (MoUs) with the host country and the selection of observers. It provides guidelines on the management of the EU EOM and covers issues relating to the security of the mission and the safety of EU observers.

Section Six outlines the *roles and responsibilities* of EU election observers. As well as offering detailed information on the tasks of core team members, long-term observers and short-term observers, the section provides guidelines for meetings with interlocutors, including a series of checklists on questions to be asked in meetings.

Section Seven provides guidance for the observation of voting and counting on *election day*, including guidelines on the development of reporting forms as well as specific points for observation when visiting polling stations. The section also provides guidelines for observing the tabulation and publication of results and the post-election environment.

Section Eight provides guidelines for EU EOM reporting, including the preliminary statement (released shortly after election day), and the final report (released after the conclusion of the electoral process), as well as the regular internal reporting.

This handbook should be used in conjunction with the second edition of the Compendium of International Standards for Elections (second edition, 2007), published by the European Commission, which provides a detailed examination of the international standards for elections, including the text, and ratification status by country, of the principal universal and regional instruments. A series of reporting materials (guidelines, templates and examples) have also been produced for use by all EU EOMs.[3]

---

1. The Communication (EC COM (2000) 191) can be found at http://europa.eu/eur-lex/en/com/cnc/2000/com2000_0191en01.pdf

2. http://ec.europa.eu/external_relations/human_rights/eu_election_ass_observ/docs/code_conduct_en.pdf

3. http://ec.europa.eu/external_relations/human_rights/eu_election_ass_observ/index.htm and http://www.needs-network.org

1. The European Union and Election Observation

1.1 The EU and Democracy and Human Rights

The commitment of the EU to supporting, developing and consolidating democracy, the rule of law and human rights is at the core of the EU's identity and is well-grounded in the various legal instruments that govern EU structures and activities. These include the Treaty on the European Union (1992),[5] which states that the EU 'is founded on the indivisible, universal values of human dignity, freedom, equality and solidarity; it is based on the principles of democracy and the rule of law.' The Treaty also provides for policies on development cooperation which will contribute towards these values.

The promotion of democracy is at the centre of the EU's Common Foreign and Security Policy (CFSP), and relations between the EU and its partners are established in recognition that the consolidation of democratic institutions and human rights is of joint value and common interest. In line with this policy, the EU provides

> *The Union is founded on the principles of liberty, democracy, respect for human rights and fundamental freedoms, and the rule of law, principles which are common to all Member States.*
>
> Treaty on European Union,

> *Respect for all human rights and fundamental freedoms, including respect for fundamental social rights, democracy based on the rule of law and transparent and accountable governance are an integral part of sustainable development.*
>
> Cotonou Agreement,
> Article 9

extensive support to initiatives and programmes that seek to promote, develop and consolidate human rights, democratic institutions and the rule of law in partner countries. Since the early 1990s, a human rights clause has been included in all EU agreements with partner countries. The Cotonou Agreement (2000) signed by the EU and partner countries in Africa, the Caribbean and Pacific (ACP) regions places strong emphasis on democracy, good governance and respect for human rights.

1.2   Rationale for EU Election Observation

Election observation expresses the EU's interest and concern in promoting democratic elections within its wider policy of support for democracy, the rule of law and human rights. It is internationally recognised that citizens have the right to participate in government and public affairs by voting or being elected at genuine periodic elections. The right to participate cannot be exercised in isolation; genuine and democratic elections can only take place where there is enjoyment by all persons, without discrimination, of their fundamental freedoms and political rights. These include the freedoms of expression, association, assembly and movement. The right to participation and other associated freedoms and rights are not achievable without the protections afforded by the rule of law.

Elections provide the means for the people's will to be freely expressed in choosing their government. For governing institutions to have democratic legitimacy they should have been granted the authority to govern in the name of the people, and be accountable to the people for the exercise of that authority, through genuine and periodic elections. Election observation by the EU reflects its commitment to supporting the democratisation process and the strengthening of democratic institutions within partner countries.

A genuine and democratic election process can contribute to ensuring sustainable peace and stability. Elections provide groups with an opportunity to express their political voice in competition with their opponents without resort to violence, and enable the peaceful transfer of political power. In this regard, election observation by the EU can complement and enhance other EU crisis management and peace-building initiatives in partner countries.

The EU also recognises that international election observation can provide an comprehensive, independent, and impartial assessment of an electoral process. As election observation enhances transparency and accountability, it can promote public confidence in the electoral process and may serve to promote electoral participation. This in turn can mitigate the potential for election-related conflict. In common with other international observation groups, an EU EOM will seek to make a positive contribution to the process, but will not interfere in the way in which an elec-

Voter education, Liberia, 2005.

tion is conducted, nor validate its result. It is only the people of the host country who can ultimately determine the credibility and legitimacy of an election process.

1.3   The Mandate for EU Election Observation

A range of election observation activities have been supported by the EU since the first such undertaking, the deployment of an *ad hoc* election mission to the Russian Federation in 1993. In 2000, in recognition of its growing role and increasing support for election observation activities, the European Commission produced the Communication on EU Election Assistance and Observation which established a systemic and consistent approach to its work in these fields. This identified a strategic approach to ensuring coherence between election observation and EU initiatives on human rights and democracy. In this regard, EU EOMs are only deployed to countries where an invitation to observe has been received from the state and/or electoral authorities.

The Communication identified the main objectives of EU election observation:
* to strengthen respect for fundamental freedoms and political rights;
* to undertake a comprehensive assessment of an election process in accordance with international standards;
* to enhance public confidence in the electoral and democratic processes, including providing a deterrence to fraud; and
* to contribute, where relevant, towards the prevention or resolution of conflict.

The Communication, which was subsequently endorsed by the Council of Ministers and the European Parliament, establishes a standard and consistent methodology for EU observers that is based on an impartial, independent and long-term assessment of an electoral process, in accordance with international standards for democratic elections. The Communication also provides a strategic and consistent approach to the programme management of election observation activities by the EU. This includes a policy on deploying missions where observation is complementary to the EU's efforts in promoting democracy and human rights, and where the EU is engaged in post-conflict stabilisation. Deployment should take place only if observation has the potential to bring added value and make a constructive contribution to the election process. An observation mission may therefore not be sent to a country where from the outset an election cannot be expected to fall substantially short of international standards, or where a country's democratic practices are considered to be generally sound. At the same time, the decision whether to send a mission should not be seen as a judgment as to whether an election will be in line with international standards.

1.4   The Scope of EU Election Observation

Since 2000, the EU has observed elections in 41 partner countries in Africa, Latin America, Asia and the Middle East (see map on page 8).

Each EU Member State is also a participating State of the Organization for Security and Cooperation in Europe (OSCE). Election observation within OSCE participating States is undertaken by the OSCE Office for Democratic Institutions and Human Rights (OSCE/ODIHR). As the EU and the OSCE/ODIHR use a comparable methodology, the EU does not deploy missions to observe elections in the OSCE region.

1.5   The Role of EU Institutions

The 2000 Communication advocated coherence among the respective approaches of the three relevant EU institutions – the European Commission, the Council of Ministers and the European Parliament – towards election observation. Close cooperation among the three institutions is well-established; EU EOMs are led by Members of the European Parliament, who act as chief observers, while Member States provide the long-term and short-term observers who take part in an EU EOM. The final decision on the composition of an EU EOM rests with the European Commission.

World map showing places of deployment for EU EOMs between 2000 and 2007. In this period 64 EOMs were deployed.

List of countries where EU EOMs have been sent 2000–2007:

Aceh/Indonesia	Ethiopia	Madagascar	Sri Lanka
Afghanistan	Fiji	Malawi	Tanzania
Bangladesh	Guatemala	Mauritania	Togo
Bolivia	Guinea Bissau	Mexico	Uganda
Burundi	Guyana	Mozambique	Venezuela
Cambodia	Haiti	Nicaragua	West Bank and Gaza Strip
Congo Brazzaville	Lebanon	Nigeria	Yemen
Democratic Republic of Congo	Liberia	Pakistan	Zambia
East Timor	Indonesia	Peru	Zimbabwe
Ecuador	Ivory Coast	Rwanda	
	Kenya	Sierra Leone	

European Commission

The European Commission leads the programming and implementation of election observation activities, and all election observation missions are funded from the European Community budget, principally the European Instrument for Democracy and Human Rights (EIDHR).[6] There are two election observation teams within the European Commission. The first, covering programming and related policy aspects of implementation and follow-up, is the Human Rights and Democratisation Unit of the Directorate General for External Relations (DG External Relations). The second, covering the practical implementation of observation missions, is the unit in charge of central management of thematic budget lines in DG EuropeAid (AIDCO). These teams work in close cooperation with the relevant geographic desks in DG External Relations and DG Development and Delegations of the European Commission.

European Union Member States

In view of the political and diplomatic nature of election observation and to ensure EU policy coherence, the European Commission consults closely with EU Member States on the planning and implementation of election observation missions in the relevant Council Working Groups. The role of the EU Member States is extremely important to the political follow-up of an EU EOM and the nomination of election observers.

European Parliament

The European Parliament, as the elected representative body of EU citizens, plays a prominent role in election observation, and deploys its own delegations to observe elections. Observer delegations from the European Parliament work in association with EU EOMs. The European Parliament's focal point for elections is the Election Coordination Group (ECG), which is co-chaired by the Chairpersons of the Parliament's Foreign Affairs Committee and Development Committee. Regular dialogue on election observation missions and related issues takes place between the European Commission and the European Parliament in the context of the ECG. Tho role of the European Parliament is also important in the political follow-up on EU EOM.

1.6 Code of Conduct for EU Election Observers

All EU observers are bound by the following EU code of conduct.[7] This is in harmony with the code of conduct accompanying the *Declaration of Principles for International Observation*, to which EU observers should also adhere.

- ☑ Observers will respect the laws of the land. They enjoy no special immunities as international observers, unless the host country so provides.
- ☑ Observers will participate in all pre-election briefings with their supervising officers.
- ☑ Observers will be subject to the direction and management of the observer team leadership, carrying out their written terms of reference and covering the geographical schedules specified by team leaders.
- ☑ Observers should be aware of the presence of other electoral observation groups, and liaise with them under the direction of the EU EOM leadership.
- ☑ Observers will carry with them prescribed identification issued by the host government or election management body, and will identify themselves to any interested authority upon request.
- ☑ Observers will maintain strict impartiality in the conduct of their duties, and shall at no time express any bias or preference in relation to national authorities, parties, candidates, or with reference to any issues in contention in the election process.
- ☑ Observers will not display or wear any partisan symbols, colours or banners.
- ☑ Observers will undertake their duties in an unobtrusive manner, and will not disrupt or interfere with the election process, polling day procedures, or the vote count.
- ☑ Observers may bring irregularities to the attention of the election officials, but will not give instructions or countermand decisions of the election officials.
- ☑ Observers will base all conclusions on well documented, factual, and verifiable evidence, and will keep a record of the polling stations and other relevant places that they visit.
- ☑ Observers will refrain from making any personal or premature comments about their observations to the media or any other interested persons, but should provide, through a designated liaison officer or spokesperson, general information about the nature of their activities as observers.
- ☑ Observers will participate in post-election de-briefings with their supervising officers and will contribute fully towards EU reports on the elections being observed.

☑ Observers must comply with all national laws and regulations. Where these limit freedom of assembly or movement about the country, they must note where such rules prevent them from carrying out their duties.

☑ At all times during the mission, including during private time away from work, each election observer should behave blamelessly, exercise sound judgement, and observe the highest level of personal discretion.

Code of Conduct Violations

In case of concern about possible code of conduct violations, the EU EOM chief observer shall conduct a fair inquiry into the matter, in consultation with the European Commission election teams. If a serious violation is found to have occurred, the observer concerned may have their accreditation withdrawn and be dismissed from the EU EOM. The authority for such decisions rests with the chief observer, and European Commission election teams.

Professional Working Environment

The code of conduct focuses on the election-related aspects of observers' conduct. Beyond the stipulations of the code of conduct, however, all EU observers are expected at all times to contribute to a professional working environment that is free from intimidation or harassment, including sexual harassment. Special care should be taken to ensure that national staff members are protected from harassment. EU EOMs will designate a focal point to whom staff members may bring any concerns in regard to the professional working environment.

EU observers should behave in a manner which respects citizens and officials of the host country. In view of the need for EU EOMs to maintain the highest level of private and public conduct, EU observers should not patronise any establishments where victims of trafficking may be employed. Likewise, in accordance with the provisions of the code of conduct, which requires observers to 'behave blamelessly, exercise sound judgement, and observe the highest level of personal discretion', for example abuse of alcohol, use of illegal drugs, and the use of prostitutes is prohibited.

1.7   EU Electoral Assistance

The EU is a leading global actor in the field of electoral assistance and provides technical and material support to electoral processes in many partner countries. The methodological approach for electoral assistans was outlined in the 2000 Communication. In recent years, there has been a significant increase in the funding and coverage of electoral assistance, which is tailored towards implementing long-term

support strategies within the framework of democratic development and support to good governance.

The European Commission works closely with partner countries to follow-up on the recommendations of EU EOMs, especially in relation to strengthening the institutional capacity of election management bodies and the long-term needs of civil society. However, an EU EOM is politically independent from any EU-funded technical assistance projects that may be taking place in the country being observed.

A comprehensive overview of the role of the European Commission in election assistance is provided by the handbook Methodological Guide on Election Assistance.[8]

1.8 Relations with Other Election Observer Organisations

1.8.1 International Observer Groups[9]
The European Commission has endorsed the *Declaration of Principles for International Election Observation* which establishes a universal code of practice for international election observation, intending to safeguard the integrity and purpose of this field of work. Under the *Declaration of Principles*, all endorsing organisations pledge to cooperate with each other in conducting international election observation missions. Therefore, EU EOMs routinely cooperate with delegations of observers from other bodies which have endorsed the *Declaration of Principles*. The EU has strongly supported the development of a common approach to election observation methodology, and is committed to increasing cooperation and links with other international bodies involved in election observation.

1.8.2 Domestic Non-Partisan Election Observers
The EU has supported the development of domestic non-partisan election observation in many countries. Such support recognises that domestic non-partisan observation can greatly enhance transparency as well as public confidence in the integrity of an election process. For example, over the election day period, domestic non-partisan observers provide an independent scrutiny of voting, counting and tabulation. Activities such as 'parallel vote tabulation' or 'quick counts' (where domestic observers track and analyse election results) can be significant deterrents against fraud and other irregularities. The European Commission provides considerable support to the development of the capacity and credibility of domestic non-partisan observer groups with a particular focus on their use of long-term and comprehensive methodology and the use of international standards in assessment and reporting. EU EOMs liaise closely with domestic election observer groups and welcome information from them on the

conduct of the election process, but draw their own assessments and conclusions, independently of domestic groups.

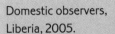

Domestic observers, Liberia, 2005.

---

5. http://eur-lex.europa.eu/en/treaties/dat/11992M/htm/11992M.html

6. The objective of the EIDHR is to work with, for and through civil society organisations, defending fundamental freedoms and helping civil society to become an effective force for dialogue, democratic reform and defence of human rights. It complements the new generation of geographical programmes, which increasingly focus primarily on public institution building and reforms.

7. The code of conduct for EU Election Observers was established by the Council Decision 9262/98 and is included as Annex III of the 2000 EC Communication on Election Assistance and Observation (COM 191).

8. http://ec.europa.eu/europeaid/projects/eidhr/EC_Methodological_Guide_on_Electoral_Assistance.pdf

9. Links to these organisations and initiatives are found at Annex 3.

2. International Standards for Elections

2.1 Key Definitions

2.1.1 International Standards

International standards for elections stem from political rights and fundamental freedoms which are enshrined in universal and regional instruments. These instruments establish legal and political commitments to meet specific standards in relation to elections. EU observers assess an election process in terms of compliance with international standards for elections.

These standards relate to the following:
• the right and opportunity, without any distinction or unreasonable restrictions, for citizens to participate in government and public affairs through:
– periodic elections,
– genuine elections,
– universal suffrage,
– equal suffrage,
– the right to stand for election,
– the right to vote,
– the right to a secret ballot,
– the free expression of the will of voters;
• the freedom of expression;
• the freedom of association;
• the freedom of assembly;

- the freedom of movement;
- the freedom from discrimination; and
- the right to an effective legal remedy.

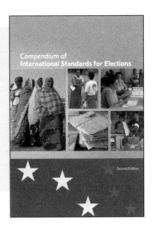

For a detailed overview of the relevant universal and regional instruments relating to elections, see the European Commission publication *Compendium of International Standards for Elections* (second edition, 2007) which includes a matrix that details, by country, the membership of international organisations and status of ratification of universal and regional instruments relevant to elections.

2.1.2 Best Practice for Democratic Elections

In its assessment of an electoral process, an EU EOM also makes reference to best practice for democratic elections. These are electoral practices which, by the extent of their use internationally, can be considered to facilitate opportunities for democratic elections. While not always specifically referred to in universal or regional instruments, many of these practices can be considered essential to a genuine and democratic electoral process. The following are key examples of best practice for democratic elections:

- there is transparency in the electoral process;
- the election administration acts in an effective, impartial, independent and accountable manner;
- there is equal access for candidates and political parties to state resources;
- there is equal access for candidates and political parties to, and balanced coverage by, any state or publicly funded media;
- the electorate is informed of its rights through civic and voter education programmes; and
- there is a peaceful atmosphere – free from violence, intimidation or reprisals – for candidates and parties to campaign and for the electorate to vote.

2.1.3 National Legal Framework

In addition, an EU EOM will also assess the extent to which an electoral process is conducted in accordance with the national legal framework and the degree to which the national laws support or inhibit compliance with international standards for elections.

2.2 Overview of the UN Human Rights System/Framework

Universal Declaration of Human Rights

Before the Second World War and the establishment of the United Nations (UN), there was no generally accepted, comprehensive set of human rights at the international level. The rights concerning political participation could only be found in national legislation, and were usually provided for in a general manner in constitutions. Following the Second World War, there was widespread international support for establishing a comprehensive and binding international human rights treaty. The first step towards this was the *Universal Declaration of Human Rights* (UDHR), adopted by the UN General Assembly in 1948. The UDHR marked a watershed by establishing a non-binding treaty, but broadly accepted list of the rights of the individual in relation to the state.[11]

The UDHR was significant in the development of political participation as a universally accepted human right. Political participation, both as a voter and as a candidate/representative, is linked to a number of other substantive human rights without which it cannot meaningfully be exercised. These include the freedoms of assembly, expression, association and movement. For example, there is no meaningful right to participate as a political representative if one's party cannot be registered, one's supporters cannot attend a rally, and one's opinions are not allowed to be published. Democracy is not specifically prescribed in the UDHR, although it does form the basis for many United Nations resolutions.

The International Covenant on Civil and Political Rights

The international human rights associated with political participation were further developed and codified by the *International Covenant on Civil and Political Rights* (ICCPR), which is binding under international law on all states that have ratified the treaty.[12] The ICCPR builds on the right to political participation, detailing the requirements associated with elections that are a key part of this right. Other important treaties in the electoral context are mentioned in Section *2.4 Other Universal Legal Instruments for Elections*.

Signing and Ratification of Human Rights Treaties

Once a state has signed and ratified a human rights treaty, it becomes bound by it and required to implement it in its national law.[13] If a state signs but has not yet ratified the treaty, the state is not legally bound by it, but it is obliged not to carry out acts that would defeat the object and purpose of the treaty. The purpose of having a time period between signature and ratification is for states to seek domestic approval of the treaty, and to enact the necessary implementing legislation, although national implementing legislation can be inacted after ratification. States may enter reservations to certain articles of a treaty when they ratify; which limits their obligations under the treaty. In many cases however, a reservation requires acceptance by all State Parties to treaty. Information on which states have signed and ratified human rights treaties can be found in the *Compendium of International Standards for Elections*, and on the UN treaty body database.[14]

Enforcement of Human Rights Treaties

One of the big challenges of international human rights law is how human rights are enforced and what actions can be taken against a State Party that is not complying with the terms of a human rights treaty.

The principle enforcement mechanism is through national courts. By ratifying a human rights treaty and implementing it into national legislation, a state agrees to ensure that the rights contained in that treaty can be fully exercised by its citizens. If a citizen considers one of his or her rights provided in the treaty has been infringed by a decision of the government or of a governmental agency, that decision can be challenged through the national courts.

Internationally, however, it is harder to ensure the protection of human rights. There are two principal enforcement mechanisms. First, each of the core international human rights treaties has a committee or monitoring body which checks compliance. In the case of the ICCPR, this is the UN Human Rights Committee.[15] These committees require periodic reports from each country on how the treaty is being implemented and enforced, and engage in a dialogue with each country over problematic areas. The committees also publish their interpretations of the treaties as General Comments. The reports and comments are publicly available on the committees' websites. Second, State Parties can choose to recognize the competence of the treaty monitoring committees to receive complaints from individuals alleging a violation of their rights.[16] The committee will make its decisions on these complaints available to the relevant parties.

In addition to the UN system, regional bodies have their own mechanisms to enforce the regional human rights treaties (see Section *2.5 Principal Regional Instruments for Elections*). These include the Inter-American Commission and Court on Human Rights, the European Court of Human Rights and the African Commission and Court on Human and Peoples' Rights.[17] Judgement delivered by these bodies although not binding on states who are not parties to that regional instrument, contribute to the case law of the international human rights system, and help to explain and interpret these rights. For further details, see Chapter 2 of the *Compendium of International Standards for Elections*, which cites case law on many aspects of the rights associated with political participation.

In reality, there are limits to the effectiveness of these enforcement measures, and if a country where rule of law is weak is prepared to face national and international disapproval, it can continue to violate human rights. Political and diplomatic pressure, both national and international, is often a more effective means to press for the enforcement of human rights treaties and to hold states accountable for failing to meet international standards.

2.3   Principal Universal Legal Instruments for Elections

The fundamental freedoms and political rights necessary for democratic elections are established by the *Universal Declaration of Human Rights* (UDHR) (1948),[18] and the *International Covenant on Civil and Political Rights* (ICCPR) (1966).[19] The UDHR has been accepted by all members of the United Nations and represents basic international standards; moreover, a number of its provisions now have the status of customary international law. The ICCPR, which has been signed and ratified by over 160 State Parties, is legally binding upon all ratifying countries.

2.3.1   *The Right to Participate in Government and Public Affairs*

UDHR Article 21	ICCPR Article 25
(1) Everyone has the right to take part in the government of his/her country, directly or through freely chosen representatives. [...] (3) The will of the people shall be the basis of the authority of government; this will shall be expressed in periodic and genuine elections which shall be by universal and equal suffrage and shall be held by secret ballot or by equivalent free voting procedures	Every citizen shall have the right and the opportunity, without any distinction [...] and without unreasonable restrictions (a) to take part in the conduct of public affairs, directly or through freely chosen representatives (b) to vote and to be elected at genuine periodic elections, which shall be by universal and equal suffrage and shall be held by secret ballot, guaranteeing the free expressions of the will of the electors (c) to have access, on general terms of equality, to public service in his country.

2.3.2 Other Fundamental Freedoms and Political Rights

The UDHR and ICCPR also establish fundamental freedoms and other political rights which relate to elections and the wider electoral environment. These include:

	UDHR	ICCPR
• freedom of opinion and expression,	Art. 19	Art. 19
• freedom of peaceful assembly,	Art. 20	Art. 21
• freedom of association,	Art. 20	Art. 22
• freedom of movement,	Art. 13	Art. 12
• freedom from discrimination,	Art. 2	Arts. 2 and 3
• the right to an effective legal remedy.	Art. 8	Art. 2

2.3.3 Interpretation of the ICCPR

The United Nations Human Rights Committee (UN HRC) issues General Comments which provide authoritative interpretations on ICCPR provisions and compliance. Particularly relevant to elections is General Comment No. 25 (1996) on Article 25 (*The right to participate in public affairs [and] voting rights*).[20] These comments provide a useful basis for interpreting the provisions and scope of the Covenant, for example by clarifying and defining the reasonableness of any restrictions upon the rights outlined in the convenant.

2.4 Other Universal Legal Instruments for Elections

Other universal human rights treaties provide additional standards for electoral processes and the wider environment in which they take place. They include:
- the International Covenant on the Elimination of Racial Discrimination (ICERD) (1966); [21]
- the Convention on the Elimination of All Forms of Discrimination Against Women (CEDAW) (1979);[22]
- the Convention on the Rights of Persons With Disabilities (CRPD) (2006).[23]

2.5 Principal Regional Instruments for Elections

There are a number of instruments providing standards relating to elections which are agreed to by states within a geographic region or as members of an international organisation. These instruments can have the status of treaties, which are legally binding upon those states that have signed and ratified the treaty. They can also have the status of declarations or political commitments, which have a persuasive impact on a country and can be considered as 'politically binding'. Some treaties required a certain number of states to ratify them before an individual treaty can enter into force internationally. For example the 2007 African Charter on Democracy, Elections and Governance requires 15 ratifications to become a binding treaty under international law. Both treaties and political commitments provide important regional sources for election standards in many countries where the EU observes elections and, where relevant, will be referred to in EU EOM reporting.

Regional Body	Treaties	Political Declarations and Commitments
African Union (AU)	African Charter on Human and Peoples' Rights (1981)	African Union Declaration on Principles Governing Democratic Elections (2007)
Economic Community of West African States (ECOWAS)		Declaration of Political Principles of ECOWAS (1991) ECOWAS Protocol on Democracy and Good Governance (2001)
Southern African Development Community (SADC)		SADC Principles and Guidelines on Democratic Elections (2004)
Organisation of American States (OAS)	American Convention on Human Rights (1969)	American Declaration of the Rights and Duties of Man (1948)
League of Arab States (LAS)		Arab Charter on Human Rights (1994)
Organization of the Islamic Conference (OIC)		Cairo Declaration on Human Rights in Islam (1990)
Commonwealth		Harare Commonwealth Declaration (1991)
Organization for Security and Cooperation in Europe (OSCE)		Document of the Copenhagen Meeting of the Conference on the Human Dimension of the CSCE (1990)
Council of Europe (CoE)	European Convention for the Protection of Human Rights and Fundamental Freedoms (1950)	European Commission for Democracy through Law (Venice Commission) Code of Good Practice on Electoral Matters (2002)

2.6   Applying International Standards

Section Four of this handbook details the structured methodology by which an EU EOM applies international standards for elections and best practice for democratic elections to its assessment of all aspects of an electoral process. In its reports, the EU EOM will identify where international standards have been met, and where they have not.

In most countries, the primary source of reference on the relevant international standards for an election will be the ICCPR, although an EU EOM will also routinely take account of the standards for elections established in the other universal and regional instruments. In countries that have not signed and/or ratified the ICCPR, EU EOMs will refer, in particular, to the provisions of the UDHR, as well as other treaties or commitments, as the source of international standards for elections.

The conduct of an election can be influenced by a range of contextual factors. In circumstances where international standards have not been reached, or where national law or international best practice has not been followed, an EU EOM will consider whether there are mitigating or aggravating factors, thus placing those circumstances into context. These factors are often described as the 'grey zone' (see table below for examples).

Both mitigating and aggravating factors will be considered carefully when an EU EOM assesses any failure to meet international standards. For example, an EU EOM may be less critical when problems are not deliberate and are addressed openly, while it will be highly critical of any election where there is dishonesty or undue political or executive interference.

Examples of contextual factors to be considered:

Towards a more positive assessment	Towards a more negative assessment
Mitigating factors	**Aggravating factors**
• post-conflict or first multi-party election	• country has an 'established' electoral history
• poor infrastructure and/or poverty preventing sufficient financial investment in elections	• no external cause
• *force majeure*	• problem was foreseeable
• no previous history of electoral problem	• persistence of problem from previous election
• problem is isolated or limited in nature	• problem is of regional or national scale
• problem is non-discriminatory	• problem affects a specific group
• willingness to admit and address problem	• refusal to acknowledge problem despite evidence of its occurrence
• independence of electoral process is intact	• undue government or partisan interference in the process
• problem is addressed with openness, transparency and includes stakeholders	• opaque problem-solving procedure
• problem is addressed through appropriate and/or lawful channels	• exclusion or repression of stakeholders
• problem caused by inadvertent error	• problem remains unaddressed or is addressed using inappropriate or unlawful means
• problem is not deliberate or dishonest	• problem caused by deliberate political action
• public confidence in system is maintained despite problem	• public confidence in the system is diminished
• peaceful atmosphere	• coercion and violence
	• dishonesty

11. Although the UDHR is not a treaty but a declaration, it represents a universally accepted standard and a number of its provisions now have the status of customary international law.

12. As of August 2007, the vast majority of states have signed and ratified the ICCPR, although Pakistan, Cuba, Malaysia and Saudi Arabia were among those that had not, and China and Lao People's Democratic Republic were among those that had signed it but not yet ratified it.

13. Accession is equivalent to ratification.

14. http://www.unhchr.ch/tbs/doc.nsf
http://www.ohchr.org/english/bodies/hrc/index.htm

15. http://www.ohchr.org/english/bodies/hrc/index.htm

16. The usual means for a State Party to accept the Committee's jurisdiction over individual complaints is to sign an optional protocol.

17. These bodies were established by the regional organisations the Organization of American States, the Council of Europe and the African Union.

18. http://www.unhchr.ch/udhr/

19. http://www.ohchr.org/english/law/ccpr.htm

20. http://www.unhchr.ch/tbs/doc.nsf/0/d0b7f023e8d6d9898025651e004bc0eb? Open document.

21. General Recommendation No. 20 of the ICERD Committee on Article 5. Also see General Recommendation No. 25 of the ICERD Committee on gender-related dimensions of racial discrimination.

22. See also General Recommendation No. 23 of the CEDAW Committee on Political and Public Life (1997).

23. The Convention, adopted in December 2006, was not in force at the time this handbook was printed.

3. EU Observation Methodology

3.1 Consistency

To ensure a consistent approach to election observation, the EU applies the same methodology in all countries where it observes elections. This methodology was established by the 2000 Communication on Election Assistance and Observation and is line with the *Declaration of Principles for International Election Observation*. The EU deploys experienced observers who come from a variety of backgrounds and provides training in the different aspects of election observation. All observers are obliged to adhere to the code of conduct for EU Election Observers (see Section *1.6 Code of Conduct for EU Election Observers*).

The EU election observation methodology ensures that information on the conduct of an election and other indicators of the wider democratic environment are gathered systematically by an EU EOM. The use of international standards for elections, as established in universal instruments, as well as, best practice for democratic elections, ensures that information gathered is assessed through a standard approach that is relevant to all countries. Assessment of an election does not involve comparison between individual countries. Safeguards are provided against subjective or par-tisan assessments of the election process.

3.2 Comprehensive and Long-Term Observation

EU election observation methodology comprehensively focuses on all aspects and stages of an election process (see Section Four). In their reports, EU EOMs will cover the following twelve areas of assessment:

(i) *political context*	(vii) *media*
(ii) *legal framework (including electoral system)*	(viii) *complaints and appeals*
	(ix) *human rights (including participation of women and minorities)*
(iii) *election administration*	
(iv) *voter registration*	(x) *role of civil society*
(v) *party and candidate registration*	(xi) *election day*
	(xii) *results and the post-election environment*
(vi) *election campaign*	

The assessment work of an EU EOM is undertaken through the direct observation of electoral events by EU observers and analysis of information obtained from relevant documents and meetings with a broad range of national and regional election stakeholders (see Section *6.3 Meetings with Interlocutors*). Observers are deployed in the capital city and regional locations across the host country to ensure that there is a balance of coverage of different regions, and urban and rural areas.

An electoral process is not a one-day event, but rather an electoral cycle that encompasses longer-term issues including the legal framework, the registration of voters, the registration of parties and candidates, the campaign, voting, counting and tabulation, and complaints and appeals.[24] The electoral process is also connected to broader issues of democracy, the rule of law and human rights. A comprehensive assessment of an electoral process therefore requires an EU EOM to have a long-term presence in the host country. Ideally, EU observers – consisting of a core team based in the capital and long-term observers (LTOs) based in regions across the host country – will be present from the opening of the campaign to the announcement of final results and the conclusion of any election-related complaints. Where electoral events such as the registration of voters and candidates takes place before EU observers are deployed, an assessment can still be made of relevant legal and procedural issues and, from the information an EU EOM receives from interlocutors, the extent to which the law and procedures were properly implemented.

If an EU EOM is able to observe the electoral process only partially (for example because of a shortened deployment period, or restrictions in accessing a specific region of a country), this fact will be explained in the statements and reports produced by an EU EOM.

3.3 Increased Coverage on Election Day

On election day, an EU EOM increases its coverage to observe voting and counting at polling stations. EU observers are deployed in mobile teams throughout the host country, and each team visits a number of different polling stations within its designated region. The number of polling stations visited nationwide is intended to provide a viable statistical sample so that an effective and credible assessment can be made of election day. To ensure the reliability and consistency of election day observation, EU observers use a standard reporting form and teams spend a minimum of 30 minutes in each polling station. EU observers will also undertake observation of the tabulation process.

3.4 Impartial and Independent Assessment

EU election observers are obliged to be strictly impartial and not to show bias towards any side in an electoral process. They will base their findings only on accurate and credible information. The EU EOM will not accept offers of assistance or support that may compromise its independence or be perceived as partisanship.

An EU EOM is independent in its findings and conclusions. Although there will be close cooperation with the EU institutions, an EU EOM will operate under a separate and distinct mandate from that of the European Commission and its Delegation present in the country being observed. An EU EOM will collaborate with other international election observers from organisations that have endorsed the *Declaration of Principles* but will base its findings and conclusions on its own observations, thus retaining its independence.

3.5 Non-Interference in the Election Process

EU observers will not interfere in the election process. Where problems are observed, an EU EOM will bring them to the attention of electoral authorities but will not intervene to correct or otherwise directly influence the proceedings. EU observers will seek to have a courteous and constructive relationship with the electoral authorities and all electoral stakeholders. An EU EOM will report on the honesty, accuracy, transparency and timely delivery of election results only, not on the political outcome of the results. In its final report, an EU EOM will offer recommendations for improving the integrity and effectiveness of future electoral processes and the wider process of democratisation.

3.6 Cooperation with the Host Country

EU observers will respect and adhere to the laws of the country being observed. An EU EOM will be deployed only after receipt of an invitation from the state and/or electoral authorities of the host country. Memorandums of understanding (MoUs) between the European Commission and the host country will outline the rights and responsibilities of both parties. The MoUs will include reference to the EU EOM's mandate to act impartially and not to interfere in the electoral process.

In return, the MoUs will provide and guarantees that an EU EOM is able to enjoy the necessary conditions for effective and credible observation. These include: unimpeded access to all aspects of the electoral process and to all persons concerned with the election; the freedom to operate without interference, including the freedom to issue public statements and reports; the freedom of movement around the country and conditions that ensure the safety and security of EU observers; the issuing of appropriate accreditation, which should be provided on a non-discriminatory basis; guarantees that there will be no adverse action against its national or foreign staff or others who assist the EU EOM with its work (see Section *5.1.3 Minimum Conditions for Effective and Credible Election Observation*).

3.7 Openness in Findings and Visibility in Work

An EU EOM issues a public preliminary statement shortly after election day (usually within two days) at a press conference, where the chief observer is open to questions. A comprehensive final report is issued within two months of the completion of the election process. In addition, the EU EOM undertakes public outreach activities during the course of its deployment to raise public awareness and understanding of its presence, mandate and role.

---

24. See 'Electoral Elements: On the International Standards of Electoral Participation', Institute of Human Rights, Åbo Akademi University, Finland (2002).

4. Areas of Assessment

This section outlines the areas of an electoral process that will be assessed by an EU EOM as part of its long-term and comprehensive observation. For each individual area of assessment, the following information is provided:

- a background description of the area being assessed, including key indicators of what is necessary for there to be a genuine and democratic election process;
- a chart identifying:
  - (a) the international standards that are relevant to the area being assessed, including references to relevant provisions and interpretations of the UN Human Rights Committee on Article 25 of the ICCPR contained in its General Comment No. 25;
  - (b) examples of best practice that facilitate the achievement of genuine democratic elections in the area being assessed;
- an indicative checklist of issues the EU EOM will consider in assessing the extent to which an electoral process is conducted in accordance with international standards.

The identified international standards relate to all elections for governing bodies, including local government. The standards are also relevant to referendums, which present an opportunity for citizens to have direct participation in government.[25]

4.1 Political Context

All citizens have the right to participate in government and to take part in the conduct of public affairs through elections that reflect the free expression of the will of the electorate. The democratic legitimacy of a government stems from the authority granted to it by the electorate, and the government is accountable to the electorate for its exercise of that authority, through genuine and periodic elections. However, while the holding of democratic elections is a necessary condition for a country to be a democracy, the conduct of an election should be assessed within the broader democratic framework of the host country.

In its assessment of the political context of the electoral process, the EU EOM will consider the background to the elections, including wider democratic and governance issues. This will include an analysis of the opportunities for citizens to participate in government and public affairs; the nature of political engagement; opportunities for pluralism and conditions for political parties. It can also extend to looking at the separation of powers and whether elected bodies exercise their authority in a democratic manner. The assessment will include issues related to respect for human rights and the rule of law. It will also focus on the periodic nature of elections (e.g., whether they take place with sufficient regularity) and the experience of previous electoral events in the host country, especially if shortcomings occurred.

In addition, the EU EOM will undertake an analysis of the political role of electoral stakeholders, identifying the primary issues of political discourse.

International Standards	Examples of Best Practice
Free Expression of Will [26]	
• Where citizens participate in the conduct of public affairs through freely chosen representatives, those representatives are able to exercise governmental power and are accountable through the electoral process for the exercise of that power.	• At least one chamber of the legislature is made up entirely of popularly elected representatives • Elected representatives win and hold their seats as individuals and cannot be removed during their mandate by their political parties.
Periodic Elections [27]	
• Genuine, periodic elections are essential to ensure the accountability of representatives for the exercise of the legislative or executive powers vested in them.	• Elections for a legislature take place every 2–5 years and for an executive president every 4–6 years.
• Elections must be held at intervals which are not unduly long and which ensure that the authority of government continues to be based on the free expression of the will of electors.	• There is provision for early elections to be called in specific circumstances, such as a parliamentary vote of no confidence in the government, and by-elections to replace vacancies amongst representatives.

Issues to be Considered by the EU EOM

- Is the authority to govern exercised by an elected body that holds democratic legitimacy?

- Are elections to the body held with sufficient regularity?

- Have the elections been called according to schedule and by the due procedures? Where early elections are taking place, have they been called according to due procedures? Where elections have been delayed but are now taking place, what were the reasons for the delay?

- Are there other political and democratic factors relevant to the conduct of the electoral process?

- Are there any conditions created by the broader environment that make it difficult for candidates/political parties to operate?

- Are human rights and fundamental freedoms respected?

- Is a broad range of opinions represented by existing candidates/political parties to ensure the voters have a genuine choice?

- Have elected officials been duly installed in office?

4.2   Legal Framework

4.2.1   Election-Related Legislation

An electoral process takes place within a framework of legislative and regulatory provisions. The national legal framework is expected to provide a basis for the conduct of an electoral process that is in accordance with international standards for genuine and democratic elections and should include guarantees for the exercise of fundamental freedoms and political rights associated with elections. The assessment of an EU EOM will therefore need to identify and refer to the relevant universal and regional instruments. These will constitute the international legal framework used to assess the election process.

In addition to specific laws that apply to electoral issues (e.g., an election law), the national legal framework may include provisions of the constitution, and laws relating to voter registration, the regulation of political parties, the media, and campaign finance, as well as criminal and administrative laws. Regulatory powers for an electoral process may also be provided by administrative decrees and secondary legislation that have the force of law. The election management body may have the power to issue administrative regulations on important aspects of the election. Whatever the source, legislation should be consistent with other laws and provide adequate detail on all aspects of the electoral process, limiting the opportunity for inconsistent or subjective interpretation. All stakeholders should have access to copies of laws and regulations.

The process for adopting election-related laws is expected to have been undertaken in a manner that ensures broad support for the legal framework for elections. There should be no discrimination against any candidate or political party. Experience has shown that confidence in the election legislation is enhanced when it is drafted in an open and inclusive manner and there is consensus on important issues, such as the electoral system and the composition of the election administration. Certainty and transparency in an electoral process is strengthened when the legal framework is established well ahead of an election date being announced. Late changes in legislation, or delays in adopting regulations on key issues, can undermine an electoral process.

Crucially, an assessment of the legal framework will also include the degree to which the relevant laws are properly implemented, so that all rights are protected, respected and fulfilled *de facto* as well as *de jure*. It is expected that all bodies with specific responsibilities to enforce the law (e.g., the election management body, public prosecutors, judiciary, media regulators, and government officials) will do so in a consistent and impartial manner. In this regard, an assessment may be made of the degree to which these bodies uphold the legal framework and international standards related to elections.

International Standards	Examples of Best Practice
Right to Participation [28] • Any conditions which apply to the exercise of electoral rights should be based on objective and reasonable criteria. Electoral rights may not be suspended or excluded except on grounds which are established by law and which are objective and reasonable. • Fundamental freedoms and political rights, including electoral rights and voting process, should be established and guaranteed by law. **Freedoms of Expression, Assembly and Association** [29] • Freedom of expression, assembly and association are essential conditions for democratic elections and must be fully protected. **Non-Discrimination** [30] • No distinctions are permitted between citizens in the enjoyment of electoral rights on the grounds of race, colour, sex, language, religion, political or other opinion, national or social origin, property, birth or other status.	• The legislative framework for elections is prepared and adopted in an inclusive and transparent process. • The primary legal source on elections has been adopted by parliament, not issued by executive decree. • The election law enjoys the support of opposition parties as well as the support of parties backing the government. • Election-related laws and regulations are easily accessible for public inspection. • The legislative and administrative framework for elections ('the rules of the game') is established well ahead of the start of the election process (preferably one year before). If changes to the legal framework are needed after an election is called, there should be consensus amongst electoral stakeholders, and any changes should be well publicised.

Issues to be Considered by the EU EOM

- Does the domestic legal framework provide a sound basis for the conduct of elections in accordance with international standards, including guarantees of fundamental freedoms and political rights?

- Are all aspects of the electoral process established in law and in adequate detail before the start of the election process?

- Are there any legal provisions which directly or indirectly discriminate against particular individuals or groups?

- What is the status of international law within the domestic system? Where international law is not directly applicable in domestic courts, have steps been taken to incorporate it in to domestic law?

- Does the legal framework for elections enjoy broad confidence among electoral stakeholders?

- Is the legal framework implemented and complied with in a consistent and impartial manner?

- Is the law being enforced in a consistent and impartial manner by the relevant authorities?

- Were there any late changes to the laws or regulations? If so, was there adequate publicity to ensure that stakeholders were aware of the changes? Was there a valid reason and general consensus behind the late changes?

4.2.2 Election System

Significance of Electoral Systems

The choice of electoral system plays a crucial role in determining the relationship between the electorate and the elected institutions and shapes the political future of the country. Each electoral system has its own distinct characteristics which impact on how complex the system is for voters to understand, how much it costs to implement, and how votes cast will be translated into electoral results. Some electoral systems will be well established over many decades, while others may have been more recently adopted, possibly as part of a post-conflict or new democratic settlement. The choice of electoral system can be controversial. For example, opposition political parties may argue that they face disadvantages under the system in place, while incumbents may argue for the *status quo*. There is no particular model of an electoral system that can be described as an 'international standard'.

Types of Electoral System

Electoral systems fall within three main categories. *Plurality-majority* systems are usually used for elections where one candidate will be elected to a single seat in an electoral district; the winning candidate must either win the largest number (i.e., the plurality) of votes (known as the simple majority), or win more than half (i.e., the majority) of the votes cast (known as the absolute majority). *Proportional* systems are usually used for elections where there is more than one seat in an electoral district. Mandates are allocated using formulae that distribute seats so that they represent the proportion of the vote won by candidates or parties. *Mixed* systems use a combination of plurality-majority and proportional systems.

Assessing the Electoral System

The EU EOM assesses whether there is public confidence in the electoral system and will consider the merits or shortcomings of an electoral system insofar as it provides for the enjoyment of fundamental freedoms and political rights.

The electoral system should ensure that there is equal suffrage through the principle of 'one person, one vote'. This principle means that every voter has the same number of votes in an election, and that each vote is equal in weight. An electoral system can create circumstances where equal suffrage is not achieved due to an imbalance in the allocation of seats or the delineation of boundaries among different electoral districts. For example, in a parliamentary election where there may be considerably more voters in constituency A than constituency B, the votes of voters in constituency A are given less 'weight'.

In proportional systems, an EU EOM will pay particular attention to how the system translates votes cast in favour of a candidate or political party into seats. The EU EOM will consider factors such as the implementation of the electoral formulae used to allocate seats, and any legally imposed minimum thresholds that parties or candidates must reach in order to win a seat. These considerations are based on an assessment of whether the system may produce disproportionate results. For example, where the number of seats per electoral district (the 'district magnitude') is small, there is risk of disproportionality. In other instances, unreasonably high thresholds may make it impossible for some parties to be elected. This may be of particular concern if the threshold is set high for the specific purpose of excluding any political parties or minority groups. A high threshold or a high district magnitude in a proportional system can also lead to 'wasted votes', where the choices of many voters are not represented. The electoral system can include a component that seeks to address previous imbalances in political representation through the use of quotas or reserved seats to promote the representation of, for example, women and minorities.

Assessing Boundary Delineation

As part of its assessment of an electoral system, the EU EOM will review the procedures for the delineation of electoral boundaries. The drawing of boundaries should be undertaken using a transparent and consistent procedure, established by law, and may include the use of criteria such as population size and geographical or administrative boundaries. Electoral boundaries should be regularly reviewed to reflect demographic changes. The drawing of electoral boundaries can be undertaken in such a way as to manipulate the outcome of an election – so-called 'gerrymandering'.

International Standards	Examples of Best Practice
Free Expression of Will [31] • Although the ICCPR does not impose any particular electoral system, any system operating in a State Party must be compatible with electoral rights and must guarantee and give effect to the free expression of the will of the electors.	• The electoral system has been chosen through wide consultation. There is general consensus among political parties and other election stakeholders on the choice of electoral system.
Equal Suffrage [32] • The principle of one person, one vote, must apply, and within the framework of each State's electoral system, the vote of one elector should be equal to the vote of another. • The drawing of electoral boundaries and the method of allocating votes should not distort the distribution of voters or discriminate against any group and should not exclude or restrict unreasonably the right of citizens to choose their representatives freely.	• The electoral system produces results that are broadly representative of the expressed will of the electorate. • The electoral system is not frequently changed and has not been changed to give advantage to a particular political party or grouping. • The delineation of electoral boundaries and the distribution of seats among electoral districts is based on justifiable and established criteria and reflects the size of the population of each district so that each elected official represents approximately the same number of electors. • Electoral boundaries are drawn by an impartial, non-political body and are reviewed periodically, for example, after a census and/or major demographic change. • Voters in the same election cast the same number of votes using similar voting procedures.
Non-Discrimination [33] • Temporary special measures aimed at accelerating de facto equality between men and women shall not be considered discriminatory but shall in no way entail the maintenance of unequal or separate standards.	• Quotas or other temporary measures are implemented to provide a more equitable representation of women or minority groups in elected office. • Legislation requires that a certain percentage of candidates of each gender appear in designated places on party candidate lists; this can ensure the election of both women and men without discriminating against either group. • Reserved seats are allocated to minorities to ensure that members of minority groups are represented in parliament.

Issues to be Considered by the EU EOM

- Is the electoral system, as well as all formulae and procedures for translating votes into results, provided for in law?

- Does the electoral system guarantee equality of suffrage?

- Does the choice of electoral system have the broad support of the key electoral stakeholders?

- Is the choice of electoral system widely understood by the public? Is there public confidence that the electoral system provides for the free expression of the will of the electorate?

- Has the electoral system, or elements of it, been changed for political purpose?

- Are there requirements to review boundary delineation on a regular basis? Are the procedures for the delineation of electoral boundaries based on transparent and justifiable criteria? Have electoral boundaries been drawn in a discriminatory or distorted manner?

- In a proportional electoral system, does the formula for seat allocation risk creating disproportionate results due to a high legal threshold?

An Overview of Different Electoral Systems [34]

	Can be used in:	
	presidential elections	legislative and local elections
Plurality-Majority Systems		
First Past the Post (FPTP) Used in single-member districts. The winning candidate is the one who gains more votes than any other candidate but not necessarily a majority of votes.	☑	☑
Two-Round System: Majority Run-Off Used in single-member districts. Voters vote for one candidate. A candidate receiving over 50 per cent of votes cast wins; otherwise, a second round election is held between the two candidates who received the most votes in the first round. The second round will produce a candidate with an absolute majority of votes.	☑	☑
Alternative Vote Used in single-member districts. Voters indicate their choices on the ballot paper in order of preference. A candidate receiving over 50 per cent of first preferences wins; otherwise, second-preference votes (and then third-preference votes, etc.) are reallocated until one candidate has an absolute majority of votes cast.	☑	☑
Block Vote Used in multi-member districts in which voters have as many votes as there are candidates to be elected. Counting is identical to the FPTP-system: candidates with the highest totals win the seats. Where votes are cast for parties, not individual candidates, it is referred to as Party Block Vote.	☐	☑
Limited Vote Used in multi-member districts. Voters have more than one vote but fewer votes than there are candidates to be elected. Counting is identical to the FPTP-system: candidates with the highest number of votes win.	☐	☑

	Can be used in:	
	presidential elections	legislative and local elections
Proportional Systems		
List Proportional Representation (List PR) Used in multi-member districts. People vote for one party and parties receive seats in proportion to their overall share of the vote. Winning candidates are taken from the lists of candidates submitted by the party. List PR may have 'closed' or 'open' party lists. • *Closed List:* electors are restricted to voting for a party only and cannot express a preference for any candidate within a party list. • *Open List:* electors can express a preference for a candidate or candidates within a party list, as well as voting for the party. Seats are distributed using a specific formula (e.g., the d'Hondt or Sainte-Laguë methods).	☐	☑
Single Transferable Vote A preferential PR system used in multi-member districts. Candidates must gain a specified quota of first-preference votes to win a seat. When a successful candidate is elected or an unsuccessful candidate excluded, the voters' preferences are reallocated to their next choice of candidates.	☐	☑
Mixed Systems		
Mixed Member Proportional (MMP) One group of seats is elected using a plurality-majority system, usually from single member districts. Another group of seats is chosen, from multi-member districts, through the proportional system. The proportionally elected seats are allocated using formulae that 'compensate' for any disproportionality produced by the plurality-majority seat results.	☐	☑
Parallel System Similar to MMP in which a proportional system is used in conjunction with a plurality-majority system, but (unlike MMP) the seats won in the proportional election do not compensate for any disproportionality that may arise from the plurality-majority system.	☐	☑
Single Non-Transferable Vote Used in multi-member districts, but (unlike Block Voting) voters can only vote for one candidate. Seats are allocated to as many of the 'highest-polling' individual candidates as there are seats allocated to the district.	☐	☑

4.3 Election Administration

4.3.1 *The Work of the Election Management Body (EMB)*

Role and Responsibilities of the EMB

The effectiveness and professionalism of the bodies responsible for administering an election is crucial to achieving a genuine electoral process. The manner in which the election administration, generically referred to as the Election Management Body (EMB),[35] conducts the election should provide a framework that ensures citizens are able to enjoy their fundamental freedoms and political rights. The EMB should work transparently, efficiently and professionally and will be expected to administer the electoral process so that it is conducted fairly, impartially and in accordance with national laws and international standards for elections. An EMB should be able to undertake its work without political interference or intimidation. The EU EOM will observe the work of all levels of the election administration, ranging upwards from polling station boards and regional bodies to the highest level of decision-making and coordination.

The EMB will be expected to plan effectively to ensure that all foreseeable electoral needs and voter requirements (e.g., the determination of voting and counting procedures, the identification of polling station locations, the printing of materials, etc.) are adequately met in a timely manner. The production and printing of sensitive electoral materials, such as ballot papers and seals, should be undertaken with the relevant security requirements but also in a transparent manner that enables stakeholders to have confidence in the integrity of the production process. All EMB personnel should be provided with instructions and/or training on their role and responsibilities, including their duty to act in a fair and impartial manner.

Types of EMBs

There is no standard model of an EMB or system for administering an election. Many countries have an *independent EMB* that is administered separately from governmental institutions. Other countries may have an *executive EMB* which operates through agencies of national or regional government, e.g., the Ministry of Interior. Alternatively, there may be a *judicial EMB* where the electoral process is overseen by judges in countries where it is constitutionally permissible for the judiciary to perform executive functions without compromising judicial independence. An EMB may often incorporate a mixture of these various models, in addition to which various branches of central and local government may be involved in the electoral process (e.g., voter registration). In some circumstances, such as a post-conflict country, an EMB may also include members of the international community. EMBs may also be recipients of international technical assistance.

The highest responsible level of an independent EMB may be composed of different kinds of members and may be appointed by different methods (e.g., nomination by parliament or open recruitment). A *non-partisan independent EMB* consists of persons who are appointed on the basis of their professional experience. The independence of these members is strengthened where defined criteria are used to ensure that a balance of interests is represented. A *partisan independent EMB* consists of persons nominated by political parties or candidates. Their presence promotes involvement and responsibility as well as extended opportunities for scrutiny. The role of partisan EMBs is greatly enhanced where its membership is representative of the political spectrum, especially participants in the election, and when those members act in a collegial, consensual and constructive manner rather than by taking decisions along party lines. A *mixed independent EMB* may include both partisan and non-partisan members.

Structure of the EMB

An EMB is usually headed by a commission, responsible for decision-making and supervision of the entire process. The EMB is likely to have lower-level supervisory bodies (especially in federal countries) that often reflect the different levels of local government (e.g., region, district, municipality). All these bodies may operate on a permanent basis, or be temporary bodies established for the electoral period only. Temporary bodies may be under-prepared for the administration of an election if they are not appointed in a timely manner. The secretariat of an EMB plans and implements the administrative and technical work. The EMB should use appropriate rules of procedure that regulate how it conducts business and makes decisions. There will need to be effective coordination and clear distinction of roles among the different branches and levels of the election administration.

EMB Working Methods

Regardless of the model chosen, an EMB should act independently and impartially. To ensure that its decisions are seen to be free from partisan interests, the EMB should act in a transparent and accountable manner. Best practice has shown that public confidence in an EMB is enhanced if all stakeholders are made fully aware of its work, and all decisions and minutes of meetings are published promptly. Transparency can be achieved through consultation with election stakeholders, regular briefings of the media, and the holding of open EMB sessions which accredited party or candidate representatives, observers and members of the media may attend.

EMBs that are independent from governmental institutions are considered particularly appropriate in countries where there is limited confidence in the ability of government bodies to act in a neutral manner, or where government has a limited functioning capacity, such as in post-conflict situations. The independence of such EMBs is usually guaranteed in law and is facilitated by control of a realistic budget rather than reliance on *ad hoc* government funding. The independence of an EMB can be undermined if its members can be arbitrarily removed or replaced.

International Standards	Examples of Best Practice
Genuine Elections [36]	
• An EMB should be established to supervise the electoral process and to ensure that it is conducted fairly, impartially and in accordance with established laws	• The EMB acts in a transparent, impartial, independent and inclusive manner, taking decisions by consensus.
• There should be independent scrutiny of the voting and counting process so that electors have confidence in the electoral process.	• The EMB is fully accountable for its activities.
	• Political representatives, observers (both domestic and international), media and other relevant stakeholders have full access to information.
	• Transparency measures include: publication of all decisions and minutes, open sessions, press conferences, and regular consultative meetings with stakeholders.
	• Election officials are provided with training on their role and responsibilities.
	• The EMB uses established rules of procedure.
	• The highest level of the EMB has the authority to issue regulations and orders to lower-level bodies to ensure consistent procedures throughout the country.
	• The EMB has an adequate budget, over which it has control.

Issues to be Considered by the EU EOM

The following areas of assessment are relevant for all levels of the work of an EMB, including the highest level body, regional bodies and polling station committees.

• Is there public confidence in the work of the EMB?

• Are the powers of the EMB — at all levels — established in law, including obligations to administer and supervise an election process fairly, impartially and in accordance with the law?

• Is the EMB acting independently (functioning in a fair and impartial manner)?

• Is the EMB adhering to the law, including complying with legal deadlines?

• Is the EMB able to work freely, without interference or intimidation?

• Does the EMB act in a transparent and inclusive manner? Is it providing access for its work to be scrutinised by accredited representatives, observers and media?

• Does the EMB function in accordance with rules of procedure?

• Does the EMB take decisions by consensus?

• Does the EMB operate efficiently and meet deadlines?

• Is the EMB communicating effectively with election stakeholders and the wider public?

• Is the EMB consulting approiately with political parties, candidates, civil socialy organisation, and other election stakeholders.

Issues to be Considered by the EU EOM (cont.)

Issues Specific to Higher-Level Bodies (i.e., those above polling station level):

- Is there effective coordination and clear distinction of roles among the different branches of the EMB?
- Is the EMB planning effectively for all foreseeable needs within an adequate timeframe, including the appointment of all necessary personnel?
- Are appropiate decisions/instructions being taken and communicated effectively to lower level bodies?
- Are sensitive electoral materials produced in a manner that guarantees their integrity?
- Is the EMB providing adequate training for its personnel?
- Does the EMB have adequate financial and other resources?
- Does the EMB have control of its own budget and staffing?

In the Case of an Executive EMB:

- Are there sufficient safeguards to ensure the EMB acts independently of partisan or political interests?

In the Case of an Independent or Judicial EMB:

- Is the independence of the EMB and its members sufficiently guaranteed in law and in practice?

In the Case of a Non-Partisan, Independent EMB:

- Does the EMB membership reflect a non-partisan balance of interests?
- Is there public confidence in the ability of the EMB to act in a non-partisan and independent manner?

In the Case of a Partisan, Independent EMB:

- Does the EMB membership provide a representative balance of the political spectrum and participants in the election?
- Are all members able to assume their position on the EMB? Do all members have equal access to information?
- Does the EMB work in a collegial, consensual and constructive manner?

4.3.2 *Voter Education*

Responsibility for impartial voter education often rests with the EMB, frequently in conjunction with civil society and the media. Voter information and education activities are necessary to ensure that all eligible citizens are aware of their political rights, including their right to vote and to be registered to vote. Voter education initiatives are of particular importance in countries with a limited democratic tradition and/or low levels of literacy. Ahead of election day, all voters will need to be provided with basic and impartial information, on matters such as the polling date, times and locations.

Voters should also be aware of their right to participate, the significance of the election, the type of election taking place, the identities of candidates and political parties and the way in which their choice should be indicated (especially where there is the right to vote for more than one candidate). Similar information should be provided ahead of voter registration initiatives. The EMB has a responsibility to ensure this information is provided without discrimination ahead of election day and to make adequate information available in polling stations on election day.

Broader civic education, providing information on wider issues of democracy and governance, is also often provided by state authorities and civil society organisations.

International Standards	Examples of Best Practice
Right of Participation [37] • Voter education campaigns are necessary to ensure the effective exercise by an informed community of their electoral rights.	• Widespread voter education campaigns are undertaken by the authorities, including the EMB, and supported by civil society. • All voter education is impartial. • The EMB cooperates with civil society and the electronic and print media on voter education. • Voter education targets groups that might be least likely to vote, including persons who have just reached voting age, women and minority populations. • Voter education is conducted in minority languages.

Issues to be Considered by the EU EOM
• Is voter education being conducted to inform citizens of their electoral rights and opportunity to participate in the electoral process? Is this effective, especially in providing voter education to groups or individuals who may face exclusion or restriction from the political processes, e.g., women, first-time voters (usually young people) and minority groups?   • Does voter education include voter registration and encourage citizens to ensure they are registered to vote?   • Are voters aware of the election and familiar with candidates, parties, and issues as well as registration and voting requirements?   • In newly established democracies, does voter education inform voters of the nature and purpose of democracy, and of their rights and responsibilities within it?   • Is voter education provided in an impartial manner? Is civic education being provided, and if so, is it conducted in an impartial manner?   • How is civil society involved in voter education? Is civil society being facilitated in this work by the EMB?   • What methods are being used to reach the non-literate part of the population? Is voter education being conducted in minority languages?   • Has any voter education been inappropiate?

4.4 Voter Registration

4.4.1 The Right to Universal Suffrage

The right to universal suffrage is an international standard for democratic elections. This right should be provided without discrimination and with only reasonable exclusions, restrictions or disqualifications.

International Standards	Examples of Best Practice
Universal Suffrage [38]	
• The right to vote at elections and referendums must be established by law. The grounds for deprivation of suffrage should be objective and reasonable.	• There are consistent legal provisions governing eligibility with respect to citizenship, age, residence and temporary absence.
• A minimum age limit is a reasonable restriction.	• The established age of majority (usually 18) is the minimum age for voting.
• Independently established mental incapacity is a ground for denying a person the right to vote.	
• It is unreasonable to restrict the right to vote on the ground of physical disability or to impose literacy, educational or property requirements.	
• Party membership should neither be a condition of eligibility to vote nor a ground of disqualification.	
• If conviction for an offence is a basis for suspending the right to vote, the period of such suspension should be proportionate to the offence and the sentence.	
• Persons who are deprived of liberty but who have not been convicted should not be excluded from exercising the right to vote.	
Non-Discrimination [39]	
• Civil and political rights are to be respected without distinction of any kind, such as race, colour, sex, language, religion, political or other opinion, national or social origin, property, birth or other status.	• Suspension of the right to vote for persons convicted of an offence should occur on exceptional grounds only and in proportion to the nature or gravity of the offence.

Issues to be Considered by the EU EOM

- Is universal and non-discriminatory suffrage provided for by law?
- If universal and non-discriminatory suffrage is provided for by law but suffrage is not de facto universally enjoyed, what are the reasons for this?
- Are all legal exclusions and/or restrictions on the right to suffrage reasonable?
- Are there consistent legal provisions governing eligibility to vote?

4.4.2 The Registration of Voters

Significance of the Voter Register
The registration of voters should enable eligible citizens to exercise their right to vote on election day. Developing and maintaining an accurate voter register and producing reliable voter lists for each polling station can be extremely complex. The accuracy and completeness of the voter register is of critical importance, as non-registration prevents citizens from enjoying their right to vote and therefore inhibits universality of suffrage.

Creating the Voter Register
The procedures for registering voters differ among countries. The voter register may be compiled by the EMB or by other state authorities. *Active registration* (sometimes called voter-initiated registration) requires voters to initiate or apply for inclusion on the voter register. *Passive registration* (sometimes called state-initiated registration) requires state authorities to initiate the compilation of the voter register. This is often done using records of residence or citizenship. In some countries, it is compulsory to be registered to vote.

A voter register may be produced centrally or by using regional sources of information that are then merged to produce a single national register. There should be no fee for citizens to be registered as voters. Voter registration may be undertaken through door-to-door visits by registration officials. Citizens may be required to prove their identity before registration using specified documentation. Registered voters may be provided with voter cards as proof of their registration. There may be legal provisions that allow non-registered eligible voters to be included on special supplementary voter lists on election day. In all cases, the procedures in place should ensure that all eligible electors are able to vote, only eligible electors are able to vote and that adequate measures are taken to prevent multiple registration that could lead to multiple voting (e.g., through changes in residence or name changes after marriage). Procedures should also be in place to ensure the removal of the names of deceased persons and the inclusion of newly eligible voters.

To prevent people from registering more than once, each person may have a finger stained with special indelible ink or ID cards may be marked.

Updating the Voter Register
A voter register has to be regularly updated to remain accurate. This can take place on an ongoing basis, at fixed regular periods, or only when an election is called. Whichever method is chosen, it should ensure that all electors who are eligible to vote on the date of the election are included in the voter register. In cases of active registration, the responsible bodies should conduct voter education to ensure the fullest participation in the registration process. In cases of passive registration, eligible electors should be provided with the opportunity to inspect the voter register to confirm their inclusion.

Procedures for Voter Registration
Voter registration procedures should be clearly stipulated

Checking the voter register, Haiti, 2006.

in law. Where citizens are registered to vote in their place of current residence, definitions of residence (such as a distinction between permanent and temporary residence) need to be clear. The voter register does not need to include personal data other than that which is required to identify a voter and establish eligibility. Any requirement for additional information, such as ethnicity, creates scope for discrimination. Suffrage for minorities and internally displaced persons (IDPs) should be guaranteed. Issues related to the legal status of non-citizens should be considered, if significant sections of the resident population are excluded from citizenship and therefore from voting. Where suffrage is permitted to citizens who reside outside of the country, opportunities should be provided to them to enable them to vote, especially in the case of refugees from that country.

Public Confidence in the Voter Registration Process
The public should have confidence in the accuracy of the voter register. The authorities should ensure that the preliminary and final voter registers are published, and that copies are available for public inspection to allow checks for inaccuracies and omissions. Political parties, in particular, should have an opportunity to access

the full voter register. Where there are strong allegations or evidence of exclusion, inconsistencies and inaccuracies in the voter register, the authorities should take constructive and transparent steps to improve its quality.

Challenges to the Voter Register

There should be effective administrative or judicial procedures that provide stakeholders with the opportunity to challenge irregularities in the voter register, including the exclusion of eligible electors, to correct errors in the register or to seek the removal of any ineligible persons. All complaints relating to voter registration should be resolved within a reasonable timeframe prior to election day.

International Standards	Examples of Best Practice
Universal Suffrage [40] • States must take effective measures to ensure that all persons entitled to vote are able to exercise that right. • Where registration of voters is required, it should be facilitated and obstacles to such registration should not be imposed. If residence requirements apply to registration, they must be reasonable, and should not be imposed in such a way as to exclude the homeless from the right to vote. • There should be no fees, taxes or other costs related to citizens being registered to vote. **Equal Suffrage** [41] • Persons must not be registered more than once or in more than one location (the principle of one person, one vote).	• There are consistent legal provisions for the method of registration, registration timetable, documentation to prove eligibility, registration forms and the format of the register. • The voter register is sufficiently recent to allow for newly eligible voters to be included and recently deceased persons to have been removed. • Where there is active registration, there is an effective voter education campaign and the method of registration is simple and accessible. Voter registration should be intensified for groups less likely to be registered (e.g., first-time voters, women, minorities, etc). • A preliminary voter register is made available for public inspection to ensure voters can confirm their inclusion and its accuracy can be assessed before it is finalised. Relevant extracts from the preliminary voter register are posted at polling stations or other convenient locations. • The voter register is computerised to avoid duplicate entries. • Political parties are able to access copies of the voter register. • The number of registered voters is published in advance of the election and that number is broken down to different levels, including by polling station. • There is a right to challenge any inaccuracies or omissions in the voter register. Corrections are made through a simple but secure procedure.

International Standards	Examples of Best Practice (cont.)
	• Where voter registration documents are provided, they are unique, secure and reliable.
	• The voter register respects privacy and excludes unnecessary and potentially discriminatory personal data, such as ethnicity.
	• Where expatriate citizens have suffrage, there are effective procedures to facilitate out-of-country voter registration.
	• Where applicable, there are effective procedures to facilitate voter registration for IDPs and refugees.

Issues to be Considered by the EU EOM

Note: Although the registration of voters is often completed before an EU EOM is deployed, EU observers will still assess the legal and procedural framework, and evaluate how effectively registration was conducted. They will also consider concerns expressed by interlocutors about the registration process.

• Are the voter registration procedures detailed in law?

• Are restrictions on registration (such as on residence) reasonable?

• Does the procedural framework provide the opportunity for all eligible citizens to be registered as voters?

• Are there suitable measures to include newly-eligible voters, prevent multiple entries, and remove the names of ineligible or deceased persons?

• Is there verifiable evidence that eligible voters are not registered, or that ineligible voters are registered? If so, are these isolated instances or do they constitute a pattern?

• Is the preliminary voter register/list available for public inspection?

• Are effective opportunities and remedies available for identified inaccuracies and omissions to be corrected?

• Is data on the number of registered voters published? Is data broken down regionally, and if so, to what level?

• Are relevant extracts of voter lists posted at polling stations or another accessible location ahead of election day?

• Is there public confidence in the accuracy and reliability of the voter register in advance of election day?

• Are problems with the voter register observed on election day?

• Are women and men registered in numbers proportional to their share of the population? If not, why not?

• Are minorities registered in numbers proportional to their share of the population? If not, why not?

• Where applicable, are effective measures in place to ensure registration of IDPs?

• Where applicable, are effective out-of-country registration procedures in place to ensure registration of expatriate citizens, including refugees?

Issues to be Considered by the EU EOM (cont.)

In the Case of Active Registration (i.e., where voters initiate registration):

- Are there suitable opportunities for the registration of all voters?

- Is there adequate voter education on the procedures for registering as a voter?

- Are the procedures simple, and are registration offices accessible, including for those with restrictions on movement or limited mobility?

In the Case of Passive Registration (i.e., where state authorities initiate registration):

- Is the source of data for registering voters clearly identifiable?

- Is the source accurate and reliable?

- Are there measures for eligible voters to be registered to vote, if they are not included in the data source?

- Are there effective procedures to ensure that women who change their name and/or place of residence after marriage are registered?

4.5 Political Party and Candidate Registration

4.5.1 Freedom of Association

Freedom of association is a prerequisite for the full enjoyment of the right to take part in government, including by forming or joining political parties. Democratic elections can only take place within a pluralistic environment, which has a range of political views and interests. Most countries have a specific legal framework for the registration and regulation of political parties or other political movements that establishes procedural requirements. The registration and regulation of political parties, which may be administered by an executive body (such as the Ministry of Justice), the judiciary or the EMB, ensures that political parties have a degree of consistency in their structure. These regulations may include requirements for internal democracy as well as a unique name and symbol for each political party. Restrictions on the right to form or join a political party should be reasonable. The law should also provide the right to challenge a decision on political party registration.

International Standards	Examples of Best Practice
Freedom of Association [42]	
• The full enjoyment of electoral rights requires freedom to engage in political activity individually or through political parties and other groups or organizations.	• Procedures for the registration and regulation of political parties follow clearly established and transparent criteria.
• The right to freedom of association, including the right to form and join organizations and associations concerned with political and public affairs, is essential for the enjoyment of electoral rights. Political parties and membership in parties play a significant role in the conduct of public affairs and the election process.	• There is no government or executive official interference in the operation of political parties.
	• Political parties are based on formal statutes that provide for internal democracy and transparent operation.
	• Political parties are required to have unique names, logos, etc.
• No restrictions may be placed on the exercise of the right to freedom of association other than those which are prescribed by law and which are necessary in a democratic society in the interests of national security or public safety, public order, the protection of public health or morals or the protection of the rights and freedoms of others. This shall not prevent the imposition of lawful restrictions on members of the armed forces and of the police in their exercise of this right.	• Decisions to refuse or withdraw the registration of a political party occur only under the most serious circumstances and can be challenged.
	• There is cooperation and consultation between the EMB and registered political parties.

Issues to be Considered by the EU EOM

- Is the right to form or join a political party guaranteed in law?

- Are restrictions or requirements for the registration and regulation of political parties reasonable?

- Are all political groups equally able to form political parties, and are all citizens equally able to join the political party of their choice?

- Is any political movement refused registration as a political party? Does the refusal of registration prevent the party or its candidates from taking part in the election? Is refusal reasonable? If a party is denied registration on technical grounds (e.g., an error in its paperwork), is it given the opportunity to correct the error before the denial becomes final?

- Is there any unreasonable official interference in the operation of political parties?

- Do political parties practice internal democracy and act in a transparent manner?

- Do requirements for the geographical distribution of members or branches inhibit political representation, in particular of regionally concentrated national minority groups?

4.5.2 The Right to Stand for Election

All persons, political parties or political groups who wish to stand for election should be free to do so without discrimination. A genuine election requires an open and inclusive registration process for political parties and candidates from across the political spectrum, contributing to presentation of a real choice to the electorate.

Individuals should be able to stand as independent candidates as well as nominees of a political party.

Responsibility for the registration of candidates usually lies with the EMB, either centrally or at a local level. Procedures should be clearly established and applied consistently in a manner that does not have the intention or effect of restricting the choice of political options for voters. Although some types of restrictions or qualifications on candidacies may be permissible, these should be reasonable and should not involve potentially discriminatory measures, such as a requirement to have excessive numbers of supporting signatures, or unreasonably large financial deposits. A requirement for cross-regional support may affect the ability of candidates or parties representing regionally concentrated minority groups to stand or could prevent independent candidates from standing. Adequate time should be provided between the opening and closing of nominations to allow candidates to prepare and submit their registration papers.

The disqualification of a candidate should be made only on the most serious grounds. Candidates should have an opportunity to rectify technical errors in their nominations and to challenge their disqualification. All complaints relating to candidate registration should be resolved within a reasonable timeframe before election day so that successful candidates have sufficient opportunity to campaign. Following their registration, candidates should not be subject to interference, including any pressure, coercion or intimidation, or attempts to force their withdrawal.

International Standards	Examples of Best Practice

Right to Stand [43]

- Any restrictions on the right to stand for election, such as minimum age, must be justifiable and based on objective and reasonable criteria.

- Persons who are otherwise eligible to stand for election should not be excluded by unreasonable or discriminatory requirements such as education, residence or descent, or by reason of political affiliation.

- The right to stand for election should not be limited unreasonably by requiring candidates to be members of parties or of specific parties.

- Established mental incapacity may be a reasonable ground for denying a person the right to hold office.

- It may be reasonable to restrict certain elective offices as incompatible with tenure of specific positions (e.g., specifically described high ranking positions in military or public service or any member of the judiciary).

- No person should suffer discrimination or disadvantage of any kind because of that person's candidacy.

- Conditions relating to nomination dates, fees or deposits should be reasonable and not discriminatory.

- If a candidate is required to have a minimum number of supporters for nomination this requirement should be reasonable and not act as a barrier to candidacy.

- Civil and political rights are to be respected without distinction of any kind, such as race, colour, sex, language, religion, political or other opinion, national or social origin, property, birth or other status

- Everyone has the right, without distinction as to race, colour or national or ethnic origin, to equality before the law and in particular the right to stand for election

- Women, on equal terms with men, shall be eligible for election to all publicly elected positions.

- Temporary special measures aimed at accelerating de facto equality between men and women shall not be considered discriminatory.

- The procedural framework and timetable for candidate registration is provided for in law and is set in advance of the opening of nominations.

- Requirements, such as a minimum period of residence, are determined using transparent and objective measures that do not seek to restrict opportunities to stand.

- Reasons are provided for a decision to refuse the nomination of a candidate.

- Challenges to a decision to refuse a candidacy are heard within an expedited timeframe ahead of election day to ensure that, if successful in the challenge, the candidate may still campaign and run for election.

- The minimum age for candidates is the same as for voting, although a higher age limit may be set for positions of high authority.

- There is a sufficient time and opportunity between the opening and closing of the nomination period for nominations to be submitted.

- Fees/deposits should be of an amount that prevents frivolous candidates but not be overly-restrictive. Fees/deposits should be refunded if a candidate gains a set proportion (e.g., five percent) of the valid votes cast.

- The procedures for the verification of supporting signatures should be reasonable and provide for opportunities to rectify technical errors.

- Lists of all registered candidates and political parties should be published at the conclusion of the registration process and available in polling stations on election day.

- Quotas or other temporary measures may be implemented to provide a more equitable representation of women in elected office.

- Specific seats may be reserved for candidates from national minority groups to ensure that the group is represented.

- Discrimination against any candidate should be dealt with using legislation.

- Efforts are undertaken to encourage candidacies from under-represented groups.

- Special support is offered to candidates facing de facto discrimination, e.g., extra funding or skills training.

Issues to be Considered by the EU EOM

Note: Where the registration of candidates takes place before an EU EOM is deployed, EU observers will still assess the legal and procedural framework, and evaluate how effectively candidate registration was conducted. This will include following-up on any complaints submitted in relation to candidate registration and concerns expressed by interlocutors.

• Does the legal and procedural framework for candidate registration provide for the right to stand for election on equal grounds?

• Are all candidates, political parties and political groups able to exercise their right to stand?

• Is the ability to run as a candidate restricted by any discriminatory practices?

• Are restrictions or qualifications on the right to stand reasonable? Are restrictions applied equally and objectively?

• Are candidates able to challenge a refusal to register their nomination? If there are any technical errors or deficiencies in a candidate's nomination, is the candidate given the opportunity to correct these before a final decision is taken?

• Are fees/deposits set at a reasonable level and are they consistently collected?

• Is there a consistent and reasonable process for checking nominations (e.g., confirming signatures)?

• Are registered candidates free from interference or pressure to withdraw?

• Do any aspects of candidate registration directly or indirectly affect the ability of women candidates or candidates from minority groups to stand?

• Were any candidates or parties refused the possibility to stand? If so, were the grounds for this reasonable?

• Were any candidates disqualified after they were registered? If so, were the grounds for this reasonable and justifiable?

4.6 Election Campaign

Prerequisites for an Open and Fair Contest

Freedoms of expression, assembly, association and movement without discrimination are prerequisites for a democratic election process. For there to be an open and fairly contested campaign, it is crucial that there is opportunity for all candidates, political parties, and their supporters – regardless of whether they are in favour of incumbents or opposition – to promote their policies, hold meetings and travel around the country. The electorate should be informed on their range of choice of parties and candidates. Thus, there should be equal opportunities for holding public rallies, producing and using electoral materials, and conducting other campaign activities, so that candidates, political parties and their supporters are able to present freely their views and qualifications for office. Violence or the threat of violence, intimidation or harassment, or incitement of such acts through hate speech and aggressive political rhetoric are incompatible with democratic elections.

Campaign Regulations

Guarantees of the right to open and fair campaigning should be established in domestic law and may need to be further regulated and supervised by administrative bodies, such as the EMB. Campaign regulations, including the setting of an official campaign period, should provide equal opportunities for all candidates and political parties. Regulations should specify equal access to state resources and prevent arbitrary administrative action which limits campaigning opportunities. Special rules often regulate media coverage and the financing of campaign activities. In addition, reasonable restrictions may be placed on certain activities during the campaign period, such as a prohibition on campaigning immediately before election day (the so-called 'campaign silence' period).

Rural campaigning in Ethiopia, 2005.

However, campaign regulations should not otherwise restrict the freedoms of association, assembly, expression and movement. Campaign activities should not be restricted to particular venues designated by the government. Political activities should also be permitted outside any fixed campaign period.

Responsible authorities should implement and enforce campaign regulations in a consistent and impartial manner. Any restrictions on campaigning, such as a requirement for advance permission for holding a public rally, will need to be applied equally to all contestants and should not be implemented in a way that limits legitimate opportunities to campaign. Where a 'campaign silence' is imposed in the period immediately before election day, it should be effectively and consistently enforced. All contestants have a duty to campaign fairly and make efforts to prevent violations of the election legislation and regulations. Promotion of self-regulation by candidates and political parties can provide a useful contribution to a fair campaign, for example, through the establishment of a code of conduct.

Campaign Financing

Regulations governing financing of electoral campaigns and the funding of political parties, should require transparency. It is common practice for candidates and political parties to be obliged to disclose funding sources and provide reports and accounts of their campaign expenditure. Where state funds are provided for campaign purposes, they should be disbursed on a fair, equitable and timely basis. Restrictions on fund raising and campaign expenditure should be reasonable and apply equally to all candidates and political parties. Reasonable restrictions on campaign funding can include limits on funding from foreign or anonymous sources. Limits on campaign spending may be necessary to prevent a disproportionate or one-sided campaign, but should not be so strict as to prevent effective campaigning. It is usual that the EMB has responsibility for supervising and enforcing campaign finance regulations.

Use of State Resources

The fairness of a campaign will be undermined where state resources are unreasonably used to favour the campaign of one candidate or political party. State resources – such as the use of public buildings for campaign events – should be available on an equitable basis to all contestants. Incumbents should not seek to use the benefits of their elected office as part of an election campaign. Public officials and civil servants should participate in campaign activities only in a personal capacity during their free time away from working hours, and should not wear a uniform of their place of employment.

Role of Security Forces

Law enforcement agencies should behave in a neutral manner. They are obliged to protect citizens from election-related violence, intimidation and coercion, including attempts to bribe voters. Candidates and their supporters should be free from harassment, including threats of job dismissals, especially for public employees. The arrest and/or detention of candidates and supporters from one political group, the disruption of rallies and meetings, or excessive police presence at a rally may indicate politically motivated activity by security forces. Attention may need to be focused on groups susceptible to pressure or coercion by persons in authority, such as students, members of the armed forces and, where applicable, members of clans or tribal groups. All citizens have the right to seek an effective legal or administrative remedy to protect their electoral rights during a campaign.

International Standards	Examples of Best Practice
Freedoms of Expression, Assembly and Movement [44]	• The campaign is regulated in law and/or by administrative regulations that ensure equal opportunity for all candidates and political parties to campaign freely without unreasonable restriction.
• The full enjoyment of rights protected by article 25 of the ICCPR requires freedom to debate public affairs, hold peaceful demonstrations and meetings, criticize and oppose, publish political material, campaign for election and advertise political ideas.	• The duration of the campaign period is long enough to enable the contestants to organise effectively and to present their policies to the electorate.
• The right of peaceful assembly shall be recognized. No restrictions may be placed on the exercise of the right to peaceful assembly other than those imposed in conformity with the law and which are necessary in a democratic society in the interests of national security or public safety, public order, the protection of public health or morals or the protection of the rights and freedoms of others.	• If use of state resources is permitted, access must be provided to contestants on an equitable basis.
	• Any advantage provided to the incumbent should be reasonable, regulated and kept to a minimum.
Free Expression of Will [45]	• All state institutions – particularly the law enforcement agencies – are required to act in a non-partisan manner.
• Persons entitled to vote must be free to support or to oppose government, without undue influence or coercion of any kind which may distort or inhibit the free expression of the elector's will. Voters should be able to form opinions independently, free of violence or threat of violence, compulsion, inducement or manipulative interference of any kind.	• Campaign financing regulation promotes transparency and requires details on the sources of funding and items expenditure. Restrictions on campaign spending are reasonable and allow for adequate campaigning.
• Reasonable limitations on campaign expenditure may be justified to ensure that the free choice of voters is not undermined or the democratic process distorted by disproportionate campaigning on behalf of any candidate or party.	• Where available, public funds for campaigns are provided on an equitable basis using fair criteria and distributed in a timely manner.

Issues to be Considered by the EU EOM

• Are the freedoms of expression, assembly, association and movement provided for by law without discrimination? Are any restrictions on these rights 'necessary in a democratic society'?

• Are all candidates and political parties able to enjoy the exercise of these rights equally so that they are able to present their views to the electorate in an open and fairly contested campaign?

• Are campaign regulations being implemented and enforced in a consistent, impartial and effective manner?

• Are regulations on campaign financing, including limits on spending, being implemented and enforced in a consistent, impartial and effective manner?

• Is the use of state resources permitted? Are state resources being used to the advantage of one or more political contestants? Is there a clear regulation preventing public servants from participating in a campaign in their official capacity?

• Are there verifiable instances of violence, intimidation or harassment, or the incitement of such acts? Are such incidents promptly, consistently and effectively addressed?

Issues to be Considered by the EU EOM (cont.)

- Are law-enforcement agencies acting in an impartial, restrained, professional and appropriate manner?

- Have contestants agreed to abide by a code of conduct for campaigning and, if so, is the code being adhered to?

- Are there direct or indirect restrictions on the ability of women candidates and their supporters to campaign?

- Where relevant, are there direct or indirect restrictions on the ability of national minority candidates and their supporters to campaign?

4.7 Media Environment

Role of the Media in an Election

Freedom of expression is an integral part of a democracy and should be guaranteed in a country's legal framework. This fundamental right guarantees that members of a society are able to impart and receive information without prior censorship, restraint or interference. The right to publish freely without constraint is a key condition of freedom of speech and a major pillar of any democratic society. An independent and diverse media sector is the best way to ensure that a wide range of opinion and viewpoints are expressed and communicated to the public. For there to be a genuine democratic electoral process, it is essential that candidates and political parties have the right to communicate their political opinions and manifestos in the media in order that voters receive a diverse range of information to enable them to make an informed choice.

During an election period, the media play a central and influential role in providing candidates and parties with a stage to engage voters. In this respect, the media will often be the main platform for debates among contestants, the central source of news and analysis on the manifestos of the contestants, and a vehicle for a whole range of information about the election process itself, including preparations, voting and the results, as well as voter education. The media therefore have a great deal of responsibility placed on them during election periods, and it is essential that the mass media of radio, television and newspapers provide a sufficient level of coverage of the elections that is fair, balanced and impartial, so that the public are informed of the whole spectrum of political opinions and ideas.

Media Regulation During an Election Campaign

Laws and regulations for media coverage of election campaigns should not limit freedom of expression unduly, but act in a supportive capacity. There are legitimate reasons for certain limits to be imposed on the media in the public interest. Regulatory tools, such as a campaign silence period to allow voters a period of reflection before election day, and limits placed on the publication of opinion polls immediately prior to elections, as well as rules prohibiting the publication of material likely to incite racial or religious hatred, reflect an overriding public interest. There may also be positive statutory or regulatory measures encouraging the media to act in a specific way to ensure the public interest is best served. Any legal measures applied to the media sector should not, however, be overly restrictive or unnecessarily impede the activities of the media, and they should be proportional and 'necessary in a democratic society'.

Any legislation or regulation of the media should reinforce the principle of equal or equitable access for candidates and political parties. For example, when there is a system of paid for political advertising, all candidates should receive the same treatment and have access to advertising space under the same conditions as every other candidate. The concept of due impartiality does not mean that broadcasters cannot provide critical coverage of the candidates and parties, but they should seek to provide different views, present facts and clearly distinguish between news and editorial positions.

Equity is also a key concept related to balance. Although a range of political parties and candidates may stand for election and should be treated equally, these parties may enjoy varying degrees of support and prominence in society. The larger parties with wider support will naturally be more prominent in the news agenda. The concept of equity provides for the notion of proportionality, in that in countries where there are many political parties, it is seen as a reasonable editorial policy decision to grant larger parties a greater degree of coverage. During an election campaign, the media should not provide disproportionate coverage of the official duties of incumbents, and should separate reports of an incumbent's official duties from any campaign activities they undertake.

The state-owned and publicly funded media have a special responsibility to be balanced and impartial during an election campaign period. Because of their unique role in society, state – owned media should provide equitable access to candidates and parties as part of their responsibilities to the public. In cases where publicly funded media provide free access to the parties for party political broadcasts, these should be broadcast without editorial interference. Broadcasters should not be liable for comments made by candidates. Free political broadcasts should be aired during peak time viewing and listening, when audiences are highest. Time should be allocated on a non-discriminatory basis – for example, by lottery – and the length of these slots clearly established before the campaign period starts. Although privately owned broadcasters tend to have fewer obligations placed on them, journalistic professionalism suggests that they should remain impartial and balanced in their news coverage. In the case of newspapers, there is a common pattern for newspaper titles to support a political party in their editorial lines; how-

ever, there should be a clear separation between news stories, opinion and edit-
orials that distinguishes between fact and opinion.

Media Supervisory Bodies

A media supervisory authority may be responsible for overseeing the implementation of the regulations for media coverage during an election period. There are
different models for such a supervisory body, including a self-regulatory model, a
traditional regulatory authority that is responsible for overseeing the activities of
the media on a permanent basis, or, sometimes, a branch of the EMB. Whatever
the model chosen, the supervisory body should act in an impartial, independent,
transparent and consistent manner in order to fulfil its mandate and ensure compliance of the media to relevant regulations. It should also investigate alleged violations and impose effective remedies when violations have occurred. There should
be an efficient complaints procedure that provides corrective measures of both a
self regulatory and statutory nature. Any sanctions imposed by the supervisory body
should be proportional to the violation committed by the media outlet, and should
include corrections and retractions of inaccurate stories as a first tier of regulation. Although a range of other measures may be at the disposal of the supervisory
body, these should not include penal sentences or any other measures that could
have a chilling effect on the media, lead to self-censorship among journalists, or
act to stifle media freedom in any other way.

Media Environment

In its assessment of the media environment, an EU EOM will consider the broader
obligations of state authorities, including the responsibility not to limit unjustifiably
the activities of the media, or impede journalists in their reporting, as well as their
responsibility to promote pluralism and freedom of the media. Administrations have
a duty to protect journalists from attacks or intimidation and to enable them to
work safely, without fear of reprisals for their reporting. Any form of violence against
journalists (including harassment and intimidation), as well as any illegal actions
interfering with media freedom, should be investigated and prosecuted.[46] The
approach of an EU EOM in its assessment of the media is therefore holistic, as it
includes an analysis of the legal framework, an assessment of the efficacy of the
regulatory institutions, an overview of the broader media landscape and issues
relating to the freedom of the media. A quantitative and qualitative analysis of the
media's coverage of the campaign is also conducted, using established media monitoring methodology to complement the level of analysis outlined above (see Section
6.4 Media Monotoring by the EU EOM).

International Standards	Examples of Best Practice

Freedom of Expression [47]

- Everyone has the right to freedom of expression. This includes freedom to seek, receive and impart information and ideas of all kinds, regardless of frontiers, either orally, in writing or in print, in the form of art, or through any other media of [their] choice.

- In order to ensure the full enjoyment of rights protected by article 25, the free communication of information and ideas about public and political issues between citizens, candidates and elected representatives is essential. This implies a free press and other media able to comment on public issues without prior censorship or restraint that informs public opinion.

- The exercise of the right to freedom of expression carries with it responsibilities. It may therefore be subject to certain restrictions but these shall only be such as are provided by law and are necessary (a) for respect of the rights or reputations of others (b) for the protection of national security or of public order or of public health or morals.

- Regulatory bodies ensure the media's coverage of elections meets legal requirements.

- All broadcast media provide balanced and impartial coverage of the election, as well as non-discriminatory and equitable levels of access for contestants.

- State-owned or publicly funded media provide free airtime or print space to the candidates or parties in a non-discriminatory and equitable manner.

- The conditions for contestants to purchase paid for political advertising are non-discriminatory with standardised rates for all contestants.

- The media airs debates among candidates following clear and mutually agreed rules and procedures.

- The media cooperates with the EMB in voter education.

- The media portrays women, as well as men, as serious candidates and political leaders.

Issues to be Considered by the EU EOM

In Relation to the Media Landscape

- Does the legal framework guarantee the freedom of the media? If so, is this freedom respected in practice?

- Is the media able to work freely and operate without prior censorship (including self-censorship), intimidation, obstruction or interference?

- Has there been any violence against journalists? If so, does it appear election-related?

- Have any media outlets been closed as a result of government action? If so, what were the circumstances and do they appear politically motivated?

- Have any media outlets been harassed by government agencies (e.g., tax audits)?

- Is libel a criminal offence? If so, have any journalists faced criminal sanctions for their reporting? Were any such cases election-related?

Issues to be Considered by the EU EOM (cont.)

- Have media outlets been subject to election-related law suits?

- Have broadcast licenses been issued impartially, without regard to political affiliation?

- Is there a pluralistic and independent media environment, which provides access to a broad range of political opinion?

- Where does the population get the majority of its election news? Television? Radio? Newspapers? Other sources?

- Does the media operate professionally?

In Relation to Media Coverage of Elections

- Is there a clear and consistent regulatory framework for the media's coverage of elections?

- Does the regulatory framework provide for the media to work freely and without prior censorship during an election campaign?

- Does the regulatory framework provide the right to equitable and non-discriminatory access for all candidates and political parties standing for election? Do contestants have the opportunity to enjoy these rights?

- Does the media provide sufficient information to enable voters to make an informed choice on the election through news reports, analysis and debates? Is this information provided in a fair, balanced and impartial manner?

- Does the media delivered objective information on the election administration and provided any voter education initiatives?

- If there is a provision for paid political advertising, are the costs and conditions reasonable, and offered on an equal basis? Are paid for political advertisements clearly labelled as such?

- Is there any preferential treatment by the media in favour of a particular candidate or political party?

- Is there discrimination in reporting based on racial, ethnic, gender or religious background? Are stereotypes of any group reinforced?

- Is there any coverage that may be regarded as hate speech? Are there instances of defamation of candidates or distortion of campaign messages?

- Where there are prohibitions on the publication of opinion polls or a pre-election 'media silence period', are these rules complied with?

- Does the law provide a prompt corrective remedy in cases where media regulations have been violated? Are such remedies effective?

In Relation to State-Owned or Publicly Funded Media

- Do all candidates and political parties receive fair, balanced and impartial coverage on the state/public media? Is there any bias shown and, if so, in favour to whom?

- Do all candidates and political parties have equitable access to airtime or print space in the state/public media? Is such access provided free of charge?

- Do the state/public media comply with their responsibility to inform the public on relevant issues on the electoral process?

- Are there any complaints of unfair coverage or interference in free airtime/print space in the state-owned or publicly funded media?

- Do the public media operate independently of the government?

Issues to be Considered by the EU EOM (cont.)

In Relation to Private Media

- Do the private media provide the public with sufficient coverage of the election campaign and election-related issues? Is the coverage impartial and balanced? If the private media demonstrates bias in their coverage, who do they favour?

- Are private media outlets owned by candidates or political parties? If so, does this affect the overall balance of media coverage of the election?

- Is ownership of private media outlets concentrated in a few owners in a manner that could lead to biased or unbalanced coverage of the election?

In Relation to the Media Supervisory Body

- Is there a media supervisory body? If so, does it act independently and function in an impartial, transparent and professional manner? Is it free to work without undue interference? Does it have the confidence of electoral stakeholders, in particular the media industry? Is it independently monitoring the media's coverage of the election? Is it effective in dealing with media related complaints?

4.8 Complaints and Appeals

All citizens have a right to an effective remedy, where their political rights have been infringed or denied. Without the opportunity to seek protection and redress in law, the political rights and freedoms related to elections may be of little value. The procedures for submitting and deciding upon election-related complaints and appeals need to be clearly established in law. Citizens should be made aware of their right to lodge complaints and appeals. Opportunities should be readily provided for citizens to submit complaints, and to follow the process of adjudication.

The adjudication of complaints should be undertaken in a transparent and impartial manner. Decisions should be based only on the available evidence and without political consideration. No adjudicator should have a conflict of interest with any party to the complaint or in the outcome of the complaint. The conduct of complaints and appeals processes is a useful indicator of the overall rule of law in the host country, and the level of public confidence in the integrity of the judiciary. This is especially relevant where the law is violated with impunity, or where the judiciary acts in a partisan or corrupt manner.

Timeframes

For each stage of the electoral process, the law should specify realistic timeframes for complaints and appeals to be submitted, and for decisions to be reached. The timeframes should provide a suitable balance between the time pressures of an election process, and ensuring that there is sufficient time to allow a complaint/appeal to be lodged and heard fairly. There should also be sufficient time to allow for any remedy to be meaningful. This is particularly important for complaints that relate to voter or candidate registration, as remedies should be enforceable before election day.

Procedures for Complaints and Appeals

The procedures for addressing complaints and appeals vary among countries but will be expected to provide for a hierarchical right of appeal. Electoral disputes may be initially handled by the election administration and appeals lodged before a court. Alternatively, complaints may be dealt with by the election administration only, or by the judiciary only. Some countries enable final appeals to be lodged with parliament, which creates a possibility for a conflict of political interest. Confidence in a complaints resolution process is greatly enhanced where there is right of appeal to a court, as election administrators may have a conflict of interest in adjudicating an election dispute. The adjudication process can be undermined where there is a lack of public confidence in the independence and impartiality of the judiciary. The complaints procedure should be undertaken in a transparent manner, including public hearings and the publication of decisions and reasons. All final decisions are expected to be enforced.

Recording complaints, Mauritania, 2007.

Violations of the Criminal Law

In many countries, election irregularities can be treated as criminal offences. Where a complaint to protect an electoral right also relates to an allegation of criminal activity, the authorities should act to ensure protection of both the electoral right and the rights of the suspect, including the right to a fair trial for the suspect, which should be guaranteed in domestic law. Any decision to prosecute should be taken on the available evidence and without political consideration. At the same time, failure to prosecute electoral offences can undermine confidence in the election and encourage further offences.

Database of Complaints

An EU EOM will maintain a record of election-related complaints submitted to the election administration and/or the judiciary as well as any resulting appeals. This will facilitate assessment of the implementation and enforcement of the relevant procedures. An EU EOM may take steps to try to verify the basis of complaints and follow how effectively they are being addressed. Separately an EU EOM can maintain a database of complaints that it receives directly but which have not been formally submitted. An EU EOM will always encourage complainants to use the prescribed procedures for complaints, and will make clear that it cannot adjudicate on any complaint.

International Standards	Examples of Best Practice

Right to an Effective Remedy [48]

- All persons whose rights or freedoms are violated shall have an effective remedy, including in circumstances where the violation has been committed by persons acting in an official capacity.

- The remedy shall be determined by competent judicial, administrative or legislative authorities, or by any other competent authority provided for by the legal system of the State.

Right to a Fair Hearing [49]

- All persons shall be equal before the courts and tribunals. Everyone shall be entitled to a fair and public hearing by a competent, independent and impartial tribunal established by law.

Genuine Elections [50]

- There should be access to judicial review or other equivalent process so that electors have confidence in the security of the ballot and the counting of the votes.

Free Expression of Will [51]

- Any interference with registration or voting as well as intimidation or coercion of voters should be prohibited by penal laws and those laws should be strictly enforced.

Examples of Best Practice

- The procedures for submitting complaints and the jurisdiction of the relevant tribunals are clearly established. The procedures incorporate reasonable timeframes for the submission and resolution of complaints and the opportunities for appeals.

- Courts have short deadlines for resolution of electoral complaints so candidates will not be disadvantaged by delays.

- Challenges to the election results are adjudicated before the final results are certified.

- The complaints procedure allows for a complainant to submit evidence (either in writing or orally) and for a defendant to respond to the evidence.

- There is a right of appeal, including a right of appeal to a court.

- There is no real or apparent conflict of interest that calls into question the impartiality of the arbiter of the case, including any familial, political or pecuniary relationship with any party to the complaint (e.g., complainant or respondent), thereby respecting the principle that 'no person shall be a judge in their own cause'.

- Full public information is available on the procedures, and full written record are archived and avialable.

Issues to be Considered by the EU EOM

- Does the law provide citizens with the right to an effective remedy in cases where their political rights have been infringed?

- Are the complaints procedures transparent?

- Do the complaint procedures provide an effective remedy?

- Are remedies provided within a realistic timeframe?

- Is there a right of appeal to a court?

- Is the judiciary independent and perceived to be so?

- Are decisions on complaints or appeals taken impartially? Do the decisions appear to be reasonable, based on the available evidence?

- Is there confidence in the complaints procedures and the role of adjudicators?

- In cases of alleged criminal acts, are decisions to prosecute taken impartially? Do the decisions appear to be reasonable, based on the available evidence?

4.9 Human Rights

4.9.1 All Human Rights

Human rights are at the heart of an electoral process and international standards relating to elections are drawn largely from international human rights instruments. As set out in more detail in the sections above, an election process should be carried out in an environment in which the population can fully enjoy all its political rights and freedoms. All human rights issues will be considered carefully by an EU EOM, since a seemingly well-run election can be meaningless, if essential civil and political rights and fundamental freedoms are not guaranteed.

In addition to the specific human rights issues described in the sections above, the violation of other human rights can result in an election that does not meet international standards. For example, the right to liberty and security of the person may be violated by the arbitrary arrest or detention of persons on election-related matters, or by threats and violence directed against those involved in an election.[52] Concerns may arise if electoral stakeholders (such as campaign activists or participants at a rally) are arrested or detained without any basis in law, or where any arrest or detention is inappropriate or disproportionate to the circumstances of the case. All such persons have the right to be brought promptly before a tribunal or else released, and the right to challenge the lawfulness of their detention.[53]

An EU EOM will identify all human rights obligations and standards that are relevant to the host country. In circumstances where there are allegations of human rights violations during an electoral process, an EU EOM will track and attempt to gather information on allegations. Domestic human rights organisations can be an important source of information for EU EOMs on the extent to which a host country respects human rights.

International Standards	Examples of Best Practice
Right to Participate [54] • Every citizen has the right to take part in public affairs and to vote and be elected in genuine elections. **Freedoms of Expression, Assembly, Association and Movement** [55] • Freedom of expression, assembly and association are essential conditions for democratic elections and must be fully protected. **Non-Discrimination** [56] • States must respect and ensure that all individuals can enjoy their rights without distinction of any kind, such as race, colour, sex, language, religion, political or other opinion, national or social origin, property, birth or other status. **Security of the Person** [57] • Everyone has the right to liberty and security of person. No one shall be deprived of his liberty […] **Fair and Public Hearing** [58] • All persons shall be equal before the courts. Everyone shall be entitled to a fair and public hearing by a competent, independent and impartial tribunal.	• All the human rights guarantees of international instruments have been fully incorporated into domestic law. • Laws are implemented in a manner that ensures all rights are respected. • Any political prisoners are released and allowed to participate in elections. • Any state of emergency rules are lifted before an election process begins. • All official agencies – and in particular law enforcement agencies – exercise restraint and do not interfere in the electoral process. • Personnel of law enforcement agencies receive training on human rights and training on appropriate conduct during an election period.

63

Issues to be Considered by the EU EOM

- Have any candidates or their supporters been detained or arrested? Are any candidates, or persons who were likely to be candidates, in exile?

- Have any prospective candidates been prevented from running because, for example, they are held in custody or are subject to administrative sanctions or a criminal investigation?

- Have any candidates, party activists, political activists, civil society representatives, electoral officials, observers, media representatives or voters been the victim of election-related violence?

- Have any campaign rallies, demonstrations, political gatherings or other activities been prohibited or obstructed by the authorities or security forces?

- Have any individuals or groups been subject to threats or intimidation, in particular by state authorities?

- Have any journalists been harassed or have any media outlets been closed or otherwise obstructed?

- Have government workers, students or others been forced or instructed to participate in campaign activities in support of ruling parties or incumbents?

- Are there any state-of-emergency laws or regulations in place? If so, how do these affect the electoral process?

- Are the military involved in politics?

4.9.2 Non-Discrimination

The enjoyment of human rights may not be restricted on grounds of race, colour, sex, language, religion, political or other opinion, national or social origin, property, birth or other status.

International Standards	Examples of Best Practice
Non-Discrimination • Civil and political rights are to be respected without distinction of any kind, such as race, colour, sex, language, religion, political or other opinion, national or social origin, property, birth or other status. [59] • Every citizen shall have the right and the opportunity, without any of the distinctions mentioned and without unreasonable restrictions, to [vote and to be elected, to take part in the conduct of public affairs]…[60] • All persons are equal before the law and are entitled without any discrimination to the equal protection of the law. [61]	• Freedom from discrimination is specifically provided for in domestic legislation. • Discriminatory acts are prohibited under relevant legislation. • The EMB acts in a non-discriminatory manner and takes steps to ensure and promote representation of diversity. • No electoral actor acts in a discriminatory manner or promotes discriminatory policies. • Affirmative action measures are in place where necessary to increase the participation of excluded groups.

Issues to be Considered by the EU EOM

- Are the political rights of citizens restricted on unreasonable or discriminatory grounds?
- Are all eligible citizens equally provided with the opportunity to enjoy their political rights as voters and/or candidates?
- Do any laws or practices result in indirect discrimination? Does the EMB include women and persons belonging to minorities at all levels?
- What affirmative action measures are in place? Are these effective?

4.9.3 The Participation of Women

Women and men have an equal right to participate in all aspects of public life. An election cannot fully comply with international standards unless women, as well as men, can fully enjoy all their political rights. The EU EOM's assessment of an electoral process will therefore carefully consider the equal rights and opportunities for women and men in regard to elections.

Women's right to participate in elections is not limited to being registered and voting, but also to stand for office, to participate fully in a campaign, and to impart and receive information freely. Women should be well represented in candidate lists, political party leadership positions, and senior government positions. Women should have equal access to positions in the election administration and as domestic election observers.

In considering the participation of women in elections, an EU EOM will have to take into account the legal, social and cultural circumstances of a country. In some countries, either traditions or laws may limit women's ability to be politically active. Women may not be able to move about freely, inhibiting any prospect for active political participation. Women may receive less education than men or be more likely to live in poverty than men, with the result that they are disadvantaged politically. Although women may be equal to men under the law, they may be subject to indirect discrimination, or suffer from cultural stereotypes that can limit their openings to political participation. In countries where women's freedoms (movement, association, assembly) are particularly restricted for cultural or other reasons, consideration should be given to whether adequate enabling measures are in place.

Every element of an electoral process can affect women differently from men. The electoral system could work to the disadvantage of women; for example, experience shows that larger numbers of women are most likely to be elected in proportional systems with closed lists. The legal framework might disadvantage women in unexpected ways; for example, if citizenship laws apply differently to women and men, some women may be disenfranchised. If political parties do not practice internal democracy, it may be more difficult for women than men to be selected as candidates. Requirements for monetary deposits for candidates could

65

Political rally in Yemen, 2006.

disproportionately disadvantage women, since women are more likely than men to be poor. Women with small children might not be registered to vote if registration centres are not easily accessible. Since women may be more likely than men to be illiterate, ballot papers without photographs or symbols of candidates could work to their disadvantage. A tradition of 'family voting' in some countries impedes women's right to a secret ballot. Women voters should be protected from intimidation, coercion and harassment. In some countries this might require separate polling stations for women. These are a few examples of the types of issues that will require an EU EOM to undertake a comprehensive assessment of how all aspects of the electoral system affect women.[62]

Article 4 of the CEDAW stipulates that 'temporary special measures aimed at accelerating the *de facto* equality of men and women shall not be considered discrimination'. This opens the possibility for countries to implement a policy of reserved seats or quotas for women. An EU EOM will assess how any such system is implemented and the extent to which it is effective in achieving its aims.

As a consequence of all these considerations, an EU EOM's assessment of women's participation in an election should include reference to indicators of equality between women and men in the wider context, including levels of literacy, access to education and employment, and social norms of behaviour, with particular reference to how these factors affect women's political rights. This assessment will be especially important where equal rights and opportunities are guaranteed in law but are not enjoyed in practice.

International Standards	Examples of Best Practice
Non-Discrimination • The equal right of men and women to the enjoyment of all civil and political rights should be ensured. [63] • Discrimination against women violates the principles of equality of rights and respect for human dignity, is an obstacle to the participation of women, on equal terms with men, in the political [and] cultural life of their countries, hampers the growth of the prosperity of society [...].[64] • States shall ensure to women, the rights, on equal terms with men, to vote in all elections and to be eligible for election to all publicly elected bodies... and to perform all public functions.[65] • Societies in which women are excluded from public life and decision-making cannot be described as democratic. The concept of democracy will have real and dynamic meaning and lasting effect only when political decision-making is shared by women and men and takes equal account of the interests of both. [66]	• Voter education promotes the participation of women in the electoral process, especially in the right to register as voters, participate as candidates and to individually cast a secret ballot. • Political parties support and encourage women candidates, including by ensuring that women are nominated as candidates in equal numbers to men and are placed in 'winnable' positions on party lists. • The legal and procedural framework for elections is reviewed to ensure that it does not have a negative impact on the participation of women. • EMBs seek to employ equal numbers of men and women at all levels. • Domestic observer groups include equal numbers of men and women. • Party agents include equal numbers of men and women • Data is collected on the number of male and female voters, candidates, agents, observers, and EMB staff. • Media portrays women as credible leaders and candidates.

Issues to be Considered by the EU EOM

- To what degree do women participate in public life?

- What societal attitudes are there to women's involvement in politics? What barriers are there to women's equal participation?

- What measures are in place to promote equality of participation?

- How many women are registered as voters? Is this an improvement over previous elections? Are women disadvantaged by factors such as registration locations, literacy requirements, the language used, and documentation requirements?

- What is the attitude of political parties towards women in politics?

- How many women are standing as candidates? Are there any special provisions for female candidates?

- Does the EMB employ equal numbers of men and women at all levels?

- Do domestic observer groups include equal numbers of men and women, and at what levels?

- Are issues of special interest to women addressed by the contestants?

- Are women attending and speaking at rallies?

- Is voter and civic education reaching women?

Issues to be Considered by the EU EOM (cont.)

- Are there signs that violence during the campaign has had a stronger disengaging effect on women?

- What time and space is given in the media to female candidates and to issues of special interest to women?

- Are there segregated male and female polling stations? If so, are the women's stations staffed by women, and are there sufficient female observers and party agents to provide effective coverage?

- Is a culture of family or group voting resulting in women having less opportunity to mark their ballot in secret?

- What proportion of women vote in relation to those who were registered, and in relation to men who voted?

- How many female candidates were elected? Is this an improvement over previous elections?

- Is there a quota for female seats? If so what is the attitude to this, and is this a productive way of promoting effective female representation and participation?

4.9.4   *The Participation of Minorities*

In countries where there are minority populations of different national, ethnic, religious, cultural or linguistic backgrounds, an assessment of an electoral process will consider the right and opportunity for them to take part in the electoral process. This will employ a similar methodology to that used for assessing the participation of women in the electoral process. In particular, it will look at the right of all eligible citizens from minority groups to be registered as voters and the right for candidates from minority backgrounds, or who represent minority political parties, to stand for office. The assessment will consider the impact of the electoral system and, for example, whether there is distortion of electoral boundaries or allocation of seats and/or votes that discriminates against the participation of any minority groups. In some countries minorities have traditionally been discriminated against and marginalised, resulting in particular problems, such as high rates of illiteracy, and low rates of obtaining citizenship documents and voter registration. Special measures may need to be taken to increase rates of participation by minorities.

Some countries have legislation that recognises the rights of minority groups, including the right to enjoy their own culture and language. States should aim to produce election materials, including voter education and ballot papers, in minority languages.

International Standards	Examples of Best Practice
Non-Discrimination • States Parties undertake to guarantee the right of everyone, without distinction as to race, colour, or national or ethnic origin, to equality before the law, notably in the enjoyment of ... the right to participate in elections and to take part in the conduct of public affairs.[67] • Where a minority exists in a country, the minority has a right to the enjoyment of its language.[68] • Information and materials about voting should be available in minority languages.[69] **Equal suffrage** • The drawing of electoral boundaries and the method of allocating votes should not distort the distribution of voters or discriminate against any group[70]	• Electoral materials, including ballot papers, are made available in minority languages. • Voter and civic education initiatives are aimed at minority groups and are conducted in minority languages. • Minorities are represented in political parties, including as candidates and party agents. Political parties support and encourage minority candidates. • EMBs seek to employ minorities at all levels. • Domestic observer groups include minorities. • The legal and procedural framework for elections is reviewed to ensure that it does not have a negative impact on the participation of minorities. • The electoral system facilitates representation of minority groups and promotes inter-communal cooperation.

Issues to be Considered by the EU EOM

• Are there reliable and up to date census figures for the percentage of minorities in the population?

• Does the constitution or legal framework provide any recognition of minorities?

• To what degree do minorities participate in public life?

• Is there an equal right and opportunity, both in law and in practice, for persons belonging to minorities to participate in the electoral process as voters, candidates, political party activists, and electoral administrators?

• If not, what measures are in place to promote equality of participation by minority groups?

• Are there any candidates who are members of minorities? If so, have they faced any particular obstacles?

• Are there restrictions on the formation of political parties representing minority groups?

• Do registration requirements for political parties, for example on geographical distribution of members, inhibit the participation of regionally concentrated minorities? Do electoral thresholds have an impact on the ability of minority political parties to win seats?

• Does the EMB make efforts to employ people from minority groups, and at what levels?

• Do domestic observer groups make efforts to include people from minority groups, and at what levels?

• Are issues of special interest to minority groups addressed by the contestants? Are they covered by the media? Do the media operate in minority languages?

Issues to be Considered by the EU EOM (cont.)

- Are people from minority groups attending and speaking at rallies?

- Is voter and civic education reaching people from minority groups?

- How many candidates from minority groups were elected? Is this an improvement over previous elections?

4.9.5 The Participation of Persons with Disabilities

Citizens with disabilities have an equal right to participate in government and in the electoral process. Restrictions on the right to suffrage and the right to stand as a candidate on the grounds of physical disability are unreasonable. Voters with disabilities should not face obstacles in enjoying their political rights, and the authorities should take measures to ensure access to polling stations, assisted voting, and, if necessary, absentee voting.

international standards	Examples of Best Practice
Non-Discrimination [71] • State Parties shall guarantee to persons with disabilities political rights and the opportunity to enjoy them on an equal basis with others and shall ensure effective and full participation in public life, including the right and opportunity for persons with disabilities to vote and be elected.	• Voting procedures and materials are easy to use by persons with disabilities. • Polling stations and voter registration facilities are accessible to persons with disabilities, for example, being located on ground floors of buildings. • Special materials are developed to enable the blind to have a secret vote (i.e., without the assistance of another person). • Where necessary, assisted voting is in place but with appropriate safeguards – that the person providing the assistance is selected by the voter and must sign an oath protecting secrecy. • Postal ballots are provided for persons who cannot visit polling stations due to physical disability or long-term illness.

Issues to be Considered by the EU EOM

- Are persons with disabilities provided with the opportunity in practice to exercise their electoral and political rights?

- What are the barriers to their participation in the electoral process?

- What measures are in place to promote and enable their participation?

- Where active registration is taking place, are efforts made to ensure inclusion of eligible people with disabilities in the voter register?

- What special voter education is taking place?

4.9.6 *The Participation of Internally Displaced Persons and Refugees*

Where relevant, an assessment of an electoral process will take account of the participation of internally displaced persons (IDPs), i.e., persons who have been forced or obliged to leave their place of residence (as a result of conflict, violence, human rights violations or natural or human disasters) but who have not crossed their country's border. As citizens of the country, IDPs should still retain all of their political rights, including the right to participate in the country's electoral process. Measures will need to be taken to ensure their enjoyment of these rights. In particular, this will include a continuation of their right to suffrage and their right to cast a vote, which may be affected by their forced change of residence or loss of documentation.

In countries with more than one constituency, the question of which constituency the IDPs may cast their vote in is often acute. Voting in the place of origin or the new residency can have considerable ethnic, religious, linguistic and political implications. Where possible, IDPs should be able to vote in their place of origin (although without being required to return there, particularly when security considerations make this too dangerous). IDPs should also be able to officially change their place of residence, in the same way as any other citizen, and without discrimination, when their decision is to re-settle in their place of new residence. In such instances, there should be no impediments to IDPs registering and voting in their new place of residence. Documentation issues are also relevant, as many IDPs may have lost their identity documents, or they may have been destroyed when they fled. This requires special efforts by the authorities to facilitate the IDPs' enjoyment of their civil and political rights.

Similarly, an assessment may need to consider whether refugees (i.e., persons who have been forced to leave their country because of a well-founded fear of violence or persecution) are able to participate in their country's electoral process. This issue will be dependent on whether the legal framework provides electoral rights to citizens resident outside the country. If this is so, it will also be dependent on how this legislation is implemented, and whether the host-country where they are living will allow this to take place. In countries from which there has been a large outflow of refugees, especially following conflict, it is reasonable to assume the host-country authorities will facilitate their participation in an electoral process. Returning refugees may face similar issues to those of IDPs in enjoying their right to vote.

International Standards	Examples of Best Practice
Universal Suffrage [72] • States must take effective measures to ensure that all persons entitled to vote are able to exercise that right. • If residence requirements apply to registration, they must be reasonable, and should not be imposed in such a way as to exclude the homeless from the right to vote.	• IDPs and refugees are provided with necessary documents to ensure they can be registered to vote, cast their vote, and run for office. • IDPs are able to vote in elections for their home district. • IDPs do not suffer adverse consequences (e.g., loss of social benefits or housing) in their current place of residence by registering to vote or casting their vote in their home districts. • Registration and voting is facilitated for refugees in their current location, with no negative repercussions for their status in the host-country. • Voter education and campaign material is provided for IDPs and refugees.

Issues to be Considered by the EU EOM

• Are there accurate figures for the number of IDPs and refugees?

• Are there issues concerning the districting of constituencies that relate to IDPs – i.e., are they properly counted in the population, and are the districts delimited and representatives allocated fairly?

• Are IDPs given the opportunity to be registered as voters, to vote and to stand as candidates in their home districts, their current locations, or their districts of new residence?

• Regarding voter registration, have special measures been undertaken to enable and/or facilitate registration of IDPs and, where necessary, facilitate personal identification and re-issuing of identity-certifying documents or voter cards? If out-of-country voting is permitted, have similar measures been taken to facilitate voter registration of refugees?

• Are appropriate and effective measures in place, i.e., legal, policy, administrative, procedural and other, to ensure participation of IDPs in all aspects of an electoral process without discrimination? If out-of-country voting is permitted, are similar measures in place for refugees?

• Are appropriate and effective measures in place to enable and ensure participation by certain vulnerable groups within the displaced population, e.g., women or minorities?

• Have appropriate voter education campaigns been designed for and reached displaced persons, whether the displaced reside in camps, collective centres or are dispersed among general population?

Issues to be Considered by the EU EOM (cont.)

- Are IDPs able to campaign or participate in a campaign, including having freedom of movement? Do security conditions allow the exercise of their participation rights, including assembly, expression and association?

- Have there been any cases of coercion and threats towards IDPs and/or any other attempts at influencing their voting choices, either during the election campaign or on election day?

- On election day, have special arrangements been made to enable and facilitate the participation of internally displaced persons in an electoral process, e.g., when distance to the polling station is long, is transport provided? If transport is necessary, is it free of charge or low-cost to enable the participation of people with no or little means?

- Has the election process coincided with incidents of forced displacement of population? If so, are there reasons to believe that the displacement aimed at changing the outcome of the elections?

- Are there any mechanisms for refugees to register and vote in their current location? What safeguards are in place for the security of such votes? What voter education and campaign information is provided? How will votes by refugees be counted?

4.10 Civil Society

All persons have a right to participate in public affairs, including in civil society activities and, through their right to freedom of association, to form and join civil society organisations. Such organisations play an essential role in democratic development through their ability to represent social interests, advocate policies, provide key services and undertake research activities, often from a non-partisan perspective. They also provide an important function of promoting accountability through their scrutiny of government activities. Any restrictions on the formation, registration and operation of civil society organisations should be reasonable.

Civil society organisations will often participate in an electoral process through domestic non-partisan election observation. Such work greatly enhances the transparency of the electoral process and can make a vital contribution to public confidence in the credibility and legitimacy of an election. A legal framework for elections should provide guarantees for the right of domestic non-partisan observer groups, in addition to similar rights provided to candidates, political parties and their agents, to observe all aspects of the electoral process. It is important that non-partisan domestic observer groups enjoy the respect and the confidence of the public. Such groups should play a clearly neutral role

Voter receiving a ballot paper, Mexico, 2006.

Photo: Sonia Sapienza

73

and report only accurate and objective findings. This will require the groups to be well-organised, adhere to a credible methodology, and provide quality training for their observers. Civil society organisations may also contribute to the electoral process in other ways, especially by delivering of voter education activities, promo-ting codes of conduct for contestants, undertaking parallel vote tabulations, hosting public meetings or debates, and proposing and commenting on electoral reform.

International Standards	Examples of Best Practice
Freedoms of Expression, Assembly and Association [73]	
• Citizens are able to take part in the conduct of public affairs by exerting influence through public debate and dialogue with their repre-sentatives or through their capacity to organize themselves. This participation is supported by ensuring freedom of expression, assembly and association.	• Election laws provide for observation of all aspects of the election process by non-partisan domestic observers. • EMBs and other authorities welcome, encourage and facilitate civil society participation in the electoral process, including through meetings and consultation with observer groups and cooperation on voter education activities.
Genuine Elections	
• There should be independent scrutiny of the voting and counting process … so that electors have confidence in the security of the ballot and the counting of the votes.	• The accreditation process for domestic observers is simple, timely and efficient.

Issues to be Considered by the EU EOM
• Are the rights to form and join a civil society organisation protected in law? • Is there an active and pluralistic civil society participating in public affairs? If so, how effective is it? Are there obstacles to its effectiveness? • Are domestic observer groups provided with the right to observe all aspects of the electoral process? • Is there active observation of the electoral process? If so, what aspects are being observed ? • Are there restrictions on who can be accredited to observe the electoral process or on their degree of access? Are the restrictions reasonable? • Is there public confidence in the work of such groups and the quality of their observation methodology? • Are civil society organisations undertaking other activities related to the electoral process? • Have civil society organisations made any constructive suggestions in relation to improving the electoral process? • Are domestic observer groups cooperating in their observation activities? • How widespread is the coverage by election observers of registration and of polling? • What is the the quality of domestic observation and reporting?

4.11 Voting and Counting

4.11.1 Polling: The Right to Vote, Equal Suffrage and the Free Expression of the Electorate's Will

All eligible citizens have the right to vote and should be provided with opportunities to exercise that right. In some countries voting is compulsory, but elsewhere voters can choose not to vote and cannot be forced to do so, or punished for not doing so.

In order exercise the right to vote, electors will need to have access to polling stations. The authorities have a responsibility to facilitate the freedom of movement of voters to polling stations. Location of polling stations is an important factor and voters should not be required to travel an unreasonably long distance, or be required to pay for transport, to reach their designated polling station. Opportunities for access to polling stations may be undermined where there is overcrowding or a failure to inform voters of their designated polling station. Arrangements should be made for persons with disabilities to have access to their designated polling stations.

The number of polling stations should be in proportion to the size of the electorate. The number of voters designated to a polling station is considered reasonable when the total number of votes cast can be processed effectively during the time available, if all voters participated. In many countries, the maximum number of voters per polling station is fixed in law. The time available for voting should be fixed in law and should be the same for all voters. Delays to the opening of polling stations or early closing undermines the right to vote.

Where voters are required to prove their eligibility through showing identification papers, documentation constituting valid proof should be outlined in law and should be the same for all voters. If electors may only vote in polling stations where they are registered, copies of the voter register should be available for public inspection prior to polling day. Nobody should be able to vote on behalf of another person (so-called *proxy voting*) unless it is defined by law for specific circumstances.

The procedures for voting should be consistent for all voters and allow electors to cast their ballots in an efficient and organised manner. There should be an adequate number of polling staff to ensure that all tasks can be undertaken at all times. Polling staff should be trained to ensure they fully understand their functions, and should be required to act in a fair and impartial manner. Eligible citizens who are prevented from voting by, for example, a decision of the polling staff or due to exclusion from the voter register, should have an opportunity to seek effective remedy. Accredited agents of political parties and candidates, as well as accredited international and domestic observers, should be permitted to observe all polling activities. No unauthorised person, including members of the security

Voting in a polling station in Liberia, 2005.

forces, agents or observers, should interfere in the conduct of polling or the exercise of an elector's right to vote.

Voters should receive the number of ballot papers to which they are entitled, and that number should be the same for all voters. *Multiple voting* – where a voter casts more ballots than permitted – should be prohibited by law. Safeguards to prevent a person from voting again in the same or another polling station should be put in place. Examples of such safeguards include: marking the voter register to indicate an elector has voted, requiring the voter to sign the register, and marking a voter's finger with ink.

There should be enough ballot papers for all registered voters at a polling station to vote, and extra ballot papers should be provided as a contingency, for example, to replace spoiled ballots. To protect the integrity of the ballot and prevent fraud in the use of ballot papers and other sensitive electoral materials, safeguards should be put in place to ensure that ballot papers are properly recorded, supervised and secured at all times, including during transfer to the polling station and storage. The security measures should be transparent and accountable. To prevent fraudulent use of ballot papers, safeguards should be applied, such as marking them with an official stamp and/or of the signatures of polling station officials.

Ballots should be designed as simply as possible and should be easy for voters to understand and fill out. Complex ballot papers can cause confusion for voters and may also delay voting and counting. The use of symbols and/or photographs to represent candidates or parties is practiced in many countries, especially where there is a high level of illiteracy. In countries with more than one official language, ballot papers should be available in all official languages. Contestants should be represented in equal size on a ballot paper, and their order of candidates should be determined in a fair manner, for example, by drawing lots.

The right to vote and the free expression of the will of the electorate may be undermined where there is intimidation, undue influence or coercion of the voter. Voters should be free from violence or the threat of violence. Instances of bribery or other unfair inducements to vote for a certain candidate also compromise the free expression of the will of the electorate. In many countries, campaigning on election day, or the immediate run-up to election day, is prohibited by a 'campaign silence' period. Campaigning or the display of partisan symbols should be banned inside polling stations. Security personnel are often present near polling stations on election day to protect against any unlawful or arbitrary interference with the voting process. At all times they should act in an appropriate and impartial manner and should not contribute in any way to an atmosphere of intimidation. Similarly, public authorities should act in a neutral manner on election day.

Assisted Voting
Electors who are unable to vote unaided under standard procedures, e.g., blind or illiterate voters, have the right to be provided with assistance. Wherever possible, however, steps should be taken to enable them to vote without assistance. Procedures for assistance should be regulated and publicised before election day. Assistance in marking a ballot paper should only be provided to those who would not otherwise be able to cast a ballot. The assistance provided should be independent, honest and protect the secrecy of the voter's choice. It is best practice that the person can choose who can assist them to vote, although there may be restrictions on the number of times an individual can provide assistance. Those providing assistance should be impartial and therefore should not be candidate or party representatives.

International Standards	Examples of Best Practice
Right to Vote [74]	• There is an adequate number of polling stations countrywide.
• Positive measures should be taken to overcome specific difficulties, such as illiteracy, language barriers and poverty which prevent persons entitled to vote from exercising their rights effectively. Specific methods, such as photographs and symbols, should be adopted to ensure that illiterate voters have adequate information on which to base their choice.	• The number of polling stations is in proportion to the size of the electorate, with a maximum number of voters per polling station which ensures that all voters can be processed efficiently.
• Assistance provided to the disabled, blind or illiterate should be independent. Electors should be fully informed of these guarantees.	• The opening hours of polling stations are established in advance and are consistently applied throughout the country. Polling station opening should be sufficiently long to enable all electors to vote without undue inconvenience.
Equal Suffrage [75]	• Ballot papers are designed as simply as possible.
• Persons must not vote more than once (the principle of one person, one vote).	• There are sufficient electoral materials, including ballot papers, to ensure that all voters are able to vote.
Freedom of Movement [76]	• Security and integrity of ballot papers and other sensitive materials is assured in a transparent manner.
• Positive measures should be taken to overcome impediments to freedom of movement which prevent persons entitled to vote from exercising their rights effectively.	• Polling stations are accessible to persons with disabilities.
Free Expression of Will [77]	• Voters who are unable to attend their designated polling station on election day are still able to vote (see Section *4.11.3 Special Voting Procedures*).
• Persons entitled to vote must be free to vote for any candidate for election without undue influence or coercion of any kind which may distort or inhibit the free expression of the elector's will.	• Appropriate security procedures are established to ensure the political rights of citizens are protected.
• Voters should be able to form opinions independently, free of violence or threat of violence, compulsion, inducement or manipulative interference of any kind.	• Campaigning inside polling stations is not permitted.
Genuine Elections [78]	• Candidate/party agents and non-partisan election observers, including those from domestic civil society groups and international organisations, are able to observe all stages of the election day process.
• There should be independent scrutiny of the voting process and access to judicial review or other equivalent process so that electors have confidence in the security of the ballot.	

Issues to be Considered by the EU EOM

- Is the right to vote restricted in any way? Do voters have difficulties with access to their designated polling stations? Are there impediments to freedom of movement? Are there problems with overcrowding, excessive delays or queues?

- Do arrangements for voting establish equal requirements and opportunities for all voters? Are voting procedures conducive to an efficient and transparent voting process?

- Is the ballot paper designed as simply as possible and suitable for use by all voters?

- Are party/candidate agents and observers able to observe all aspects of polling?

- Is impartial assistance provided to voters who require such support?

- Do polling officials conduct voting efficiently, impartially and in accordance with the law?

- Are only authorised people present in the polling station?

- Are appropriate steps taken to guarantee the integrity of the ballot and to prevent fraud?

- Is there evidence that the integrity of the ballot has been compromised through error and/or fraud? If so, what is the scale of the problem, is it isolated or systematic, and what steps are taken to stop it?

- Are appropriate steps taken to prevent intimidation or coercion of voters and unlawful interference in polling?

- Is there evidence that intimidation or coercion of voters has taken place? If so, what steps are taken to enforce the law?

- Is there a peaceful atmosphere on election day?

- Are security forces behaving in an appropriate manner?

4.11.2 Polling: the Right to a Secret Ballot

All voters have the right to vote in secret. It is the responsibility of the authorities to guarantee this right through provision of polling booths that allow ballot papers to be marked in private. Marked ballots should not be inspected before being placed into a ballot box, or contain any identifying features that would enable the ballot paper to be traced back to the voter who marked it. Voters should not be intimidated or coerced into revealing for whom they voted. Except in cases where a voter is being lawfully assisted, a voter cannot waive their right to vote in secret. Voting at the same time as another person in the same polling booth (so-called *family/ group voting*) and voting outside a polling booth (*open voting*) should be prohibited.

An EU observer examines a ballot box, Ethiopia, 2005.

International Standards	Examples of Best Practice
Right to a Secret Ballot [79]	
• States should take measures to guarantee the requirement of the secrecy of the vote during elections.	• Polling stations ensure privacy through a sufficient number of polling booths, of an appropriate design and quality that are suitably positioned.
• Voters should be protected from any form of coercion or compulsion to disclose how they intend to vote or how they voted	• The law prohibits 'open voting' and 'group voting' unless the voter is being lawfully assisted, and this is effectively enforced.
• The security of ballot boxes must be guaranteed.	• Polling procedures ensure that a marked ballot cannot be viewed before being cast. A ballot paper is not traceable back to the voter who cast it.

Issues to be Considered by the EU EOM
• Is the right to secrecy of the ballot guaranteed in law and in practice?
• What steps are being taken to prevent group voting and open voting?
• Is group voting and open voting occurring, and if so, how frequently, and how is it responded to?
• Are persons requiring assistance provided with it in a manner that supports the secrecy of the ballot?

4.11.3 Special Voting Procedures

Special voting procedures should be applied to enable electors who are unable to attend polling stations to cast their ballot. *Absentee voting* is a term also used to describe special voting procedures by which electors are allowed to vote in a location other than their designated polling station. These include:

- *mobile voting*, where polling officials transport a mobile ballot box to voters who cannot attend their designated polling station (e.g., ill or elderly voters can cast their ballot at home or a hospital). Mobile voting usually takes place on election day but may also happen in advance;
- *postal voting*, where voters cast their ballots by post in advance of election day;
- *early voting*, where voters unable to attend their designated polling station on election day (e.g., election officials or security personnel) cast their ballot early;
- *prison-voting*, where prisoners who retain suffrage cast their ballots in special polling stations within the prison;
- *out-of-country voting*, where expatriate citizens entitled to suffrage cast their ballots at special polling stations, often at their country's embassy or by post; and
- *military voting*, where members of the armed forces vote at a designated local civilian polling station or in their barracks.

Absentee voting can strengthen an electoral process by providing all eligible citizens with opportunities to vote. However, as absentee voting often takes place outside a controlled voting environment and without the presence of observers, there is increased scope for fraudulent practices. Electors who benefit from special voting procedures, such as soldiers or persons with illnesses, can be particularly vulnerable to intimidation from persons in authority. Further concerns may arise relating to the security and integrity of ballots cast outside of a controlled environment. For example, there are increased opportunities for fraud and manipulation in postal voting. Safeguards should be put in place to ensure that the secrecy of ballots of absentee voters is maintained.

International Standards	Examples of Best Practice
The same standards apply for special voting procedures as for regular voting.	• Special voting procedures are in place to ensure that all eligible citizens can exercise their right to vote. • Where there is voting with mobile ballot boxes, this is limited to the homebound and hospitalised. Observers are allowed to accompany the mobile ballot box. • Where postal voting is permitted, there are safeguards in place to promote the secrecy of the ballot (e.g., a double envelope). Postal ballots are distributed in sufficient time to ensure that they can be returned by election day. • Where there is early voting, special measures are in place to ensure the security of ballot boxes. • No one is deprived of registration or the right to vote as a result of being homeless. • No absentee ballot is counted before the close of polling on election day.

Issues to be Considered by the EU EOM
• Do special voting procedures provide appropriate safeguards to protect the electoral rights of absentee voters?   • Is there any evidence of irregularities related to the implementation of the special voting procedures?   • Is there public awareness and confidence in the special voting procedures?   • Are observers and party/candidate agents able to observe all aspects of special voting procedures?   • What arrangements are there for the counting and aggregation of ballots cast by special voting procedures?

4.11.4 Closing of Polling and Counting of Votes

Closing and counting procedures should be established in law and provide safeguards that guarantee a transparent, prompt and accurate count. Only authorised staff should be involved in the closing of polling and the counting of votes. All staff should follow procedures specified in the law and regulations. Counting officials will need to record data using standard documentation, which is often referred to as the results protocol. All stages of the closing and counting process should take place in the presence and in full wiew of party/candidate representatives, as well as international and domestic observers if they are present. Counting should not take place in an atmosphere of intimidation.

Counting the votes, Guinea Bissau, 2005.

The time for closing the poll should be fixed. Any decision to extend voting hours should be based on objective criteria which are applied in a consistent manner. All persons who are waiting in line at the close of polls should be allowed to cast their ballot. Procedures for closing should include immediately sealing of the ballot box, and securing the unused ballot papers. Reconciliation should then be undertaken, which includes counting the number of voters who received ballot papers, the number of unused ballot papers, and any spoilt and returned ballots. The sealed ballot box should not be opened before these steps are completed.

The counting of votes should take place promptly after the closing of the poll in order to minimise opportunities for interference with the ballots. Counting may take place at the polling station or at a district or regional counting centre, following transfer of the sealed ballot box. At a district or regional counting centre, results may be counted by polling station or mixed. The counting of ballot papers at polling stations can have the benefit of enhancing transparency and accountability. However, a counting centre can create a more controlled environment for counting and, through the mixing of ballot papers from different polling stations, can address concern that retribution may be taken against voters where the results of individual polling stations are known. If the ballot box is transferred to a counting centre, it is crucial that it is supervised and accounted for at every stage. Party or candidate representatives and observers, should be permitted to accompy the ballot box while in transit.

After the opening of the sealed ballot box, the total number of ballots inside should be counted. The number of ballots inside the ballot box should be reconciled with the number of ballot papers that were issued to voters. The number of ballots inside the ballot box should not be more than the number of voters who cast their ballot.

As they are counted, ballot papers should be available for inspection by those present. All ballots that indicate the intended choice of the voter should be considered as valid, provided they contain no marks that could indicate who cast the ballot. Where there are discrepancies, the result is close, or the number of invalid votes is significant, an immediate recount may be required. The results of the count should be recorded in the official results protocol and copies of the protocol should be provided to all party/candidate agents and observers. An official copy of the results should be posted at the polling station (e.g., pinned to the door) as soon as the counting is completed, to provide an opportunity for results to be publicly inspected. There should be opportunities to seek a remedy in the event of objections against decisions or activities of the counting staff. Following the count, all polling materials should be secured and transported in an appropriate manner.

International Standards	Examples of Best Practice
Free Expression of the Will of the Electorate	
• Votes should be counted honestly and accurately.	• All ballot papers that show the clear intention of the voter are considered valid.
	• Ballot papers that reveal the identity of the voter are considered invalid.
	• The counting process begins immediately after the end of the polling.
	• Results are immediately publicly posted at the polling station or counting centre at the completion of the count.
	• Precautions are taken to prevent interference with marked ballots.
Genuine Elections [80]	
• Votes should be counted in the presence of the candidates or their agents.	• Candidate and party agents and observers are able to observe all stages of the counting process.
• There should be independent scrutiny of the counting process so that electors have confidence in the security of the ballot and the counting of the votes.	• Candidate and party agents and observers are issued with a copy of the results protocol.

> **Issues to be Considered by the EU EOM**
>
> • Are the procedures for the closing of polls and counting of votes established in law, and do they provide transparent safeguards to protect the integrity of the process and accuracy of the results?
>
> • Are the closing, reconciliation and counting procedures properly followed? Do counting officials act in an impartial manner and in accordance with the law?
>
> • Is the counting of votes and recording of results honest and accurate?
>
> • Are party/candidate agents and domestic and international observers able to observe all aspects of the counting process?
>
> • Are party/candidate agents and observers issued with a copy of the results protocol?
>
> • Are results immediately publicly posted at the polling station or counting centre upon the completion of the count?

4.11.5 Electronic Voting

Electronic voting (e-voting) is becoming established in many countries. New voting technologies can enhance voter participation, including through absentee voting, as well as provide faster counting which is less prone to human error. It can also result in cost savings. However, the use of e-voting may raise serious concerns over the transparency of the voting process and the accountability of election officials. E-voting removes many of the transparency protections that come with paper ballots. In addition, e-voting can raise concerns as to whether an individual's vote can be traced. E-voting systems linked to the internet or other computer networks may be susceptible to hacking or outside manipulation. As such, e-voting is most appropriate in countries with very high levels of public confidence in the integrity of the voting, counting and tabulation processes. In countries where public confidence in the electoral process is low, e-voting may further diminish trust. Public confidence in the use of e-voting is enhanced where there have been inclusive and transparent attempts by the authorities to test, verify and certify the equipment used.

E-voting can include the use of optical scanning machines, which scan marked ballot papers and tally results. It may also involve direct recording electronic voting equipment, such as touch-screen machines, where a voter indicates his/her choice, the choice is recorded electronically, and the results tallied. E-voting equipment should be easy to use, and voters should be able to confirm their choice of voting. Both software and hardware should include the best possible safeguards against any form of manipulation or hacking. If e-voting does not take place in controlled environments, through the use of dedicated e-voting equipment in polling stations or in other locations appropriately safeguarded, but is done in uncontrolled environments, such as via the internet, this will greatly increase the risk of hacking, and undermine the secrecy of the vote.

E-voting equipment may also be used to transfer and tabulate results data among the different levels of the EMB. Equipment used should allow for the possibility of cross-checking results, and should establish a paper trail to allow for results verification by tracing results to source, through an auditable paper record.

The use of e-voting equipment, including software operating under confidentiality agreements, may reduce the transparency of an electoral process, and potentially limit the opportunities for independent observation by party/candidate agents and observers. Observation of e-voting can be challenging as it requires specialist expertise, and can be less readily accessible to scrutiny. However, the standards for assessing elections using traditional ballot papers apply equally to e-voting. Thus, all eligible voters should have the right to vote, the secrecy of the ballot should be guaranteed, and results tallied by e-voting equipment should accurately reflect voter intention.

International observation missions will generally not be in a position to undertake a full verification of the technical aspects of an e-voting system, such as software applications and security systems. It will therefore be important for an EU EOM to make clear in its statements and reports the extent to which it was or was not able to assess these important aspects of the electoral process.

International Standards	Examples of Best Practice
The same standards apply for e-voting procedures as for regular voting.	• E-voting is introduced with the broad consensus of electoral stakeholders. • There is public confidence in the use of e-voting. • E-voting equipment is simple to use. • There is an auditable paper trail to verify results. • It is not possible to trace a ballot to the voter. • The means of e-voting do not prevent observation of the process by candidate agents or observers. • There are spot checks of the results against the auditable paper trail to verify the integrity of the system.

Issues to be Considered by the EU EOM

- Is there broad confidence of the public and other electoral stakeholders in e-voting?
- Does the e-voting system used facilitate an election that is in accordance with international standards?
- Does the e-voting system used require the use of an auditable paper trail to verify the voting results?
- Are there suitable safeguards against manipulation or interference in the e-voting process?
- Does the use of e-voting equipment allow for effective and credible observation to take place?
- Is there suitable voter education on the use of electronic equipment?
- Are staff satisfactorily trained, and is sufficient technical assistance available?
- What procedures are in place for securing and safeguarding the electronic data?

4.12 Tabulation and Publication of Results, and the Post-Election Environment

An election process climaxes in the announcement and implementation of the final results. This is likely to be the responsibility of the EMB, which should ensure that the procedures for the tabulation and publication of results are clearly established in advance of election day. Detailed information on the results from individual polling stations (or, if there are counting centres, from the lowest possible level to which results can be broken down) is a basic transparency requirement and is crucial for any results audit that may take place in the event of a challenge.

Best practice has shown that confidence in the credibility and accuracy of election results is greatly enhanced where the process is undertaken in a fully transparent and prompt manner. In particular, the EMB should ensure that:

- detailed results from the counting of votes are immediately posted for public inspection at the polling station/counting centre, and copies of the results are provided to party/candidate agents and observers;
- detailed results are published at every stage of the aggregation and tabulation process as soon as they are available, indicating how many votes have been won by each candidate or political party and the number of invalid votes;
- results are published in full, including a breakdown of results by individual polling station/counting centre, as well as regional constituencies, to allow for cross-checking of results; and
- the results process is fully accessible to candidates, political parties, their agents, domestic and international observers and the media.

It is best practice that the tabulation of results is undertaken using computer equipment, and that detailed results down to polling station level are announced in the media and posted on the internet as soon as they are available. The EMB should be able to show the connection between the votes cast and the results of the election and is expected to account for any discrepancies in the published results. An EU EOM will report on any discrepancies that it observes in the results process.

Partial results may be announced during the course of the tabulation process. If released, they should always be clearly referred to as representing only a proportion of the votes cast. An EMB will be expected to announce *preliminary results* as soon as the tabulation of results is completed at a regional or countrywide level. There may be a deadline for the announcement of preliminary results.

Final results should be declared after the deadline

Observing counting at a polling station, Uganda, 2006.

for the submission of any challenges to the preliminary results has passed. In some instances, the outcome of the results is implemented even when there are challenges that remain outstanding. In other countries, the declaration of final results is made only after such challenges have been resolved. Where successful candidates in an election are determined by a proportion of the votes cast – e.g., where a candidate is required to have more than 50 per cent of the votes, or a party is required to pass a threshold of 5 per cent – it is best practice that the proportion is calculated from the number of valid votes only. Many countries have a two-stage process for some elected positions, under which a second round of voting may be held if no candidate receives the required number of votes in the first round.

Candidates and political parties have the right to challenge the validity of election results. Procedures should be established to allow challenges to be made within an appropriate timeframe to an independent body, such as a court. Challenges should be dealt with impartially, and decisions should be based on the available evidence and made without political consideration. Where results have been successfully challenged, for example because of proven violations of voting procedures, voting should be repeated in the polling stations affected within a suitable timeframe. However, repeat polling may not be required if the total number of registered voters in the polling station(s) is of an insufficient number to change the allocation of a mandate.

Successful candidates should be installed in office and allowed to take up the authority of their position without undue delay. They are entitled to stay in office for the valid term of the mandate, and no attempts should be made to disqualify or remove them from elected office, except using grounds provided for in law and which meet international standards.

International Standards	Examples of Best Practice
Genuine elections [81] • There should be independent scrutiny of the results process and access to judicial review or other equivalent process so that electors have confidence that the results reflect the votes cast and the counting of the votes. **Free Expression of Will** [82] • The results of genuine elections should be respected and implemented. • The grounds for the removal of elected office holders should be established by law based on objective and reasonable criteria and incorporating fair procedures.	• Election officials ensure that the results of the counting of votes are aggregated, recorded and transmitted accurately. • All votes are counted and results aggregated promptly. • Detailed results data is provided to candidates or their agents, observers, the media and the general public. • Detailed results, broken down to the polling station level (or counting centre where this is the lowest level), are swiftly and publicly displayed at all levels of the EMB as well as on the internet. • In determining proportions of votes cast, the proportion is calculated from the number of valid votes only. • There are procedures that allow for election results to be challenged in an effective and timely manner. • Courts make rulings on challenges before the final results are certified.

Issues to be Considered by the EU EOM

- Are the procedures for tabulating and publishing results clearly established in advance of the election?

- Is the results process undertaken in a prompt and fully transparent manner? Can the process be fully observed by party/candidate agents and by domestic or international observers?

- Are results published within stipulated timeframes and using appropriate procedures? Are the results announced and published promptly in the media and on the internet? Are the results publicly posted at every level of the election administration, including at the polling station?

- Does each level of results aggregation include a breakdown of results by polling station or counting centre, to enable an independent audit to be conducted?

- Are there any discrepancies between the counted votes and the published results? Can the EMB account for them?

- Are candidates and political parties able to challenge the validity of election results to a court? Are challenges dealt with in an impartial manner and decided upon based on available evidence and without political consideration?

- Where results are found to be invalid, under what circumstances are repeat elections held?

- Are elected candidates installed in office?

- Is there any post-election day violence and/or intimidation or fear of this taking place?

- Is there acceptance by election stakeholders of the conduct and results of the election?

---

25. UN HRC General Comment No. 25 paragraph 6.

26. UN HRC General Comment No. 25 paragraph 7.

27. UN HRC General Comment No. 25 paragraph 9.

28. ICCPR Article 2(2) and UN HRC General Comment No. 25 paragraphs 4 and 8.

29. UN HRC General Comment No. 25 paragraph 12.

30. UN HRC General Comment No. 25 paragraph 8.

31. UN HRC General Comment No. 25 paragraph 21.

32. UN HRC General Comment No. 25 paragraph 21.

33. CEDAW Article 4(1).

34. See Electoral System Design: The New International IDEA Handbook (2005) at http://www.idea.int/publications/esd/index.cfm

35. In many countries the EMB is known as the election commission.

36. UN HRC General Comment No. 25 paragraph 20.

37. UN HRC General Comment No. 25 paragraph 11.

38. UN HRC General Comment No. 25 paragraphs 4, 10, 11, 13.

39. ICCPR Articles 2 and 3. See also ICERD Article 5 and CEDAW Article 7.

40. UN HRC General Comment No. 25 paragraphs 4, 10, 11, 13.

41. UN HRC General Comment No. 25 paragraph 21.

42. UN HRC General Comment No. 25 paragraph 25 and ICCPR Article 22.

43. ICCPR Arts 2 and 3; ICERD Article 5; CEDAW Articles 4 and 7; and UN HRC General Comment No 25 paragraph 20.

44. ICCPR Article 21 and UN HRC General Comment No. 25 paragraph 25.

45. UN HRC General Comment No. 25 paragraphs 19 and 25.

46. A Joint Declaration by the UN Special Rapporteur on Freedom of Opinion and Expression, the OSCE Representative on Freedom of the Media, the OAS Special Rapporteur on Freedom of Expression, and the ACHPR Special Rapporteur on Freedom of Expression, in December 2006 stresses that "states have an obligation to take effective measures to prevent such illegal attempts to limit the right to freedom of expression", i.e., violence against journalists in any form.

47. ICCPR Article 19(2) and (3) and UN HRC General Comment No. 25 paragraph 25.

48. ICCPR Article 2(3)(a) and (c).

49. ICCPR Article 14(1) and UN HRC General Comment No. 25 paragraphs 11 and 20.

50. UN HRC General Comment No. 25 paragraph 20.

51. UN HRC General Comment No. 25 paragraph 11.

52. ICCPR Article 9(1).

53. ICCPR Articles 9(3) and 9(4).

54. ICCPR Article 25.

55. ICCPR Articles 12, 19, 21 and 22.

56. ICCPR Articles 2 and 3.

57. ICCPR Article 9.

58. ICCPR Article 14.

59. ICCPR Article 2(1).

60. ICCPR Article 25.

61. ICCPR Article 26.

62. A more comprehensive overview of issues that affect women's participation can be found in the UN handbook Women and Elections, Guide to Promoting the Participation of Women in Elections, http://www.un.org/womenwatch/osagi/wps/womenandelections.html See also OSCE/ODIHR's publication Handbook for Monitoring Women's Participation in Elections.

63. ICCPR Article 3.

64. CEDAW Preamble.

65. CEDAW Article 7.

66. CEDAW Committee's General Comment No. 23.

67. ICERD Article 5.

68. ICCPR Article 27.

69. UN HRC General Comment No. 25 paragraph 12.

70. UN HRC General Comment No. 25 paragraph 21.

71. CRPD Article 29. The Convention, adopted in December 2006, was not in force at the time of print. For information on issues related to disabilities, see also the Bill of Electoral Rights for People with Disabilities, developed by IFES, IDEA and disability organisations. This can be found at http://www.idea.int/elections/uni_rights_02.cfm

72. UN HRC General Comment No. 25 paragraph 11. Also ICERD General Recommendation No. 22, paragraph 2(d) on refugees and displaced persons, which stipulates that all "refugees and displaced persons have, after their return to their homes of origin, the right to participate fully and equally in public affairs at all levels." This provision, however, only relates to refugees and displaced persons after their return to their homes. http://www.unhchr.ch/tbs/doc.nsf/(Symbol)/fed5109c180658d58025651e004e3744?Opendocument
In addition, see UN Guiding Principles on Internal Displacement, principle 22, which reiterates that IDPs shall not be discriminated against as a result of their displacement in the enjoyment of the right to vote and to participate in governmental and public affairs. http://www.unhchr.ch/html/menu2/7/b/principles_lang.htm

The International Organization on Migration (IOM) has produced a best practices document: Enfranchising Conflict Forced Migrants: Issues, Standards and Best Practices (September 2003) http://www.geneseo.edu/~iompress/?pg=press_pep_outputs.html

73. UN HRC General Comment No. 25 paragraphs 8 and 20.
74. UN HRC General Comment No. 25 paragraphs 12 and 20.
75. UN HRC General Comment No. 25 paragraph 20.
76. UN HRC General Comment No. 25 paragraph 12.
77. UN HRC General Comment No. 25 paragraph 19.
78. UN HRC General Comment No. 25 paragraph 20.
79. UN HRC General Comment No. 25 paragraphs 12, 19, 20.
80. UN HRC General Comment No. 25 paragraph 20.
81. UN HRC General Comment No. 25 paragraph 20.
82. UN HRC General Comment No. 25 paragraph 19.

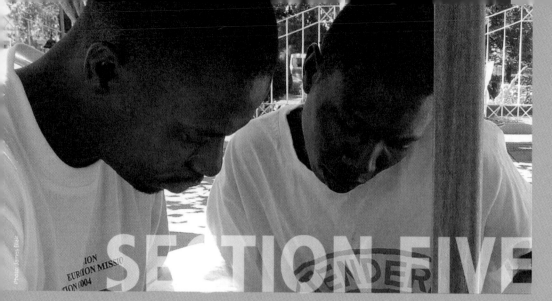

5. Establishing an EU Election Observation Mission

5.1 Deciding whether to Observe an Election

The European Commission Communication on Election Observation and Assistance of 2000 established a consistent approach for the programming of election observation by the EU. The decision on whether or not to deploy an EU EOM is made by the Commissioner for External Relations, who considers the recommendations of an exploratory mission. A decision to deploy an EU EOM does not mean that the European Commission deems an election process to be either problematic or credible. Likewise a decision not to deploy an EU EOM does not mean that a prior judgement on the electoral process has been made or that the EU has no interest in the conduct or in the outcome of the election.

5.1.1 Identification of Priority Countries
The first stage of the process leading to the decision on whether an EU EOM will be deployed is the identification of potential countries for election observation. A rolling calendar of upcoming elections is maintained by DG External Relations. In consultation with relevant Directorates in DG External Relations, DG EuropeAid and DG Development, a list is produced of countries where election observation should be considered. Discussions then take place in Council Working Groups and with the European Parliament Election Coordination Group before the list is confirmed, with countries placed in two categories, priority countries and countries 'to be followed'.

In most instances, the EU has chosen to prioritise countries holding presidential or parliamentary elections, although countries holding local elections and referendums can also be prioritised, especially where they are part of a post-conflict peace initiative, or are considered to be a particularly important indicator of democratic development. Local elections and referendums may also be observed, if they coincide with another election that is being observed by an EU EOM. Countries are categorised as 'priority' based on a range of factors, which include:

- constructive engagement through an EU EOM could result in an improved election, for example, by increasing voter confidence in the process;
- deployment of an EU EOM would complement and enhance EU democratisation and/or crisis management and peace-building initiatives in the country;
- the presence of an EU EOM would demonstrate EU support for an important political process or democratic transition;
- a geographical balance is maintained among the countries where EU EOMs are deployed.

The selection of priority countries is also necessary to make best use of the human and financial resources available for observation missions. EU EOMs are financed from the European Instrument for Democracy and Human Rights (EIDHR), a funding mechanism for the global promotion of democracy and human rights. EIDHR-funded projects are independent from the authorities of the host country.

5.1.2 *The Exploratory Mission*
Once a country is identified as a priority, the second stage in the process is the deployment of an exploratory mission to advise whether deployment of an EU EOM would be *useful*, *feasible* and *advisable*. Questions considered by the exploratory mission include:

Useful?	
	• Would the presence of an EU EOM be a constructive contribution to the electoral process?
	• Would the presence of an EU EOM contribute to deterring fraud and election-related violence?
	• Would the presence of an EU EOM support the role of civil society in the election process?
	• Would the presence of an EU EOM contribute to stakeholder confidence to participate in the election process?

Feasible?	• Can suitable logistical arrangements be made to enable an EU EOM to undertake credible election observation?
	• Is there a potentially suitable implementing partner?
	• Do security conditions provide for the safe deployment of EU observers? Can acceptable security arrangements be put in place?
	• Is it likely that the EU will receive a written invitation to observe from the host country's authorities?
	• Is it likely that the state and electoral authorities will each agree to sign a separate memorandum of understanding (MoU) with the European Commission in advance of deployment?
	• Does a preliminary assessment (of the electoral framework, the pre-election preparations, the political atmosphere and the wider democratic environment) indicate the possibility of a credible election process?
Advisable?	• Do minimum conditions for effective and credible election observation exist (see Section *5.1.3 Minimum Conditions for Effective and Credible Election Observation*)?
	• Can an EU EOM be deployed without taking any unnecessary risks and while maintaining a duty of care to EU observers?
	• Is there interest and support from election stakeholders, including the host authorities, political parties and civil society, as well as EU Member States and the wider international community, in the deployment of an EU EOM?
	• Will a critical assessment of the electoral process create political problems?
	• Is there a likelihood that final report recommendations produced by an EU EOM will be considered and implemented before the next election?

The exploratory mission is normally conducted between six and four months in advance of the scheduled election date, and usually lasts for around two weeks. It is composed of between five and nine persons, including European Commission officials, external experts on elections, security and logistics, and up to two seconded experts from Member States. The mission is led by the DG External Relations election team representative. In order to gather information and identify issues that are likely to affect the election process, members of the exploratory mission meet with a wide range of interlocutors, including the state and electoral authorities, election stakeholders (political actors, civil society, media) and representatives of EU Member States and wider international organisations. The assessment of the election framework and political environment by the exploratory mission uses the methodology detailed in Section Four.

As part of its duties, the exploratory mission also meets with relevant interlocutors (including government agencies, security advisers, health specialists, international organisations and communication and transport providers) to identify whether there are suitable logistical and security conditions for the deployment of an EU EOM. In addition, the exploratory mission will seek to prepare an indicative budget and identify a potential implementing partner (IP), that will be responsible for delivering the administrative aspects of the EU EOM.

The exploratory mission produces an internal report of its findings, based on which it makes a recommendation as to whether the deployment of an EU EOM is useful, feasible and advisable. The report provides an assessment of the election framework and environment and considers preparations that have been undertaken to date. The report can also include recommendations to improve the framework and conditions for elections that can be undertaken in advance of election day. It also outlines the scope and scale of a prospective EU EOM, including the size of core team, number of observers, deployment timing, accreditation procedures and logistical requirements. The report also provides an initial security risk assessment, proposed security measures and assesses whether or not minimum conditions for credible election observation are present. On the basis of the report a recommendation is sent by the Director General of DG External Relations to the Commissioner for External Relations, who after considering the report and its recommendation decides whether an EU EOM should be deployed. The European Commission then shares the exploratory mission report with the Council, Member States and the European Parliament.

5.1.3 Minimum Conditions for Effective and Credible Election Observation

An EU EOM requires certain minimum conditions to allow it to undertake effective and credible election observation.[83] These conditions are usually contained in the memorandums of understanding signed with the host country authorities. Conditions include:

- the host country's authorities have issued a written invitation sufficiently in advance of the election to allow an assessment to be made about whether the deployment of an EU EOM would be useful, feasible and advisable;

- EU observers will be guaranteed unimpeded access to all stages of the election process and will have full access to electoral information in a timely manner;
- EU observers will be guaranteed unimpeded access to all persons concerned with the electoral process, including:
  - electoral officials at all levels;
  - state workers, including security officials, whose functions are relevant to the organisation of elections;
  - all political parties and individuals that have sought to compete in the elections, as well as any who were disqualified, withdrew or abstained;
  - civil society representatives;
  - media personnel;
  - any other organisations and individuals that are interested or have a role to play in the election process;
- EU observers will be guaranteed freedom of movement around the country and will not be required to provide unreasonable prior notification;
- EU observers and EU EOM national staff will be provided with accreditation in a timely manner;
- the host authorities will not interfere in EU decisions relating to the size of the EU EOM, selection of EU observers and national staff, or timeframe of deployment;
- government, security or electoral authorities will not interfere in the activities of the EU EOM;
- the security situation is sufficiently stable for EU observers to be deployed and, if required, acceptable security arrangements can be put in place by the state and regional authorities;
- the EU EOM will be guaranteed the freedom to issue, without interference, public statements and reports on its assessment of the election process; and
- the state or any electoral authorities will not pressure, threaten action against or make any reprisal against national or foreign citizen who works for, assists or provides information to the EU EOM.

The absence of any of these conditions may lead to an EU EOM not being deployed. A mission can be withdrawn after deployment, if problems with these conditions arise or if a mission no longer considered useful, feasible and advisable.

5.2 Planning and Preparation for an Election Observation Mission

5.2.1 Memorandums of Understanding

Following a decision to deploy an EU EOM, the European Commission seeks to sign memorandums of understanding (MoU) with the state and electoral authorities of the host country (see Section *3.6 Cooperation with the Host Country*). The memorandums set out the role and responsibilities of the EU EOM and EU observers and the corresponding role and responsibilities of the host country authorities. Separate memorandums are agreed with the Ministry of Foreign Affairs of the host country, and the Election Management Body. An EU EOM is unlikely to be deployed before the MoUs are signed. When appropriate, for ex-ample for security reasons, special agreements such as an MoU may also be negotiated with the UN.

5.2.2 Terms of Reference

Based on the report of the exploratory mission, the European Commission prepares terms of reference which provide the basis for the structure of the EU EOM. These detail the timeframe of the mission, provisional deployment plans, the composition and tasks of the EU EOM core team, the number of observers, and the budget. An implementing partner (IP) will be contracted to provide the administrative and logistical services that are required to ensure the implementation of the EU EOM. For details on the IP terms of reference, see Section *5.3.1 The Role of the Implementing Partner or Service Provider.*

5.2.3 Appointment of a Chief Observer

The Commissioner for External Relations appoints a chief observer (CO) to lead the EU EOM. The CO is a Member of the European Parliament. There will be regular communication between the Commissioner and the CO before, during and after the mission.

5.2.4 Selection of Observers

After the decision to deploy an EU EOM, the European Commission commences selection of core team members and long- and short-term observers (LTOs and STOs). In order to be considered for selection, a candidate should be registered on the Election Observer Roster, managed by DG EuropeAid (AIDCO) at the European Commission.[84]

Criteria for EU Observers[85]

Observers participating in EU EOMs are expected to fulfill the following criteria:

- previous experience as an election observer and/or relevant experience or specific training (at national or international level);
- professional capacity in particular mission working languages wich can be English, French, Portuguese or Spanish;
- interpersonal skills (capacity for balanced judgement, ability to work in teams, ability to cope with difficult situations, respect for local attitudes and customs, good communication skills, readiness to work in a multi-cultural environment);
- ability to maintain professional independence and strict impartiality in the conduct of duties in the host country;
- ability to work with computers, internet and technological equipment (including satellite phones, radios, etc.);
- commitment to the support and promotion of democratic governance and human rights; and
- EU Member State citizenship.

All EU EOMs should also ensure, as much as possible, a gender and nationality balance.

The following additional criteria are taken into account when selecting core team members and LTOs:

- familiarity and experience with electoral laws and procedures (including experience with administrative and legislative procedures for elections), preferably in different electoral traditions;
- knowledge of human rights and democratisation issues;
- basic knowledge of EU institutions;
- analytical and drafting skills;
- participation in and successful completion of training seminars;
- appraisal(s) from previous missions and training courses included on the roster; and
- experience of training, co-ordination and people management where relevant for management postitions.

Specific requirements for all EU observers can include:

- ability to communicate fully in the working language/s of the mission;
- knowledge of the host country or region and/or the political situation;
- knowledge of relevant languages in the host country;
- experience of challenging working and living conditions;

- good physical condition; and
- previous security training and experience of diffucult security environments.

Selection Procedures

Candidates for core team positions apply directly to the European Commission. A call for applications is issued on the European Commission website.[86] Candidates may apply for up to two positions, and should sign a statement that confirms their availability for the duration of the EU EOM as indicated on the website. LTOs and STOs are nominated by each Member State's Ministry of Foreign Affairs, following a request from the Commission. Persons interested in discovering more on how to apply to be an EU observer should contact the focal point in their Ministry of Foreign Affairs.[87] A list of candidates is submitted by Member States to the Commission's selection committee. LTOs are generally expected to be available for approximately two months and STOs for up to fourteen days.

The working language of an EU EOM will be decided by the Commission, and could be English, French, Portuguese or Spanish, depending on the particular circumstances of the country being observed. All members of the EU EOM will need to be able to communicate professionally in the working language of the mission. Core team members will also need to be fluent in English and/or French as these are the languages in which EU EOM reports are produced.

Selection Committee

A selection committee consisting of representatives from the election teams of DG External Relations and DG EuropeAid, as well as the country geographical desk will select the core team, LTOs and STOs. Candidates are considered on the basis of their roster CV and the criteria for observers. The selection committee seeks to achieve a balance between nationalities, gender, age and experience of observers. Candidates for core team positions are informed directly whether or not they have been selected. LTOs and STOs are informed through their focal points whether they have been selected, placed on a reserve list or not selected.

Appraisal of Observers

All EU observers are appraised at the end of their work with the EU EOM, using criteria established by the European Commission. The deputy chief observer (DCO) and the observer coordinator will oversee the appraisal of LTOs and STOs, and this is then included in the Election Observer Roster. The core team is appraised by the CO, DCO, and European Commission election teams.

The appraisal system is intended to check the performance of observers. It should identify recommended observers, those that need more skills development, as well as those who are inappropriate for such mission work. In exceptional circumstances observers can be identified as highly recommended. Appraisals also provide feedback to observers and enable the European Commission to plan skills development activities. Criteria considered include:

- knowledge and understanding of elections, and the role of an EU EOM;
- ability to collect and analyse information;
- ability to write and communicate clearly in the mission working language/s; and
- ability to work in a team, to adhere to instructions and to behave in an appropriate manner.

5.2.5 Mission Structure

The structure and size of an EU EOM is based on the recommendation of the exploratory mission, which will propose an appropriate number of core team, LTO and STO positions, in relation to the geographical size of the country, political significance or technical complex-ity of the election process and established criteria for determining field deployment.

Missions typically consist of the folllowing positions:
- Chief observer
- Deputy chief observer
- Election analyst
- Legal analyst
- Political analyst
- Human rights analyst *
- Media analyst
- Press and public outreach officer *
- Observer coordinator
- Statistical analyst *
- Operations expert
- Security expert *

- Long-term observers
- Short-term observers

Positions marked (*) may not always be included in smaller missions. When this is the case, the responsibilites of positions not included will be assigned to other mission members. In larger missions, the core team will be strengthened by deputy analysts, experts and coordinators.

5.2.6 Criteria for Deployment of Observers

Five main criteria are used to determine the locations for the field deployment of LTOs and STOs:

- *Balanced geographical coverage:* observer teams are deployed in a way that provides a balanced coverage of the country given the number of teams being deployed;
- *Population centres:* major urban centres of the country are covered. There is also balance between urban and rural areas;
- *Areas of specific relevance:* this may include post-conflict, minority and IDP areas or other political hot spots;
- *Logistical restrictions:* observer teams may not be deployed to certain regions if there are logistical problems, such as poor transport and communication infrastructure and unsuitable accommodation; and
- *Security restrictions:* observer teams will not be deployed to areas where there are significant security risks or where security risks cannot be reasonably managed.

5.2.7 Overview of EU EOM Programming Timetable

The following table presents an indicative schedule of election observation activities from preparation to follow-up. The schedule is based on a single round election, but it is possible for the deployment period to be extended where there are more rounds, or if extended coverage is required as a result of post-election developments such as electoral appeals. This timetable may need to be adjusted according to circumstance, for example, when elections are called at short notice.

A: Preparatory Stage	
12–6 months prior to election day (E-Day)	*Consultation* between the European Commission, the Council, and the European Parliament on priority countries.
6–4 months prior to E-Day	*Exploratory mission* deployed to the country.
	Decision on deployment by the Commissioner for External Relations.
	Recruitment for the mission begins. Core team positions advertised. The European Commission informs Member States of the planned EU EOM and invites nominations of candidates for LTO and STO positions.
	Chief observer appointed by the Commissioner for External Relations.
2.5 months prior to E-Day	*Observers* selected by the European Commission.
	Implementing partner contracted.
	Memorandums of understanding signed between the state and electoral authorities of the host country and the European Commission.

B: Deployment Stage	
8-6 weeks prior to E-Day	*Announcement of EU EOM deployment by* the Commissioner for External Relations.
	Chief observer and core team arrive in country after a briefing from the European Commission and hold initial meetings.
	Press conference is held in the host country to formally announce the opening of the mission.
5 weeks prior to E-Day	*Long-term observers arrive* in country. They attend a briefing before being deployed in pairs to regional locations.
	Observation of pre-election day environment, including election administration, candidate registration, voter registration, campaign activities, the media and complaints.
7 days prior to E-Day	*Short-term observers arrive* in country. They attend a two-day briefing before being deployed in pairs to regional locations.
E-Day	*Observation of voting, counting and tabulation* by EU observers, usually including locally-recruited diplomats from EU Member States, and a delegation of Members of the European Parliament.
1–3 days after E-Day	*Preliminary statement* issued.
	Observation of the post-election environment, including tabulation of results and complaints.
3–6 days after E-Day	*Debriefing of short-term observers* and return to Europe.
10–15 days after E-Day	*Debriefing of long-term observers* and return to Europe.
2–4 weeks after E-Day (or the publication of final results, whichever is later)	*Closedown* of the mission. *Core team departs.*
3–8 weeks after E-Day	*Debriefing of core team* by the European Commission in Brussels.

C: Final Report Stage and Follow-Up	
Up to 2 months after completion of electoral process	*Final report* is presented in country by the chief observer, usually accompanied by the deputy chief observer. Organisation of a round-table in the host country to discuss the report, in particular *recommendations for the future*.
3 months after conclusion of electoral process onwards	*Follow-up technical advice and assistance* may be provided by the European Commission, taking account of EU EOM recommendations.

5.3 Deploying an EU Election Observation Mission

5.3.1 The Role of the Implementing Partner or Service Provider

Logistical and administrative support for an EU EOM is provided by an implementing partner (IP) or a service provider. This is an organisation that acts on behalf of the European Commission and takes responsibility for the administrative and financial implementation of an EU EOM. The agency is referred to as an implementing partner when it is an international agency, such as the International Organisation for Migration (IOM) or the United Nations Development Programme (UNDP), and as a service provider when it is a non-governmental organisation or a private company. In this handbook, the term IP is used synonymously for either an implementing partner or a service provider.

The IP acts on the basis of terms of reference prepared by the European Commission (EuropeAid). This includes:

- issuing contracts/letters of assignment and making payments to core team members and LTO/STOs;
- making travel arrangements including flights, visas and insurance (medical, accident and evacuation);
- providing advance practical information on the country of deployment;
- arranging initial accommodation;
- providing security information, equipment and related services;
- contracting and paying of national staff;
- arranging local transportation, including vehicle rental, airport transfers and/or internal flights;
- renting EU EOM headquarters, room bookings for briefings, press conferences, etc.;
- procuring computer and communication equipment, including internet service and office supplies;
- providing visibility material;
- developing and maintaining the EU EOM website;
- managing the EU EOM budget; and
- reporting on their activities to the European Commission.

The role of the IP is critical, especially given the tight and inflexible timetable of an EU EOM. The IP should work to the highest professional standards. In country, it is represented by a project manager and a team of support staff, including accountants and IT specialists. The IP also has a Europe-based task manager. The EU EOM operations and security experts work closely with the IP project manager to ensure that all logistical and administrative needs of the EU EOM are met.

STO travel in Democratic Republic of Congo, 2006.

Given that the role of the IP is primarily about operational and financial matters, it should not have any public profile or be involved in any decision-making on issues related to the assessment of the electoral process. Any logistical matters relating to the IP, which may have a political or security dimension, should be discussed with the CO or the DCO. Any conflicting opinion on these matters should be taken to the Commission for a final decision.

5.3.2 Mission Opening, Start-Up and Closure

The IP will arrange suitable office space for the EU EOM headquarters two weeks ahead of the arrival of the core team to allow the work of observers to start immediately. The EU EOM headquarters should be in a convenient location, which is secure and does not have any political connections. The EU EOM may also have sub-offices in other key locations. LTO teams are not provided with specific office space but are expected to work from their accommodation. All EU observers are provided with hotel accommodation upon arrival. Dependent on the situation, core team members and LTOs may be permitted to rent accommodation privately.

All local transport will be arranged by the IP, and vehicles will be hired in advance for the core team and each LTO and STO team. All vehicles should be in good working condition, fully insured, fitted with seatbelts front and back, and suitable for the terrain and distances to be covered. While safety must remain the priority at all times, to promote a positive public profile, the use of luxury vehicles will be avoided wherever possible. Where air travel is necessary, the safety record of the airline and aircraft must be considered.

The CVs of suitable national support staff will be identified by the IP ahead of the core team arrival. The IP will also arrange accreditation for all EU observers and national support staff with the relevant bodies. EU observers are provided with visibility material bearing the EU logo and the name of the mission. This includes clothing, business cards, bags and vehicle identification material. These items will comply with EU guidelines on visibility materials and will, wherever possible, be locally sourced.[88]

The EU EOM headquarters will be supplied with all necessary office equipment (computers, printers, photocopiers etc.), communications facilities and media monitoring equipment. LTO teams will be supplied with computers, printers and basic office supplies. Observers will be provided with the appropriate communication equipment, including mobile telephones, internet access and a mission e-mail address. Where necessary, the core team and observers will be provided with satellite telephones and/or radio equipment. In such cases, training in their use will also be provided.

In consultation with the media analyst, the IP will supply the equipment for the EU EOM's media monitoring unit. This includes television sets, recording equipment, cables, videotapes or DVDs, headphones, stopwatches, rulers, computers, radios and required software.

The EU EOM usually closes some three weeks after election day, unless for example there is a delay in the publication of final results or in the resolution of complaints and appeals. Points of concern in the post-election period, such as violence and intimidation, may result in some of the core team and a selection of LTOs remaining in-country for an extended period of time. Where a series of elections takes place over a short period of time, the EU EOM may remain in-country for the duration.

Before the closure of an EU EOM, the CO and the DCO will undertake a series of farewell meetings with interlocutors. A final debriefing will be provided for local EU representatives. The DCO and the operations expert are responsible for the archiving of reports and other work produced by the EU EOM. All observers are individually appraised and are required to complete an evaluation on the functioning of the mission, including the performance of the core team and IP.

5.4 Mission Security

Security is the priority on all EU EOMs. The EU often observes elections in regions and countries where there may be an increased security risk. This can be due to conflict, terrorism, criminal activity, kidnapping, natural disasters and disease. Other risks include election-related violence and transportation dangers. An EU EOM may also face risk of theft of its property or illegal interference in its work. Maintaining a duty of care to observers is paramount and is a critical factor in the decision of the Commissioner for External Relations on whether or not to deploy a mission. All EU observers have a responsibility for their own personal safety and the safety of their colleagues.

5.4.1 Risk Assessment

An initial assessment of the risks is undertaken by the exploratory mission, which identifies the potential impact of security problems on election observation. The EU EOM terms of reference establish a framework for the security of the mission that seeks to prevent, alleviate or manage risks, for example, through the provision of security equipment or protection.

An ongoing assessment of security risks to the EU EOM will be made by the core team in consultation with the European Commission (EC Delegation, DG EuropeAid and DG External Relations). The security expert will liaise with national security agencies and relevant international presences in the country, such as the United Nations (including its Department of Safety and Security) and embassies of EU Member States, to design appropriate security procedures. The security expert provides regular internal risk assessment reports to track developments, such as election-related violence, which may impact on the security of EU observers. For this reason, all EU observers are required to provide the security expert with regular security information relating to their area of responsibility.

5.4.2 Security Planning and Procedures

Based on the risk assessment, the security expert designs a security plan for the EU EOM, including security procedures and an evacuation plan. Generally, the EU EOM incorporates the standard security procedures used by other international agencies in the host country as its Minimum Operational Security Standards (MOSS). This covers matters such as communications, protection by security personnel, accommodation and transport. The security expert establishes a security operations room and a warden system to ensure coordination on security issues.

All EU observers are required to implement the security planning and procedures in their area of responsibility. All mission members are briefed and/or trained by the security expert on security procedures upon their arrival. The IP will also contribute to the briefing on security, in particular relating to the use of equipment. All mission members are expected to report regularly on their security situation.

In cases where there is significant risk, the EU EOM may require the use of armed escorts or decide to limit its areas of coverage. Where the coverage by an EU EOM is restricted, this will be stated in mission statements and reports. In cases of escalating risk towards EU observers, a partial or full evacuation may take place.

5.4.3 Security Responsibilities

The CO has responsibility for security matters in coordination with the IP and the European Commission. This responsibility is carried out in consultation with the DCO and the security expert. The European Commission election desks will be kept informed on security conditions and arrangements. Senior European Commission officials will be available at any time throughout the mission and should be fully consulted on all significant security related decisions. If at any time there is disagreement on security, the matter will be referred to senior European Commission officials in Brussels, to be resolved in consultation with all concerned parties.

The security expert advises the CO on security issues, including risk assessment and appropriate responses. The DCO advises on the impact of security risks on the political, methodological and operational aspects of the EU EOM. The security and operations experts and the IP ensure that security requirements are accommodated in logistical planning. Implementation of security procedures is overseen by the security expert. There is close coordination on security issues between the EU EOM and the IP, especially where the IP is an international agency operating under UN security regulations.

The obligation of all EU observers to strictly follow security instructions issued by the core team is part of the code of conduct for EU observers, and must be adhered to at all times. Guidelines and advice on personal security are developed for each EU EOM to reflect specific risks in the host country. It is the responsibility of all EU observers to follow these guidelines in order to minimise risk to themselves and their colleagues. Personal security requires common sense and precautionary behaviour. EU observers are required to act in an appropriate and discreet manner at all times, including when not working. Local customs and rules should be respected.

When deployed, EU observers should carry at all times their passport, EU EOM identification card, host country accreditation documents (issued by the EMB), mobile phone (with emergency contact numbers), and any other documentation stipulated by the EU EOM or IP.

In general, the highest security risk for election observers comes from travelling by road, especially as road conditions in many countries observed may be poor. Travel guidelines will be provided. These will require EU observers to use only authorised vehicles and will prohibit observers from driving a vehicle, except in an emergency. EU EOM drivers are obliged to drive safely, and seatbelts must be worn at all times by all persons in the vehicle. EU observers and national support staff will wear visibility materials (jackets, caps, etc.), and EU EOM vehicles will also be marked to ensure that they are identifiable, unless such visibility could increase the security risk. In general, EU EOM vehicles will not be permitted to travel at night outside urban areas, although exceptions are likely to be possible over the election day period.

Prior to deployment, the Commission and the IP informs EU observers of relevant medical issues in the host country and advance precautions that should be taken, including vaccinations. In addition, the IP provides medical kits, and makes arrangements for medical insurance and evacuation. EU observers should be in good health and physical condition, as they may undertake relatively strenuous tasks in often difficult conditions. EU observers who require specific medication should ensure they have sufficient quantity to cover the full deployment period plus extra to allow for loss or damage. The security expert should be informed of such requrements in advance of arrival.

5.5 Managing an Election Observation Mission

5.5.1 Relations with the Host Country

The EU EOM will establish working relations with the state authorities of the host country. Upon arrival, the CO will hold introductory meetings with the Ministry of Foreign Affairs and the EMB, bodies with which the European Commission has agreed memorandums of understanding. At these meetings, the CO will introduce the mandate and role of the EU EOM and will establish points of contact. Introductory meetings may also be held with the Head of State, the Head of Government, other representatives of the state authorities and the Speaker of Parliament. Further, introductory meetings will be held with the main political parties and may also be held with key candidates and other relevant election stakeholders. All introductory meetings are organised in advance of the arrival of the EU EOM by the Delegation of the European Commission, in consultation with the DG External Relations election team.

The EU EOM will meet regularly with the EMB and other interlocutors, such as political parties, candidates, the judiciary, civil society and the media (see Section *6.3 Meetings with Interlocutors*). In addition, further meetings will be with state authorities to discuss issues relating to the assessment and operational work of the mission. These meetings, coordinated by the DCO, may include:

- *Ministry of Foreign Affairs,* to ensure relevant accreditation and visa arrangements are made for EU observers, as well as to obtain information on issues such as voting by expatriate citizens;
- *Ministry of Justice,* to obtain information on the legislative framework, complaints and appeals processes, registration of political parties and other legislative issues;
- *Ministry of Interior* and *policing bodies,* to exchange security information relevant to ensuring the safety of EU observers. Additionally, information is gathered on the structure of the security forces and their role during the election process, as well as arrangements for voting in prisons and by security personnel;
- *Ministry of Defence,* to obtain information on voting by members of the armed forces;

- *the Ombudsman and/or National Human Rights Commission,* to obtain information on issues such as freedom of movement, expression, association and assembly, and discrimination against women and minorities;
- *state media supervisory bodies* to assess activities relating to media regulation, monitoring and enforcement.

5.5.2 Coordination with the Delegation of the European Commission and Resident Diplomatic Representatives

The CO and the DCO will meet frequently with the Head of the European Commission Delegation, the EU Presidency, and other EU Heads of Mission. The CO, accompanied by the DCO, provides regular diplomatic briefings to EU Heads of Mission outlining EOM methodology, activities and developing assessment. Such meetings provide an opportunity for the EU EOM and the other EU structures present in country to have close dialogue on the electoral process and to share relevant information. However, at all times the EU EOM retains political independence in its findings and conclusions. These briefings also enable the EU EOM to inform EU Member State embassies of procedures for the potential recruitment of a limited number of diplomatic staff for participation as locally-recruited STOs. The CO and the DCO will also meet with diplomatic representatives of non-EU countries and international organisations.

5.5.3 Coordination with other International Observer Delegations

The 2000 European Commission Communication on Election Assistance and Observation, and the 2005 *Declaration of Principles for International Election Observation* commit EU EOMs to cooperate and coordinate with other international observer groups. Such an approach can help to find common positions on the electoral process and maximise the contribution of international election observation to the host country. In addition, coordination with other observer groups should aim to maximise the coverage and impact of international observation. Cooperation can include the sharing of information, e.g., the election process, observation findings, and on security, and the holding of joint meetings with interlocutors. The EU EOM will ensure that such cooperation does not compromise its independence, and will base its conclusions on the findings of its own observers. In light of this, joint statements should in principle not be sought. Relations with other international observer groups are co-ordinated by the DCO and involve other members of the core team, in particular the observer coordinator and the security expert.

109

5.6 Mission Visibility

An important task of the EU EOM is to raise awareness and understanding of its work, including its mandate and purpose as well as the EU's wider work in support of democracy, the rule of law and human rights. The EU EOM will develop a public outreach and media strategy to build and sustain a positive reputation in-country and internationally. In doing so, it shall take steps to:

- encourage a positive attitude towards democratic processes;
- promote understanding of the important and constructive role that can be played by election observers, both national and international;
- explain the EU EOM's mandate, referring to the principles of neutrality and impartiality, as well as the duration and composition of the mission;
- provide information on EU election observation and assessment methodology;
- ensure that any public statements on the conduct of the election process are widely distributed to media outlets and other interested parties; and
- maximise visibility and transparency of the mission's work in-country and internationally.

5.6.1 Media Relations

The work of EU observers often attracts considerable national and international attention. The EU EOM media strategy should respond to this with a view to maximising the positive impact of the mission. The CO acts as the principal spokesperson of the EU EOM, and works closely with the DCO and the press and public outreach officer in developing media relations. Only the CO and DCO are mandated to speak about the conduct of the electoral process. Other EU EOM members may only speak about the mandate, structure and activities of the mission (see Section *5.6.3 Dealing with the Media*).

Opening Press Release and Press Conference

The Commissioner for External Relations will issue a press release announcing the deployment of the EU EOM. Subsequently, upon arrival the EU EOM will issue a press release to announce its formal opening. This will explain that the mission has been invited by the host country authorities to observe the election process, and emphasise the independence of the EU EOM from EU institutions, in particular its separate mandate from the Delegation of the European Commission and embassies of EU Member States. It will provide information on the composition and duration of the EU EOM as well as contact details. The press release will be sent to the elections team at DG External Relations for comment before being translated (if required), and then distributed to national and international media including press agencies.

The press release is issued at a press conference, which announces the formal opening of the EU EOM. A press advisory notice to inform the resident media of the timing and location of the press conference will be issued by the EU EOM. This will normally take place shortly after the arrival in country of the CO, and will be organised after the mission has held courtesy introductory meetings with key electoral actors. The CO will outline the information contained in the opening press release together with additional relevant information, related to the role and mandate especially the principle of non-interference in the electoral process, before answering questions.

Media Interviews, Briefings and Events
Throughout the duration of the EU EOM, there will be further opportunities for media coverage. The CO is encouraged to give interviews and to hold media briefings with journalists. The EU EOM will also issue further press releases related to mission activities. The EU EOM will invite journalists to cover mission events, including deployment of LTOs and STOs, CO activities, field trips and visits to polling stations on election day. In addition, media outlets may be invited to meet with LTO and STO teams in their areas of responsibility.

Speaking to the media, Fiji, 2006.

Where press releases are issued in relation to electoral events that may be politically sensitive (for example, if violence occurs during a campaign), care will be taken to ensure that such statements are impartial, responsible and constructive in tone. All EU EOM press releases will be sent to the DG External Relations election desk for comment before being issued.

Post-Election Press Conference to Release Preliminary Statement
A key event for the EU EOM is the release of its preliminary statement shortly after election day (see Section *8.3 Preliminary Statement*). In deciding when to release this statement, the EU EOM should balance the expectation and interest in a prompt assessment with the need for time to produce an accurate and comprehensive analysis

of its preliminary findings. The press conference usually takes place within 48 hours of the close of the polls.

At the press conference, the CO delivers a summary of the preliminary statement, outlining the findings and conclusions of the EU EOM on the conduct of the electoral process, and then answers questions. The CO highlights that the EU EOM is continuing to observe the post-election period and will produce its overall assessment in its final report, issued within two months of the completion of the electoral process. Where a delegation of observers from the European Parliament is also present, the leader of the delegation may also speak at the press conference, after the CO. When necessary, the EU EOM will ensure that professional translation is provided at the press conference. The mission will also issue a press release to accompany the release of the preliminary statement. This will be consistent in content and tone to the preliminary statement and will include quotes from the CO. It may also contain a quote from the leader of the European Parliament delegation. Statements may also be issued by the EU Presidency and the Commissioners for External Relations and/or Development in the post-election day period.

Closing Press Release

The EU EOM issues a press release to announce the closure of the mission and the likely date for release of the final report.

Press Events for the Release of the Final Report

The final report is usually issued within two months of the completion of the entire election process. It is released during a return visit of the CO an DCO to the host country after being presented to the state and electoral authorities and other election stakeholders, including representatives of political parties, civil society and the media. The report is also given to EU Heads of Mission and other representatives of the international community. A press conference will be organised by the Delegation of the European Commission, at wich the CO will present a summary outline and key recommendations of the final report (see Section *8.4 The Final Report*).

5.6.2　*Public Outreach Activities*

In addition to direct contacts with the media, the EU EOM will develop a public outreach strategy that seeks to engage and build relations with electoral stakeholders and to broaden their awareness of the mandate and role of election observation. The public outreach strategy, will be coordinated by the press and public outreach officer, and make use of a variety of mediums and structures, including community radio, and civil society networks. LTOs will be involved in regional public outreach activities.

Meeting the media, Indonesia, 2004.

EU EOM Fact Sheet

Upon arrival, the EU EOM will prepare a fact sheet, providing information on its mandate, role and activities, and background information on the EU. The fact sheet will be professionally printed and translated into all relevant languages. Copies will then be distributed widely through meetings with interlocutors and other public outreach activities.

EU EOM Website

An essential element for public outreach is the EU EOM website. This provides information on the mission, including its composition and contact details. It also contains information on the EU and its observation policy and documentation related to EU observation methodology (including this handbook and the accompanying Compendium of International Standards for Elections). The *Declaration of Principles for International Election Observation* will also be posted on the website. In addition, the website will contain all EU EOM press releases and public reports, and other election-related information. The website design will use a standard template and be maintained by the IP under direction of the EU EOM press and public outreach officer. The website will be used to provide briefing material for EU observers, and will remain available for a period of five years.

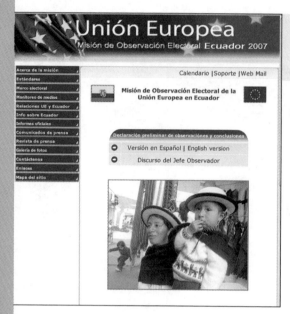

Website of the EU EOM to Ecuador, 2007

5.6.3 Dealing with the Media

Occasions when EU observers are asked by the media for interviews on their work provide important opportunities for transparency and public outreach on the work of the EU EOM. In order to ensure that an accurate and consistent message is given, the EU EOM press and public outreach officer will provide EU observers with guidelines on dealing with the media.

In principle EU observers may speak to the media only with the approval of the CO, and any requests for interviews should be referred to the press and public outreach officer. However, in circumstances where observers are directly approached by journalists, EU observers are permitted to speak on behalf of the EU EOM on the following topics only:

- to express pleasure at being in the host country and to note that the presence of international observers is indicative of the level of international interest in the country's election process;
- to introduce the role and mandate of the EU EOM, specifically the commitment of EU observers to impartiality and non-interference. It should be emphasised that the EU EOM operates in accordance with the *Declaration of Principles for International Election Observation* and its assessment is based on international standards for elections;
- to describe the policy of election observation by the EU as part of its support for democratic development, including in the host country;
- to indicate the duration and coverage of the EU EOM, the number of EU observers and the backgrounds and experience of the individual observers being interviewed; and
- to explain that EU election observation methodology is based on long-term comprehensive observation of all aspects of the election process and involves meeting with a broad range of interlocutors across the country.

If asked for details on the assessment of the electoral process, the observer should emphasise that:

- the preliminary findings and conclusions of the EU EOM will be outlined in a statement issued at a press conference, within three days of the close of polling;
- it would not be appropriate to comment on substance, since observers are seeing only a limited part of the electoral process, which may or may not be reflective of wider trends around the country. For a single observer to comment on his or her own observations might therefore give a distorted impression of the EOM's findings;
- the EU EOM will publish a comprehensive final report within two months of the completion of the electoral process; and
- the CO/DCO may be contacted for further details via the EU EOM press and public outreach officer.

When speaking with the media or indeed any interlocutor, EU observers *should not:*

- offer any kind of assessment of the electoral process;
- express their personal opinion on any aspects of the electoral process;
- make any statement that is, or which could be perceived to be, partisan in nature;
- speculate on any aspect of the electoral process, such as the conduct of election day or the results;
- compare the electoral process of the country being observed with any other country (including their own country, or other countries where they may have observed);
- make any policical comments; and
- make any comments that are critical of the host country.

---

83. Council Decision 9262/98 (Annex III of European Commission Communication 2000).

84. The roster is found at http://ec.europa.eu/europeaid/observer/index_en.htm

85. These draw on EU Guidelines on Common Criteria for the Selection of Election Observers (Council Decision 8728/99) (EC Communication on Election Assistance and Observation Annex IV).

86. http://ec.europa.eu/europeaid/projects/eidhr/elections_observation-request-candidatures_en.htm

87. A list of focal points can be found at http://ec.europa.eu/europeaid/observer/focal_point_list_en.cfm

88. EU Visibility Guidelines for External Actions http://ec.europa.eu/europeaid/visibility/index_en.htm

Photo: Sonia Sal...

SECTION SIX

6. The Roles of EU Observers

6.1 The Core Team

6.1.1 Chief Observer

The EU EOM is led by a chief observer (CO) who is a Member of the European Parliament (MEP), appointed by the Commissioner for External Relations. The CO has overall responsibility for the EU EOM, which is independent in its findings and conclusions. S/he works in close cooperation with the European Commission and other EU institutions. The CO will adhere to guidelines provided by the Commission, which requires that s/he:

- ensures that the EOM abides by the *Declaration of Principles for International Election Observation*, commemorated at the United Nations in October 2005, as well as memorandums of understanding signed with the relevant authorities;
- ensures that the EU EOM carefully follows standard EU methodology and best practice in election observation outlined in this handbook and the accompanying guidelines;
- abides by the code of conduct for EU Observers and the *Code of Conduct for International Election Observers*, contained in the *Declaration of Principles for International Election Observation*, and ensures that core team members and observers are made fully aware of the need to abide by these documents;
- ensures that the EU EOM evaluates the conduct of the electoral process in accordance with international standards for democratic elections;

- ensures that the mission maintains a 'duty of care' towards observers, and takes decisions relating to security jointly with the Commission;
- ensures that the EU EOM's independence in findings and conclusions as well as political neutrality are maintained throughout the deployment of the mission;
- represents the EU EOM in contacts with a broad range of interlocutors, liaises regularly with other credible international observation missions and domestic observer groups, and keeps Member State embassies and the European Commission Delegation informed of the EU EOM's work, findings and conclusions;
- maintains regular contact with the media in order to develop a high profile for the mission on both domestic and international levels;
- ensures that reporting by the EU EOM is of high quality, fully adhering to the guidelines and standard formats provided;
- ensures that all findings and conclusions of the EU EOM are based on carefully verified factual information gathered by the core team and observers; and
- returns to the country to present the final report, containing detailed recommendations for the future, to election stakeholders and the wider public.

As a working MEP, the CO is unlikely to be able to be present for the entire duration of the mission. During a period of absence, the CO retains overall authority, but the DCO is designated with day-to-day management responsibility. The CO should aim to be present in the host country for key electoral and mission events, including the opening of the mission, the briefing and deployment of observers, and the election day period.

6.1.2 Core Team Members

All core team members report to and work under the supervision of the CO and DCO. Specific descriptions of the role and responsibilities of core team members are provided in the EU EOM terms of reference. Prior to deployment, EU EOM core team attend a briefing at the European Commission in Brussels. All core team members contribute to mission reports and briefings for EU observers. The following provides a general description of their work.

Deputy Chief Observer (DCO)

The DCO is the principal political and technical advisor to the CO and deputises for the CO in his or her absence. In coordination with the CO, the DCO has management responsibility for the political, analytical, methodological, operational and security aspects of the EU EOM and for coordinating of the activities of all mission members and the IP. S/he is the focal point for communication with the European Commission, the resident international and diplomatic community, and national stakeholders. In addition, the DCO:

- ensures the EU EOM adheres to the memorandums of understanding agreed with state and electoral authorities;
- ensures the consistent implementation of EU election methodology (as outlined in this handbook and the accompanying Compendium of International Standards for Elections) for assessing and observing an election in accordance with international standards for democratic elections;
- provides day to day guidance and instructions to all members of the core team;
- prepares interim reports, the preliminary statement and the final report based on core team contributions and in accordance with guidelines and templates provided by the Commission, and ensures that reports are produced to the highest professional standards;
- establishes core team and EU EOM procedures, including those for contacting interlocutors, schedules of internal meetings, and produces a mission timetable detailing key events, including reporting deadlines;
- coordinates preparation of observer briefings, materials and forms, as well as operational planning for observer deployment and election day coverage;
- acts as a contact point for other international election observer groups, including an observer delegation from the European Parliament and locally recruited EU observers;
- oversees the observer appraisal process;
- retains regular contact with the CO when s/he is not present in country;
- informs the European Commission about electoral and political developments outside of reporting cycles;
- maintains close contact with the DG External Relations and DG EuropeAid election desks; and
- returns to the host country with the CO for the presentation of the final report.

Election Analyst

The election analyst is responsible for assessing the work of election management bodies, voter registration and the procedures for voting, counting and the tabulation of results. S/he leads the preparation of election day observer report forms. The election analyst may be required to have particular expertise, for example in e-voting or voter registration. Additional analysts may also be brought in to provide further expertise in specialist areas. S/he works in close cooperation with the DCO, the legal analyst and other members of the core team, and draws on reports and anlysis from LTOs and STOs. The election analyst is the focal point for relations with the election management body, other relevant administrative agencies and domestic observer groups.

Legal Analyst

The legal analyst is responsible for assessing the compliance of the legal framework with international standards for democratic elections, the implementation and enforcement of national laws, and the implementation of complaints and appeals procedures. S/he identifies the universal and regional legal and political instruments that are relevant to the host country. S/he is responsible for ensuring that mission members are familiar with the relevant international standards and that these are used by the EU EOM in its assessment. S/he should become fully conversant with host country laws and ensure that all members of the core team and LTOs understand the legal provisions relevant to their areas of assessment. The legal analyst tracks election-related complaints and appeals, maintains a database of election-related complaints, attends court cases when necessary, and provides the CO with legal opinions on relevant issues. S/he ensures that the EU EOM has copies of all relevant legislation and regulations, liaises closely with the DCO, the election analyst and other members of the core team, and analyses the reports from LTOs and STOs. The legal analyst is the focal point for relations with the judiciary and other relevant legal stakeholders.

Political Analyst

The political analyst is responsible for assessing political developments and campaign activities related to the electoral process. In addition, the political analyst provides the EU EOM with background on the politics, culture and history of the host country. The political analyst is responsible for providing a cultural awareness briefing for mission members, taking into consideration any customary, social and/or religious practices that are relevant to the electoral process and election observation. The political analyst tracks any incidents or reports of election-related violence. The political analyst works in close cooperation with the DCO, the election analyst and other members of the core team. S/he is the focal point for relations with political parties, candidates and their campaign teams, as well as for general civil society activity.

Human Rights Analyst

The human rights analyst is responsible for providing analysis and advice on the human rights context and environment in the host country. S/he analyses reports of politically motivated intimidation, arrests, discriminatory practices or human rights violations. The human rights analyst also covers issues related to the participation of women, minorities, disabled persons, and disadvantaged groups in the electoral process. The human rights analyst works closely with other core team members to mainstream human rights issues into the EU EOM's analytical work.

119

This includes close liaison with LTOs on related issues. S/he is the focal point for relations with relevant state institutions and civil society organisations.

Media Analyst

The media analyst is responsible for assessing the role of the media in the electoral process, the legal framework for media coverage, the wider environment for media, and freedom of expression. In particular, the media analyst establishes a media monitoring unit (MMU), to undertake quantitative and qualitative analysis of media coverage of the election. The MMU will consist of national staff who are trained in media monitoring methodology. The media analyst assesses compliance of the media with national laws, tracks media-related complaints, and liaises closely with the election, legal, political and human rights analysts. S/he liaises with long-term observers on regional media activity. The media analyst produces media monitoring data for inclusion in mission reports. The media analyst is the focal point for relations with media bodies, and works closely with the press and public outreach officer, including by monitoring coverage of the EU EOM in the local media.

Press and Public Outreach Officer

The press and public outreach officer is responsible for developing strategies for maximising visibility of the EU EOM through media coverage and public outreach. The press and public outreach officer establishes and maintains contact with the national and international media, and develops a comprehensive media contacts database. S/he organises all press events, identifies events of media interest, and prepares and distributes EU EOM press releases in consultation with the CO, DCO and DG External Relations. S/he is responsible for preparing content for the EU EOM website and, in this regard, will liaise closely with the IP who is responsible for maintaining the website. The press and public outreach officer oversees public outreach activities, including the development of an EU EOM fact sheet. S/he ensures that the mission follows the EU Visibility Guidelines for External Action. The press and public outreach officer will make public or press statements on behalf of the EU EOM only with the specific approval of the CO or DCO.

Observer Coordinator

The observer coordinator is responsible for coordination of long- and short-term observers (LTOs and STOs) and, in particular, the gathering and initial analysis of observer reports from the field. S/he acts as the core team focal point for all LTOs and STOs, tasks and guides observers on their operational and reporting responsibilities, and brings relevant matters to the attention of observers and the core team. Working closely with the DCO and other core team members, the observer coordinator manages the preparation of deployment plans, observer briefings, briefing materials, debriefings and other events. S/he oversees compliance with relevant codes of conduct for election observers and EU election observation methodology. In conjunction with the DCO, conducts the appraisal of observers. The observer coordinator consolidates and analyses observer reports from the field, identifying emerging issues and regional patterns, and shares relevant information with core team members. S/he is the focal point for observer deployment on election day and the return and analysis of observer forms. The observer coordinator will visit LTO teams in the field, as circumstances and work pressures permit. In larger missions, s/he may be supported by, and be responsible for a deputy observer coordinator.

Operations Expert

The operations expert is responsible for all operational aspects of the EU EOM and is the principal point of contact between the mission and the IP. The operations expert advises the IP on the implementation of the administrative and logistical requirements of the EU EOM (national staff recruitment, office space, drivers, vehicles, accommodation, room bookings, equipment, visibility materials, communications, medical kits, observer transportation, etc.). The operations expert works closely with the observer coordinator and security expert on arrangements for the deployment of observers. S/he oversees the work of the IP in the delivery of the logistical requirements and other services, including accreditation of observers and the management of finances, and ensures a smooth start-up and close-down of the EU EOM. In larger missions, s/he may be supported by, and be responsible for, a deputy operations expert.

Security Expert

The security expert advises the CO and the DCO on all security issues and is responsible for on-going security risk assessments, security planning and the implementation of the EU EOM security plan and procedures. The security expert monitors relevant security developments, including election violence, in close coordination with the political analyst. S/he establishes relations with national security structures (i.e., police, military) and international actors, including EU Member State embassies, in order to optain information on the security situation and develop contingency plans for crisis situations, inclu-ding possible evacuations. S/he establishes security reporting and warden systems, provides security clearance for the deployment plan and, where relevant, clearance for observer movement. The security expert works closely with the DCO, operations expert and IP on logistical requirements for security standards (staff, offices, accommodation, and communications equipment), and ensures EU EOM compliance with Minimum Operating Security Standards (MOSS). S/he provides a security briefing for all observers upon arrival. The security expert reports regularly to the CO and the DCO, and produces a regular security assessment report. In larger missions, s/he may be supported by, and be responsible for, a deputy security expert.

Statistical Analyst

The statistical analyst joins the mission shortly before election day to oversee the statistical analysis of observer report forms and management of the statistics team consisting of national staff. In advance of his/her arrival in country, s/he contributes to the preparation of observer forms and the development of an analytical computer programme.

6.2 National Support Staff

6.2.1 Recruitment of National Support Staff

National support staff are an essential part of an EU EOM. The number of positions for national staff is identified in the terms of reference, based on the recommendation of the exploratory mission. Suitable candidates will be identified by the IP for core team members to interview and decide on selection. The IP will then contract those who are chosen. Every reasonable effort should be made to enable national staff to vote on election day. Where there are different official languages spoken in the host country, it will be necessary to ensure that the mission has interpreters able to speak all languages. Consideration should be given to recruiting a gender and ethnic balance of national support staff.

6.2.2 National Staff Roles and Responsibilities

National staff will be briefed by the core team on their role and responsibilities, with particular emphasis on requirements for confidentiality and neutrality and the need for flexibility in terms of working hours. National staff should conduct themselves in a politically impartial and objective manner at all times, regardless of their private political opinion or views on the electoral process. Throughout their employment with the EU EOM, national staff should not be involved in partisan campaign activities or take any action that could cause the mission's impartiality to be questioned.

National staff should adhere to all domestic laws. Their employment contract will respect international labour law standards and provide a wage comparable with those for local staff in international agencies. The contract will also include a confidentiality clause and require the member of staff to give an undertaking that s/he has no conflicts of interest. National staff should be treated with respect and in accordance with their contract. They must have the right to lodge a complaint with the DCO if problems arise about the way in which they are managed.

6.2.3 *National Staff Positions*

Core team assistants/interpreters are responsible for supporting the designated core team member in their functions. Core team assistants/interpreters should have relevant professional experience (e.g., legal training if working with the legal analyst), be able to communicate professionally in the working language of the EU EOM and be able to interpret/translate as necessary. Each assistant/interpreter is managed by a core team member under the supervision of the DCO. All interpreters should be provided with a glossary of election terms translated into the relevant language(s).

Media monitors are responsible for preparing quantitative and qualitative data on the media coverage of the election. They will be trained and managed by the EU EOM media analyst. As well as possessing relevant language skills, they should be familiar with data-processing software, acquainted with the political system and media environment, and have experience in media studies or social research. They should not work as journalists during the election campaign.

LTO assistants/interpreters and *STO assistants/interpreters* are responsible for supporting LTO or STO teams in the field. They should have relevant professional experience, and, where possible, good local knowledge of the area of responsibility. They should be able to communicate effectively in the working language of the EU EOM, and be able to interpret/translate as necessary. Each LTO assistant is managed jointly by the LTO team under the supervision of the operations expert. STO assistants are managed by the STO team under the supervision of the LTO team.

Core team administrative support staff (e.g., receptionist, guards, etc.) should be able to communicate effectively in the working language of the EU EOM and are managed by the IP under instruction of the core team.

Drivers (for the core team, LTO and STO teams) are required to be licensed and prove their competence to drive safely. They should be able to communicate in the working language of the EU EOM and will be issued with driving guidelines which should be adhered to. Core team drivers usually operate from a 'pool', managed by the operations expert under the supervision of the DCO. LTO and STO drivers are managed by the relevant LTO and STO team under the supervision of the operations expert. LTO and STO drivers should be familiar with the area of responsibility.

There may also be a need to hire national staff on a temporary basis for a specific professional tasks such as translation of public reports, interpretation at media events, and provision of expert advice on the domestic legal framework.

6.3 Meetings with Interlocutors

6.3.1 *Guidelines for Meetings*

The EU EOM seeks to engage in dialogue and develop effective working relationships with a broad range of interlocutors. Meetings with interlocutors provide opportunities to obtain information and discuss election-related issues, as well as being a useful public outreach activity. It is important that all EU observers are courteous, considerate and sensitive to local customs. Observers should try to maintain good relations with all interlocutors, including when meeting with negative reactions.

No personal opinions on election-related issues are to be expressed at any time. EU observers should ensure their questions are neutral in tone and should pay particular attention to balance their meetings, engaging with political representatives from government and a broad range of opposition parties. For all meetings, EU observers should:

- be aware of relevant background information;
- prepare questions and discussion points in advance;
- be considerate of interlocutors' time and not obstruct the process of their work;
- avoid leading questions and use open questions where possible;
- ask for specific information (what, where, who, why, when, and how often);
- check the accuracy of information (by confirming their understanding with interviewees, cross-checking with other interlocutors, and by direct observation); and
- allow interlocutors the opportunity to bring up issues, ask questions and follow-up suggested recommendations.

Introductory Meetings

At initial meetings with all interlocutors, EU observers should use the following structure for presenting the EU EOM:

- introduce the EU EOM members present, including national staff, providing names, nationalities, positions, area of coverage, and location base;
- describe the background of the EU EOM, including the duration and size of the mission;
- outline the methodological basis of an EU EOM, which is in accordance with the *Declaration of Principles for International Election Observation*. Emphasise the EU EOM's long-term, countrywide coverage, as well as the independence of the mission and the role of the chief observer;
- explain that the EU EOM has been invited to observe by the host authorities and that EU observers are impartial, will not interfere in the electoral process, and will asses the elections in accordance with international standards for elections as well as in compliance with national legislation;

- explain the process and timing for publication of the mission's reports (the preliminary statement shortly after election day, and a detailed final report including recommendations two months after the completion of the election process);
- provide contact details for those present and for the EU EOM; and
- confirm the names, positions and contact details of each interlocutor (including telephone and e-mail), and confirm interlocutors' availability for future meetings.

6.3.2 Meetings with Public/Government Officials

EU observers will regularly meet regularly with a wide range of public/governmental officials (see Section *5.5.1 Relations with the Host Country*). LTO teams, in particular, will often meet with senior officials from regional or local government to obtain useful information. However, public officials may also have a partisan role to play in the electoral process, and EU observers should clarify whether meetings are held in the interlocutor's official capacity or in their partisan political role.

Possible Issues to Raise in Meetings with Public Officials

- What role and responsibilities does the public official or the office s/he represents have in the electoral process?
- Has the public official identified any problems with the electoral process?
- Does the public official have any concerns about election day?
- What is his/her impression of the election campaign?
- Does the public official perceive any difference between this election and previous elections? If so, what?
- If the public official has any responsibility for security, can the EU EOM count on his/her cooperation in the event that any security issue arises?

It may be necessary at meetings with public officials to raise allegations received, or irregularities observed, by the EU EOM, on areas over which they have responsibility. This may include the misuse of public resources, interference in campaign activities, or particular human rights concerns. The EU EOM should enquire about how the issue will be addressed by the public official, and request to be kept updated by the public official on progress in this regard.

6.3.3 Meetings with the Election Management Body (EMB)

Meetings with the EMB on Electoral Preparations

The EMB is the primary source of much information on the electoral process, such as administrative preparations, candidate registration and procedures for voting, counting, tabulation and publication of results. During their work, the core team, LTOs and STOs will meet frequently with the different hierarchical levels of the EMB. It is important for the EU EOM to meet with a cross-section of the EMB membership where there are party representatives on the EMB, as well as with members of the EMB secretariat. In accordance with the code of conduct for EU Observers, the mission may bring irregularities to the attention of the EMB but may not give instructions or seek to countermand the decisions of the EMB.

The openness of the EMB in its relationship with the EU EOM can be a useful indicator of the transparency of the work of the election administration in general. If it is permissible by law and/or is part of the memorandum of understanding between the European Commission and the EMB, the EU EOM should request permission for the election analyst and LTO teams to attend working sessions of the EMB. Contact details for the EMB should be requested at all levels.

Possible Issues to Raise in Meetings with the EMB (at all levels)

The Organisational Structure of the EMB

- How and when were the EMB members appointed? Was there any problem with the appointment of any member?

- Are the EMB members experienced? Have they received induction and training?

- How often does the EMB meet in session? How are members informed of sessions? Are these meetings open to others to attend?

- What is the representation of women (and, where relevant, minorities) within the EMB?

- How are political parties and candidates included in the work of the EMB?

- Are domestic observer groups and media accredited to follow the work of the EMB?

Decisions of the EMB

- How are decisions made by this EMB, e.g., by consensus or by vote?

- Where decisions are taken by a vote, is there a partisan split in how the votes are cast?

- Are decisions published and made available promptly to parties/candidates? Are minutes of its sessions published?

- For lower-level EMBs: how is the local level EMB made aware of the instructions and decisions of higher-level EMB?

Possible Issues to Raise in Meetings with the EMB (at all levels) (cont.)

The Responsibilities of the EMB

- What are the EMB's implementation and supervisory responsibilities?

- How has the EMB implemented its responsibilities? Have all deadlines been met? Have there been any problems?

- Is the EMB provided with sufficient resources to carry out its responsibilities?

- Is there a secretariat, and if so, what is its structure, and how is it funded and managed?

- Does the EMB supervise lower-level bodies? If so, how are staff recruited and managed? Is recruitment being undertaken in good time? What training activities of lower-level bodies are taking place?

Complaints and Appeals

- Has the EMB received any complaints, or is the EMB aware of any formal complaints or appeals that have been made? If so, what do they relate to, and how are they being handled?

Election Day and Results

- What role will this level of EMB play on election day and in the results process?

- How prepared is this EMB for ensuring transparency during the results tabulation and publication processes?

- How is security for election materials being ensured?

Relevant Information

- Can the EMB provide the EU EOM with information on lower level bodies (e.g., contact details, lists of polling stations, etc.) and relevant data (such as number of registered voters per polling station)?

- Can the EMB provide the EU EOM with copies of regulations, decisions, minutes, etc?

Possible Issues to Raise in Meetings with other Interlocutors on the Work of the EMB

- Has the EMB been working fairly, impartially and in accordance with the law?

- Have there been examples of apparent interference in the work of the EMB?

- Is there confidence in the work of the EMB? Where there is a lack of confidence, is there any issue the EU EOM may need to follow-up with the EMB, either at a local or national level?

- What reasons, examples or evidence is provided to support the interlocutor's opinions?

Meetings with the EMB on Voter Registration

The EU EOM will meet with the EMB (or, on occasions, a different state agency, such as the Ministry of Interior) to obtain information on voter registration procedures and their implementation, as well as data from the voter register itself. The EMB should be asked to provide voter registration data broken down by region/district/polling station, and disaggregated by gender (i.e., divided into male/female categories).

The core team and LTOs will undertake an assessment of the quality of the voter register. Where voter registration is taking place during the period of deployment, EU observers may also observe the implementation of procedures for registering voters. This is particularly important where there is limited public confidence in the voter register. EU observers should obtain access to a computerised version of the voter register or extracts from it to undertake an assessment of the quality and accuracy of the voter register and the voter registration process in general. The voter register should be cross-checked with the available national and regional population registration data. The most recent census or other population statistics, assuming they are accurate, can be used to compare broadly the size of the registered electorate with the number of citizens who are above voting age and are eligible to vote.

The EU EOM does not have the time or resources to undertake a full check of the voter register. However, where there are specific allegations of false or incorrect entries, the EU EOM should ask for verifying evidence of the claim for follow-up by LTOs. Where there is such evidence, the EU EOM may be able to check a sample of names included on the voter register and then locate the persons listed to check the accuracy of the data. EU observers may also check the voter register where there are allegations of exclusion of eligible voters, even when (in an active registration system) they have attempted to register, or (in a passive registration system) they are able to prove their eligibility. The EU EOM may also observe any computerised cross-checking of voter registration data.

It is extremely difficult for even the best-intentioned government agencies to produce flawless voter lists. The EU EOM assessment of a voter list will attempt to determine if errors are isolated instances or part of a systemic pattern. If the latter is the case, the EU EOM will try to discover the likely reasons for this.

Possible Issues to Raise in Meetings on the Voter Register

Procedures for Voter Registration

- Which bodies have responsibilities for compiling and updating the voter register?

- How have the registration procedures been implemented? Have there been any problems? Were all deadlines respected?

- What measures are in place for the public to inspect the voter register? Are the voter lists posted at polling stations or other convenient locations so that voters can review their entries?

- What measures are in place for parties/candidates to inspect the voter register? Are parties/candidates able to purchase or otherwise obtain a copy of the lists?

- What measures are in place for civil society organisations and other stakeholders to inspect the voter register?

- Is the voter register available for inspection by LTOs?

Possible Issues to Raise in Meetings on the Voter Register (cont.)

- What measures are in place to update the voter register, add the names of eligible citizens or to remove ineligible or deceased persons? Are there effective provisions to ensure that voters who change their place of residence, or women who change their names when they marry, are not omitted from the lists?

- Where necessary, are there any special procedures to ensure IDPs are registered and able to vote?

- Have there been any complaints about persons being wrongly excluded from or included on the voter register? If so, how many complaints? How were those complaints resolved?

Voter Registration Data

- LTOs should try to obtain the full voter registration data that is available, preferably broken down by district/polling station and, where possible, disaggregated by gender.

- Have there been any significant changes in the numbers of registered voters in different areas? If so, what are the possible explanations?

Possible Issues to Raise in Meetings with other Interlocutors on the Voter Register

- Do they have confidence in the quality and accuracy of the voter register? Have they been able to access the voter register? Where problems are identified, on what scale are these? What examples or evidence can be provided to support their opinions?

The core team or LTOs may need to follow-up with the body responsible.

Meetings with the EMB on Candidate and Political Party Lists Registration

The EMB will usually have responsibility for the registration of candidates and political party lists for an election. In instances of parliamentary or local elections, the regional or district EMBs may have a delegated responsibility for party/candidate registration. Meetings with the EMB provide the main source of information on the implementation of procedures for registration of candidates and political party lists, and whether any nominations were refused. The EMB should be asked for relevant, gender-disaggregated data on party/candidate registration, broken down by party and region.

EU observers use this information to assess whether registration procedures have provided for the right to stand for election and have been implemented fairly and impartially. Political parties and candidates should also be questioned on the registration process. In any cases of refused nominations, LTOs should meet with the rejected candidate(s) and track any related challenges to the decision.

Possible Issues to Raise in Meetings on Candidate and Political Party List Registration

Procedures for Candidate and Political Party List Registration

- Which bodies have responsibilities for registering candidates/lists for the election?

- How have the registration procedures been implemented? Have there been any problems? Have deadlines been adhered to?

- Have any candidates/lists been refused registration? If so, why? Were the grounds for refusal legal, reasonable and consistently applied? If any candidates/lists were refused registration because of problems with registration papers, were they given an opportunity to correct errors before final refusal? If candidates were required to submit a number of voter signatures in order to register, how were the signatures checked?

- Was the registration process carried out in an impartial and transparent manner?

- Did the registration of all candidates/lists take effect on the same date so that no candidate gained advantage (or was disadvantaged) by having a longer (or shorter) time to campaign?

- If symbols were allocated to candidates/lists by the EMB, how was the allocation process carried out?

- Have there been any complaints about decisions on registration? If so, how many complaints have been made? How have those complaints been resolved? Have any decisions on complaints been appealed to a higher body? (If so, the core team or LTO team should ask for further information.)

- When and how was the final register of candidates/lists published?

Candidate Registration Data

- The EU EOM (core team and LTOs) should obtain full details of the candidates who have been registered. Data should be broken down by district, political party and gender. Candidate contact details should also be requested.

- Is information on candidates and party lists made widely available to the public?

Possible Issues to Raise in Meetings with other Interlocutors on Candidate Registration

- Was the candidate registration process carried out in a fair and transparent manner?

- Are any requirements for signatures and/or monetary deposits reasonable? Have these requirements disadvantaged women interested in standing for office?

6.3.4 Meetings with the Judiciary

The EU EOM will hold meetings with members of the judiciary, prosecutors, lawyers and other experts to discuss election-related legal issues in order to assess the national legal framework and the extent to which it is in accordance with international standards. The EU EOM will also assess how election crimes are handled by the legal system (the prosecutor's office and the courts, as well as the police). There will be specific focus on the complaints and appeals processes and the independence of the judiciary with regard to dealing with election cases. Mission activities on legal issues are coordinated by the legal analyst.

A key objective for the mission is to seek information on whether the complaints procedure provides a timely and effective remedy for complaints. Complaints may be handled by a judicial tribunal, or a specialised election complaints commission or, in some cases, by the EMB itself. It will be important to assess how independent the complaints handling body is. Where possible, EU observers should obtain copies of official documentation related to any complaints, attend the hearings, and report on how it was resolved. When a decision on a complaint is appealed, the EU EOM should track its progress. The legal analyst, in coordination with LTO teams, will maintain a database of election-related complaints that will usually include the following information:

- date and location of complaint;
- date of submission and tribunal to which the complaint was submitted;
- complainant and respondent;
- whether there is factual substance (basis or substantiation) for allegation;
- legal basis for complaint;
- whether supporting evidence was submitted;
- whether the complaint has been verified by EU EOM;
- whether the complaint was submitted in accordance with procedures. If not, why not and how the receiving body dealt with it;
- how the complaint was resolved;
- whether the decision was appealed;
- whether the decision was fully in line with the national law and international standards; and
- if the complaint appeared valid, whether the process provides a timely and effective remedy.

The EU EOM will separately record the complaints that it receives directly from political parties and candidates which have not been formally submitted. EU observers should always encourage complainants to use the existing channels for complaints and should enquire why any complaints have not been formally submitted. The EU EOM will not adjudicate on any complaints but may take steps to assess the credibility of the complaint.

Possible Issues to Raise in Meetings with the Judiciary

- Which courts are responsible for election complaints? Do different branches of the judiciary deal with different types of complaints, appeals and criminal cases (e.g., administrative courts with complaints against the government agencies, criminal courts with allegations of election fraud and other election crimes, the constitutional court with constitutional matters)?

- If a complainant disagrees with a court decision, what is the appeals process, and what levels of appeal are possible?

- Can election stakeholders, including individuals, appeal to the highest responsible court?

- Does the judicial system have the personnel and financial resources to deal with large numbers of election complaints, should they arise?

- Is there a deadline for dealing with election cases? If so, what is the deadline? From the judicial perspective, is the deadline sufficiently long to deal effectively with a case? Is the deadline sufficiently short to ensure that the complainant has an effective remedy? Can the courts meet the prescribed deadlines?

- Can the courts overturn an election result after the final results have been announced?

- Have the courts ever overturned an election result?

- Have the courts ever handed down penalties for election offences? What penalties are available to the courts, for example, fines, candidate suspension or disqualification? Which penalties have been issued and how frequently?

- Have any complaints been filed with the courts for this election? If so, what is the nature of the cases? If any rulings have been handed down, what have they been?

- How are judges appointed? What is their term of office?

- What is the status in law of the international human rights instruments to which the host country is a party? Have they been incorporated into domestic law?

Possible Issues to Raise in Meetings with other Interlocutors Concerning the Judiciary

- Is there general confidence in the independence and impartiality of the judiciary?

- Is there good knowledge among election stakeholders of the judicial system?

- Is the judicial system regarded as effective and efficient?

- Is the judicial system considered to act in a timely manner?

6.3.5 Meetings with Political Parties and Candidates

The EU EOM will meet with the leading candidates and representatives of the main political parties taking part in the election. EU observers will attend campaign events such as rallies, public meetings, and debates among candidates. To ensure that the mission maintains its image of impartiality, the EU EOM will meet with parties/candidates from across the political spectrum. Where there are many parties/candidates, the mission will meet with as many of their representatives as possible.

These meetings allow EU observers to enquire about campaign-related issues and views of the party/candidate representative on the election process, including the legal framework, the electoral system and the political context of the election.

An important issue that should be the considered carefully is the degree to which parties/canditates have confidence in the election administration and other official bodies with election responsibilities. When a genuine lack of confidence is expressed, the EU EOM should seek substantiating reasons, e.g., specific examples of officials not acting in an even-handed or professional manner. The candidates and parties should also be asked, if they have any other election-related complaints, for which they can provide supporting evidence, and for their views on the media coverage of the election.

In addition, EU observers will seek to obtain information on the political platforms of the party/candidate, as well as the membership and organisational structures of political parties, as part of its assessment of the political context of the election. In particular, the EU EOM will review the internal democracy of political parties, including the decision-making processes of the party leadership in relation to, for example, its selection process for candidates, and whether women are encouraged as leaders, members and candidates within the party.

Possible Issues to Raise in Meetings with Candidates and Political Parties

Campaign Opportunities

- What are the main platforms for the party/candidate's campaign for the election? Does the campaign address the interests of women or minorities?

- What campaigning methods are being used by the party/candidate?

- Does the party/candidate have access to media coverage? Where there is regulated media coverage, e.g., candidates are entitled to free airtime, is access provided to the party/candidate and is it equal?

- Has the party/candidate been able to campaign freely, including organising public meetings or rallies, without difficulties?

- Has the party/candidate experienced interference, for example from the authorities or security forces?

- Has the party/candidate experienced any problems in relation to violence, intimidation or interference in their campaign activities? Have any candidates, supporters or activists been arrested or detained?

- How is the party/candidate funded? Are there any problems with the campaign financing regulations?

- Has there been any misuse of public resources in campaigns?

- Does the party/candidate believe that the playing field for the election is level?

- What is the opinion of the party/candidate on the wider election campaign?

Candidate Registration

- Did the party/candidate experience any problems with the registration process? If so, what was the problem and how was it resolved?

Possible Issues to Raise in Meetings with Candidates and Political Parties (cont.)

Election Framework

- Does the party/candidate have an opinion or concerns on the quality of the legal framework for elections, including the electoral system?

- Does the party/candidate have confidence in the work of the EMB?

Election Day

- Does the party/candidate plan to field agents in polling stations? How many agents will be fielded? Will training be provided?

- Does the party/candidate have any specific concerns about election day?

- Does the party/candidate anticipate any fraud or manipulation on election day? If so, what type of fraud or manipulation? Are any particular locations or specific polling stations of special concern?

- Will the party/candidate track election results from individual polling stations?

Possible Issues to Raise in Meetings with Political Parties

Party Background and Organisational Structure

- How is the party aligned? What is its constituency of support (e.g., is it a national party, a regional party, or does it represent a national minority)?

- How long has the party been registered? Is it in coalition with other parties? Has the party experienced problems with registration?

- What is its status in elected office (e.g., members of parliament, local councils, mayors)?

- What is the size of the party's membership?

- What is the proportion of women members? Are there women in the party leadership? How many and in what positions (e.g., are they confined to social/welfare/childcare/family issues)? Is there a women's section of the party?

- Do party members experience any problems or intimidation because of their membership?

- Does the party practice internal democracy in terms of decision-making? If so, how?

- How is the party funded?

- Does the party run its own media (e.g., newspaper, radio) or receive support from a media outlet?

- How does the party consider its chance of success in the election? If low, for what reasons?

Nomination Process for Candidates

- How did the party select candidates (e.g., did the regional/local party select the regional/local candidates or were they selected by the national party leadership)? Was it a public process with open participation by party members?

- What is the proportion of women and minority candidates?

Attending Campaign Events

EU observers will attend campaign events, such as rallies and public meetings or debates, as part of their observation of the campaign period. In this context EU observers should ensure political balance, attending events representing a broad range of parties, including both government parties and opposition. Attendance at such events will allow an assessment of whether:

- contestants and their supporters are able to enjoy opportunities for the exercise of the freedoms of expression, assembly and movement;
- campaign regulations, such as requirements for permission to hold rallies, are being consistently implemented;
- the general atmosphere is positive and peaceful;
- speakers use appropriate non-inflammatory language; and
- security forces are present and behave appropriately.

When attending campaign events, EU observers should not act in a manner that could be interpreted as a display of partisanship. Attendance at campaign events is dependent on a security risk assessment by the observer team in consultation with the EU EOM security expert. Where the personal safety of the observers or their national staff becomes in danger, they should all leave immediately.

Election-Related Violence

The EU EOM will record and follow-up on reports of election-related violence and intimidation. In meetings with interlocutors where such reports are made, the EU EOM needs to ensure that the information it receives is accurate and credible. Reports on intimidation against candidates, supporters or voters are often very difficult to substantiate, and EU observers may need to give their opinion on the reliability of the persons making the claims.

6.3.6 Meetings with Civil Society

The EU EOM will meet regularly with a range of civil society organisations (CSOs) particulary those involved in the field of domestic non-partisan election observation and/or human rights. The EU EOM will also meet women's groups, minority groups, community leaders and research institutions. Non-partisan election observer groups may be particularly well-informed on election issues. CSOs often play an important role in providing voter education and it is important to assess the receptiveness and cooperation of the EMB to their efforts. CSOs active in governmental reform, countering corruption, the media, public opinion surveys and other election-related matters can often provide useful perspectives. Academics may have useful specialised knowledge of electoral issues. CSO reports can be extremely useful to an EU EOM in identifying issues to be aware of in an electoral process. Any reference to the findings of CSO reports by the EOM in its own reporting should be clearly identified.

Possible Issues to Raise in Meetings with CSOs

Opinions on the Electoral Process

- What is the opinion of the CSO on the election process and the campaign? How does the current election compare with previous elections?

- What are the key issues in the election? Is the campaign addressing these issues?

- Does the CSO consider that women are participating equally in the electoral process?

- Does the CSO have opinions or concerns about the quality of the legal framework for elections, including the electoral system?

- Does the CSO believe there is public confidence in the elected institutions, the work of the EMB, the judiciary, the security forces and other governmental institutions?

- Does the CSO have any specific concerns on the election process?

Organisational Background

- What are the objectives and main fields of interest of the CSO? Does it seek to represent any particular group? Is the CSO represented countrywide and/or regionally?

- Is the CSO non-partisan or is it aligned with a specific political party or political movement?

- What are the main activities of the CSO?

- Is the CSO formally registered and, if so, for how long has it been registered? Did the CSO experience problems with registration?

- What is the size of the membership of the CSO? What is the proportion of women members? Are there women or representatives of minorities in the CSO's leadership?

- Has the CSO experienced interference in its work from the authorities, political parties or others? Do activists or members of the CSO experience problems because of its work?

- How is the CSO funded? Does it receive government contributions? Are its staff volunteers?

- Does the CSO produce its own media (newspaper, radio, reports, etc.)?

Possible Issues to Raise in Meetings with CSOs Involved in Domestic Non-Partisan Election Observation

Preparations for Election Day

- Does the CSO undertake long-term election observation?

- How many observers will it deploy on election day? In which areas will it deploy?

- Will the CSO observe voting, counting and the tabulation of the results? Will it be recording results? Will it be conducting a parallel vote tabulation?

- Will the CSOs observers be mobile or stationary, remaining in the same polling station all day?

- Has the CSO received the necessary accreditation documentation for its observers? Were there any difficulties with this process?

- Is the CSO part of a network of election observer groups?

- How is the election observation funded?

Possible Issues to Raise in Meetings with CSOs Involved in Domestic Non-Partisan Election Observation

- Has the CSO received training and related material on election observation? If so, who provided the training and materials? Is the CSO providing training for its observers?

- What are the CSO's assessments or impressions to date on the election process?

- Has the CSO issued any substantive reports or statements on the election? If so, is it willing to share them with the EU EOM?

- Will the CSO prepare a report on its findings? What issues will it cover? When will it be published? Would the CSO be willing to share its preliminary election day findings with the EU EOM on election day even before they are publicly released?

Possible Issues to Raise in Meetings with CSOs Involved in Voter Education

Voter Education Initiatives

- What activities have been undertaken for voter education? What was the focus of the voter education?

- Were any of the CSO's voter education campaigns aimed at specific groups, such as first-time voters, women or minority groups? How does the CSO assess the effectiveness of their voter education work?

- Did the CSO seek to cooperate with the EMB when preparing and delivering its voter education programme? Was the EMB helpful and cooperative?

- How was the voter education funded? Were materials produced? Are spare copies available to give to LTOs?

- Have any problems been experienced in carrying out voter education activities?

- What steps are taken to ensure voter education reaches women equally?

6.3.7 *Meetings with the Media*

In addition to its dealings with the media as part of the mission visibility strategy, the EU EOM will hold meetings with representatives of the electronic and print media, including journalists and media outlet owners or editors, to obtain information on the media environment and the media's coverage of the election process. Since various media outlets may be perceived to support a particular candidate or political party, the EU EOM should take care to ensure that it meets with a broad range of media representatives from across the political spectrum, including state/public and private media. This ensures the mission is balanced and perceived to be balanced in its approach. Meetings with media associations and trade unions can also be useful in discerning how the media views its own role and responsibilities, any restrictions it faces and whether self-censorship is a problem. The EU EOM should also meet with media regulatory or supervisory bodies (whether state or private) to assess how effectively they handle election-related complaints against the media. If there have been any relevant licensing issues or problems, the EU EOM should meet authorities with responsibility for issuing broadcasting licences.

LTO teams often meet with representatives of the regional media. Mission activities on media issues are coordinated by the media analyst.

Possible Issues to Raise in Meetings with Media Representatives

Media Environment

- Is the media free to operate without official interference?

- Have there been any cases of violence against journalists or media outlets? Have there been any threats or intimidation?

- Is self-censorship a problem?

- How effective are any media regulatory or supervisorty bodies that exist?

Background to the Media Outlet

- Is the outlet privately owned (if so, by whom?) or publicly funded?

- What is the geographical coverage and estimated audience/readership of the media outlet? How many journalists work for it? Are the journalists professionally trained?

- What level of coverage does the media outlet give to reporting on news items?

Media Coverage of the Campaign

- To what degree is its news reports covering the election-related issues?

- Are candidates and political parties provided with free access (airtime or print space) to carry their campaign platform?

- Has the outlet been carrying paid election-related advertising? Are all candidates and political parties advertising in the outlet? Has the outlet refused to carry any election-related advertising?

- What rates is the outlet charging for election-related advertising? Are these the same as for non-election related advertising? Are all contestants offered the same rate?

- Have there been any complaints about the outlet's coverage of the election campaign?

- Does the outlet have a policy to support (or to criticise/marginalise) any specific political party or candidate?

- Is the outlet carrying any voter education advertising or other election-related initiatives?

- Has the media outlet experienced any difficulties in relation to its coverage of the election campaign?

- Has there been any instance of intimidation or harassment of journalists during the election campaign?

- What coverage and profile does the outlet give to women and minorities?

Opinions on the Electoral Process

- What is the media representative's opinion of the electoral process and the campaign? How does the current election compare with previous electoral processes?

- What are the key issues in the election? Is the campaign addressing these issues?

- Are there any concerns on the quality of the legal and media framework for elections?

- Does the media outlet believe there is public confidence in the work of the EMB and other official institutions?

- Is the media outlet aware of any election irregularities?

6.4   Media Monitoring by the EU EOM

The EU EOM assesses the role of the electronic and print media during the election campaign using quantitative and qualitative methodology. This assessment considers:

- whether political parties and candidates gain fair and equitable access to the media;
- whether political parties and candidates are covered in a balanced and unbiased manner;
- whether the media and the authorities adhere to the regulations on coverage of an election campaign; and
- whether the media give sufficient coverage of electoral issues to provide for the electorate making an informed choice on election day. If the media does not, the reasons for this will be considered.

The media monitoring methodology used by an EU EOM will produce an analysis of the distribution of media time and space given to each political contestant, and the tone of coverage. The results will be analysed in the context of the specific media environment, including the regulatory framework and the overall coverage of the election.

The media analyst should be familiar with the media landscape of the country before deciding which media outlets will be monitored. Those selected should include state/public and privately-owned media outlets, and ensure a varied balance taking into account, for example, political leanings and target audiences. Media aimed at minorities should be considered for monitoring, and the geographical balance of the regional media should also be taken into account. For electronic media, the media analyst will monitor coverage of primetime broadcasts and other election-related programming for the entire period of the defined campaign period. Television and radio programmes will be recorded by the EU EOM and stored until the end of the mission.

Quantitative Analysis
The methodology used involves analysis of the quantitative coverage given to individual political actors: candidates and political parties, heads of state, heads of government, ministers, members of parliaments as well as local authorities and representatives of political parties. The data collected for the quantitative analysis are: date of coverage, media outlet, time coverage starts, duration, programme type, gender of individual political actor being covered, and issue covered. Coverage is measured in seconds of airtime or square centimetres of print-space devoted to

each individual and political party. Direct speech time/print-space – i.e., when political actors have direct access to media – is also measured.

The quantitive analysis also assesses the tone of the coverage, i.e., whether it is neutral, positive or negative. This is measured by taking into account a number of elements, including whether journalists express explicit opinions on the subject, and the context in which the subject is covered.

Qualitative Analysis
The methodology also includes a qualitative analysis of media's role. In so doing, the EU EOM considers the entire range of media activities, including:
- use or reporting of instances of hate speech and inflammatory language;
- professional standards of journalism, including the level of accuracy in news reporting, and the prevalence of biased, defamatory or partisan reporting;
- whether media outlets omit to report on certain important news items;
- whether any media outlets display support to specific parties/candidates;
- whether incumbents exploit their institutional position to gain unfair advantage during the campaign;
- whether media outlets respect the 'campaign silence' and any restrictions on the reporting of opinion polls;
- whether coverage of the EMB in the media contributes to increased confidence in its work;
- level of coverage and quality of voter education in the media;
- formats used by the media in covering election issues (candidate debates, interviews, etc.);
- whether women receive coverage in proportion to their presence, and whether gender stereotypes are portrayed (e.g., women candidates in their role as wife/mother/homemaker);
- where relevant, how much coverage the media give to issues relating to minorities, and whether they broadcast/publish in minority languages; and
- the role of new media, such as newsgroups, electronic newspapers, and blogs, in covering the election.

In some EU EOMs, where the election process entails significant regional media activity, LTO teams may also be asked by the media analyst to assist with the monitoring of regional/local media coverage of the election campaign, for example by recording local programmes.

6.5   Long-Term Observers (LTOs)

6.5.1   *Roles and Responsibilities of LTOs*

An essential element of EU election observation methodology is its long-term, comprehensive coverage of the entire election process countrywide. Observation, assessment and reporting on election-related activities and events by teams of LTOs across the country are vital to the overall collective assessment of the EU EOM.

LTOs undertake an assessment of the same broad range of issues in their areas of responsibility (AoR) that the core team follows at the national level. These include:

- *regional political context*: the role of key political and electoral actors in the process and any political developments arising;
- *election administration:* the performance of the regional/local EMBs in preparing and implementing the election process;
- *voter registration:* the level of public confidence in the quality and accuracy of the voter register, the efficiency and reliability of the voter registration process, and the tracking of any related complaints;
- *candidate registration*: the implementation of procedures for the regional registration of candidates;
- *campaign:* the range of campaign activities taking place, and whether there are any restrictions on the freedoms of expression, assembly and movement;
- *media:* the role of local media and its coverage of the election campaign:
- *human rights:* whether there are human rights issues impacting on the electoral process, including those issues relating to discrimination and the participation of women, minorities and other groups;
- *civil society:* the range of local civil society activities related to the election, especially domestic non-partisan observers;
- *complaints and appeals:* the credibility of election-related complaints and the effectiveness of processes for managing complaints and appeals;
- *election day:* the implementation of voting and counting procedures and the wider polling environment; and
- *results and post-election issues:* the aggregation, tabulation and publication of election results and the environment during the post-election period.

In addition, LTOs are responsible for preparing and managing the deployment of STO teams in their AoR for expanded mission coverage on election day. LTO teams are required to follow all management, operational and security guidelines, including on public outreach activities. Each LTO team produces a weekly report on developments in their AoR (and may also produce *ad hoc* reports on relevant situations as they arise), using reporting templates provided by the EU EOM.

LTOs work in international teams of two. The pairing of individuals is based on ensuring a balance in the team of nationalities, previous observation experience, other relevant experiences, and language skills. Where possible, there will also be a gender mix in a team. LTOs work in pairs to enhance the credibility and reliability of their observations and to ensure a balance of analysis. As the representatives of the EU EOM in their AoR, LTOs should work to the highest professional standards, maintaining the integrity of the mission. Each LTO should adhere strictly to the code of conduct for EU Observers and other relevant codes of conduct.

Ideally, LTOs are in-country for approximately seven weeks, arriving five weeks before election day and remaining in their AoR for up to two weeks after election day. LTO teams work closely with, and under the supervision of, the observer coordinator.

6.5.2 *LTO Meetings with Interlocutors*
The LTO team is the focal point for all regional interlocutors of the mission. These will include the following electoral stakeholders:
- regional and local branches of the EMB;
- senior officials from regional and local government (e.g., regional governors, municipal mayors);
- political parties from the region or the representatives/branches of national parties;
- candidates standing in the region, or the regional representatives of national candidates;
- journalists and representatives of regional and national media;
- civil society organisations active in the fields of human rights and elections in the region, including domestic observer groups, women's groups and minority groups;
- senior police officials;
- community leaders, religious leaders, academics, and others who may have useful knowledge of elections; and
- representatives of international organisations operating in the region, including other international election observer groups.

The LTO team will meet regularly with interlocutors across their AoR. (For detailed guidelines on the conduct and content of meetings for LTOs, see Section *6.3 Meetings with Interlocutors*). Both members of the LTO team will attend all meetings together.

6.5.3 LTO Orientation and Activities

Pre-Deployment
Following their selection to an EU EOM, each LTO will be contacted by the IP to confirm flight arrangements, visas, contracts, insurance, and any other administrative matters. The IP will also provide key practical information on the country where the election is being observed, as well as other requirements for LTO preparation, inclu-

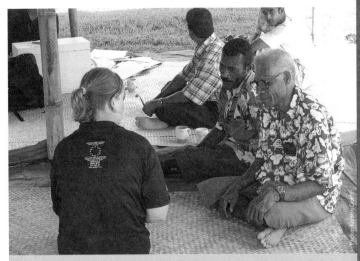

LTOs meeting election stakeholders, Fiji, 2006.

ding medical information, financial arrangements, and recommendations for suitable clothing. Each LTO supplies the IP with passport photographs and personal data for accreditation documentation, as well as next-of-kin information. LTOs may also require personal insurance, if they plan to bring their own equipment, as such items will not be insured for damage or loss by the IP.

After the core team has been deployed, each LTO will be contacted by e-mail by the observer coordinator. LTOs will be sent election-related information, including advance LTO briefing materials. LTOs are expected to familiarise themselves with this material before arriving in country.

Briefing Upon Arrival
LTOs are met at the airport by the core team representatives and the IP, before being transferred to a hotel usually in the capital city. Each LTO is provided with mission identification, accreditation, and a briefing pack. A comprehensive two-day briefing for LTOs takes place covering: EU EOM methodology, the code of conduct, all areas of assessment, relevant security issues and standard security procedures, and reporting and coordination issues. In addition, explanation is provided on administrative and logistical matters, including communications, and there is a handover of equipment and materials.

Deployment of LTO Teams
The criteria for the field deployment of LTO teams is outlined above in Section *5.2.6 Criteria for Deployment of Observers.* Ideally, all regions of the host country will be covered by LTO teams, unless logistical or security reasons restrict deploy-

ment or coverage in specific areas. The LTO team is usually based in the administrative capital of their designated region, and will travel extensively to other locations throughout their AoR. Where possible, each LTO team is deployed by road with their interpreter/assistant and driver. In larger countries, LTO teams may be deployed by air and meet their support staff upon arrival at an airport near to their deployment base.

Equipment and Funds

The equipment provided to LTO teams varies among missions. LTOs receive a laptop computer, printer, stationary, phones, visibility materials and medical kits. Where necessary, LTOs are provided with satellite phones and/or radio equipment. This equipment may be used for EU EOM purposes only. Each LTO is provided with a daily allowance to cover living costs such as accommodation and food. Funds are also provided to cover operational needs during the course of deployment. Teams should account for these funds in accordance with the financial reporting procedures of the IP.

Accommodation

Hotel accommodation is arranged for LTOs by the IP in the capital city and at their deployment base. Occasionally, an LTO team's deployment base may be outside of their AoR, if suitable accommodation is not available within it. A team may also need to stay outside their deployment base when visiting distant parts of their AoR. LTOs may arrange alternative long-term accommodation as long as it meets security standards of the mission. Generally, LTOs will not be provided with office space and will need to use their accommodation for such purposes. The core team security expert should always be informed of the address where each LTO is staying.

Mid-Term Briefing

A briefing is often held midway during the deployment of the EU EOM. The mid-term briefing enables the core team and LTOs to discuss electoral developments, clarify observation issues and confirm preparations for the deployment of STOs.

6.5.4 LTO National Support Staff

Each LTO team has an interpreter/assistant and a driver (see Section *6.2 National Support Staff*). Each support staff member is managed jointly by the LTO team members, who are responsible for providing a briefing on the work of the EU EOM and the roles and responsibilities of LTOs and the support staff. All contractual matters in relation to the support staff should be referred to the core team and the IP. LTOs should make every reasonable effort to enable their national staff to vote on election day.

6.5.5 Security for LTOs

LTOs receive a comprehensive security briefing and training upon arrival, which will include a thorough explanation of the security operating procedures and instructions applying to the mission. The security expert will provide each team with a specific briefing on the security environment in their AoR. In some cases, certain locations may be declared out of bounds.

The security expert establishes a warden structure within the EU EOM, which usually involves designating one member of an LTO team as the contact point for security issues within the AoR. The designated LTO is responsible for ensuring compliance with security requirements, such as requesting movement authorisation or submitting location reports. LTO teams provide regular (often daily) situation reports on their location, and include reports on election-related security issues as part of their standard reporting routine.

For further information, see Section *5.4 Mission Security*.

6.5.6 Preparing for STOs

During the election day period, each LTO team is likely to be joined by several teams of STOs. They may also be joined by one or more teams of locally-recruited STOs, and members of an observer delegation from the European Parliament. The core team will issue guidelines to LTOs on the specific tasks to be undertaken in order to prepare for the deployment of STOs.

The number of STOs to be deployed to the host country is considered during the exploratory mission and finalised by the European Commission in Brussels. The core team prepares a provisional deployment plan for STO teams to each AoR, using the criteria outlined in Section *5.2.6 Criteria for Deployment of Observers*. The deployment plan is finalised after consultation with each LTO team, who will be asked to indicate the optimum number of STO teams for their AoR.

Preparing a Regional STO Deployment Plan

When the number of STO teams to be deployed to each AoR is known, the LTO team will prepare a regional deployment plan for their AoR. This will include the following information:

- the AoRs covered by each STO team and their deployment base;
- a list of polling stations in each STO team's area of deployment, including identification of 20–40 that may be visited on election day. Background information on the polling stations (e.g., number of voters) should be provided;
- a list of any specific polling stations or specific areas that the STOs are directed to visit (e.g., special polling stations or problematic areas);

- suggested routes between locations in the AoR, including estimated times of travel; and
- a list of the locations of regional EMB offices and/or regional tabulation centres.

Preparing a Regional STO Briefing

A regional briefing pack of relevant materials will also be prepared, using a template provided by the observer coordinator. The regional briefing pack will include general background information on the AoR, such as the regional political context and the work of the EMB, and will highlight any specific issues that are relevant to STOs. It will also detail logistical arrangements, including a timeframe for the STOs over the election day period, procedures for the return of reporting forms, any specific security issues and a list of contact names and addresses. The regional briefing pack should also include relevant regional documentation such as maps, lists of polling stations, the numbers of registered voters at each polling station, and lists of regional candidates. This information should be available from the regional EMB. Upon the arrival of the STOs in the AoR, the LTO team will provide a regional briefing to present and explain the information contained in the briefing pack and to allow for an opportunity for questions and team-building.

Preparing STO Logistical Arrangements

The LTO team prepares regional logistical arrangements for the STOs in its AoR under the direction of the core team operations expert. This includes identifying suitable accommodation for STOs and assisting the IP with the recruitment of suitable candidates for interpreters/assistants and drivers for the STO teams. LTOs should provide a group briefing for all national support staff on their role and responsibilities.

6.5.7 Planning for Election Day and Post-Election Day Observation

Each LTO team will undertake the following tasks in planning for election day:
- confirm with the core team a schedule for reporting regional information;
- establish a schedule for STO teams on election day, covering fixed contact times with LTOs (including after final return to accommodation), the return of observer forms, and procedures for reporting serious irregularities or emergencies;
- designate 'duty' LTOs and STOs to be called in an emergency or if queries arise;
- prepare a list of contact details for key local interlocutors;
- prepare a schedule for the debriefing of STOs; and
- prepare a schedule for STOs over the immediate post-election period, including observation of the tabulation process.

Individual debriefings with STOs will normally take place at various times on election day and at the end of their observation. This is an important task for LTOs, as it ensures that the core team can be made immediately aware of key observations and allows the LTO team to clarify the information provided. It is also common for a group debriefing to take place very soon after election day, so that STOs can review and compare their findings, and the LTO team can gather further information from across their AoR.

Further information on election day and post-election preparations is found in Section Seven.

6.5.8 End of Mission

Tasks before Leaving the AoR
Ahead of their departure from the AoR, LTOs will hold farewell meetings with all key interlocutors, at which time they can distribute copies of the EU EOM preliminary statement. LTOs will also prepare a final report on the team's work and produce an electronic archive of all relevant documents for submission to the core team. Copies of complaints and other original documents should be filed and returned to the observer coordinator or legal analyst. The LTO team should also produce a contact list of its interlocutors, which may be of use to future EU EOMs. References for all national support staff (including those working for STOs) should be written, and national staff should be given the contact details of the European Commission Delegation, in case intimidation or security issues arise as a result of their work with the EU EOM.

Appraisal
LTO and STO performance are appraised by the observer coordinator in consultation with all members of the core team. The appraisal process is based on criteria established by the European Commission. All observers are given the opportunity to evaluate all aspects of the mission, including core team and IP performance (see Section *5.2.4 Selection of Observers*).

End of Mission Debriefing
LTO teams take part in a debriefing at the end of their mission. This is led by the DCO and provides an opportunity for the core team and LTOs to share and discuss their findings on the election process, and organisation of the mission. In this context LTOs will be asked to identify possible recommendations for the mission final report and improvements for future missions.

6.6   LTO Reporting

Reporting by LTOs to the core team is a cornerstone of the work of all EU EOMs. The quality of the findings of the EU EOM will, to a large extent, depend on the accuracy and usefulness of the reports produced by LTO teams, as they should provide concrete regional examples that substantiate the broader findings of the mission. The observer coordinator is in charge of managing and supervising LTO reporting. The information provided by LTOs will be used in the EU EOM interim reports, preliminary statement and final report. Guidelines for reporting by EU observers and background to EU EOM reporting are outlined in Section Eight.

Some information from interlocutors may be sensitive and need to be treated in confidence, protecting their anonymity. The LTO team should discuss these cases with the core team on an individual basis and consider whether the LTO report should include such information. If not included, it should be passed to the core team in an appropiate confidential manner.

LTO reports are submitted by the team as a joint report, reflecting the combined observations of the team. However, it is usual for the team to have a 'division of labour' in report writing, with each team member covering different issues. If the two team members disagree on a substantive issue, they may report both points of view and explain why their opinions differ.

6.6.1   LTO Weekly Reports
Each LTO team will produce weekly reports that provide information and preliminary analysis on all issues relevant to the electoral process within their AoR. The core team will establish a reporting schedule and provide a template structure, including checklists. The LTO weekly reports should contain factual information and descriptions of events, along with analysis of these facts within the regional context. Concrete examples should be provided wherever possible. Speculation, commentary or personal opinions by the LTOs should be identified as such.

As well as providing a comprehensive description of findings and electoral developments in the AoR over the reporting period, the LTO weekly report should cover relevant operational and security issues, including preparations for STO deployment, and information on any incidents of violence that have taken place. The LTO weekly report should also be used to highlight areas of concern that the LTOs consider may require action by the core team, including investigation with national authorities, and to request for further information from the core team.

As soon as LTO reports are received, the observer coordinator distributes copies to the CO and the core team. A summary of all the weekly reports is produced by the observer coordinator and circulated to the core team and LTOs. The LTO weekly reports and their summaries are internal mission documents that should not be circulated more widely. All internal mission reports should be considered confidential documents, the content of which may have political implications. If LTO weekly reports are 'leaked', this could be harmful to the mission, especially if they contain assessments that are premature.

Model Structure for the LTO Weekly Report (some issues will not have to be addressed each week)

- Executive Summary
- Background
- Election Administration
- Voter Registration
- Registration of Candidates/Political Parties
- Election Campaign
- Media Environment
- Complaints and Appeals
- Participation of Women
- Participation of Minorities
- Civil Society
- Polling, Counting and Tabulation
- Operational Issues and Preparations for STO Deployment
- Security Issues
- Action Required by the Core Team

6.6.2 Other LTO Reports
There are other reports which LTO teams may be required to submit in different circumstances. Templates for these reports will be provided to the LTO team by the core team.

Spot/Incident Reports
These reports cover important or urgent issues (e.g., a violent incident or coverage of a prominent court case). The issue covered by the spot/incident report should also be included in the next scheduled weekly LTO report.

Campaign Rally Reports
The template for these reports provides a checklist for issues to be reported on, when LTOs attend a campaign event, (e.g., a rally or public debate).

Report on the Pre-election Atmosphere
LTOs may be asked to provide a last-minute report on issues of particular interest to the core team, including the political atmosphere in the days before the election,

the technical preparations for polling, and final arrangements for the arrival of short-term observers.

LTO Final Report

At the end of their deployment in their AoR, LTO teams will provide a final report on their main findings and conclusions on the electoral process, as well as issues related to the organisation of the mission. The final LTO report may include recommendations for the core team to consider for inclusion in the EU EOM final report.

6.7 Short-Term Observers (STOs)

6.7.1 Roles and Responsibilities of STOs

The EU EOM extends the scope of its observation coverage on election day through the deployment of STO teams across the country. Their observation of voting, counting, and the tabulation process is an important part of the EU EOM's findings and overall assessment of the electoral process.

STOs will observe, assess and report on the following aspects of the electoral process:

- *election environment*, including the atmosphere over the election day period, and whether there are instances of intimidation, restrictions on freedom of movement, or other problems;
- *implementation of voting procedures*, including compliance with national laws, whether the right to vote and the right to a secret ballot are enjoyed in practice, and whether polling officials act in an impartial manner;
- *implementation of the procedures for the counting of votes*, including compliance with national laws, whether the votes are counted promptly, accurately and honestly, counting officials act in an impartial manner, and the process is transparent; and
- *tabulation and publication of results*, including whether there is a transparent, accurate and prompt transfer, tabulation and publication of results, and whether there are problems with the wider post-election environment.

Each STO team completes report forms that contain checklists for the evaluation of voting, counting, and tabulation procedures. These are returned to the EU EOM headquarters for statistical analysis. In addition, STOs provide narrative reports and regular updates to their designated LTO team. This is especially important where an STO team observes serious irregularities or problematic events. In addition, the

STO team may have separate security and logistical reporting requirements, including movement reports.

STOs work in international teams of two. The pairing of individuals is based on ensuring a balance amongst teams of nationalities, previous observation experience, other relevant experiences and language skills. Where possible, there will also be a gender mix in a team. STOs work in pairs to enhance the credibility and reliability of their observations and to ensure a balance of analysis. As representatives of the EU EOM, STOs should work to the highest professional standards and maintain the integrity of the mission. Each STO should adhere strictly to the code of conduct for EU Observers, and any other relevant codes of conduct.

Ideally, STOs will be in country for 10–12 days, arriving around a week before election day. All STOs work under the supervision of the observer coordinator and their designated LTO team.

For detailed guidelines on the work of EU observers on election day, see Section Seven.

6.7.2 STO Meetings with Interlocutors

During their work over the election day period, an STO team will meet a number of local interlocutors and electoral stakeholders, including:
- members of the local EMB, polling station officials, and counting officials;
- candidate agents and political party representatives in polling stations;
- domestic and international non-partisan election observers;
- officials from local government (e.g., municipal mayors) and police; and
- journalists.

Detailed guidelines on meetings with interlocutors over the election day period are provided in Section Seven.

6.7.3 STO Orientation and Activities

Pre-Deployment

Following their selection, each STO will be contacted by the IP to confirm flight arrangements, visas, contracts, insurance, and any other administrative matters. The IP will also provide key practical information on the country where the election is being observed, as well as other requirements for STO preparation, including medical information, financial arrangements, and recommendations for suitable clothing. Each STO supplies the IP with passport photographs and personal data for accreditation documentation, as well as next-of-kin information. STOs may also take out their own personal insurance, if they plan to bring their own equipment, as such items will not be insured for damage or loss by the IP.

Ahead of their departure, each STO will be contacted by e-mail by the observer coordinator. Whenever possible, they will be sent election-related information, including advance briefing materials. STOs are expected to familiarise themselves with this material before arriving in-country.

Briefing Upon Arrival

STOs are met at the airport by core team representatives and the IP, before being transferred to a hotel, usually in the capital city. Each STO is provided with mission identification, accreditation, and a briefing pack. A two-day briefing for STOs takes place, the agenda for which includes:

- a welcome from the chief observer and the core team;
- comprehensive briefings on EU methodology for election observation, the code of conduct for EU Observers and background information on all areas of assessment being undertaken by the EU EOM;
- a specific briefing and/or training on relevant security issues and standard security procedures;
- guidelines on dealing with media enquiries;
- detailed information on voting, counting, and tabulation procedures, observer report forms, reporting procedures and coordination issues;
- an overview of logistical, coordination and administrative issues, including a handover of equipment and materials; and
- meetings with each STO national support staff.

Deployment of STO Teams

The criteria for the field deployment of STO teams are outlined above in Section *5.2.6 Criteria for Deployment of Observers*. Once issued, the deployment plan will not be changed, except in cases of emergency. Generally, there will be more than one STO team in each of the AoRs covered by an LTO team. Each STO team will be provided with their own area of deployment. Ideally, all regions of the host country will be covered by STO teams, unless there are logistical or security reasons that restrict deployment or coverage in specific areas. The STO team is usually initially based in the administrative capital of the AoR but may later be relocated closer to their area of deployment. Where possible, each STO team is deployed by road, with their interpreter/assistant and driver. In larger countries, STO teams may be deployed by air and meet their support staff upon arrival.

Equipment and Funds

Equipment provided to STO teams will vary among missions. As a minimum, each STO will receive a mobile phone and the EU EOM's visibility material. Where necessary, STO teams may also be provided with satellite phones and/or radios.

This equipment may be used for EU EOM purposes only. Each STO will be provided by the IP with an allowance to cover living costs, e.g., accommodation and food.

Accommodation
Hotel accommodation is arranged for STOs by the IP and the EU EOM usually in the capital city and deployment base(s). Occasionally, accommodation may be outside of the STO's area of deployment, if suitable facilities are not available. STOs should stay in the accommodation that has been booked for them.

Regional STO Briefings
STOs receive a regional briefing from their designated LTO team, which will cover:
- general background information on the AoR, such as the regional political context and the work of the EMB, as well as any specific issues that are relevant to STOs;
- logistical arrangements, including a timeframe for the STOs over the election day period, procedures for the return of report forms, specific security issues, and a list of contact names and addresses; and
- relevant regional documentation, such as maps and lists of regional candidates.

Each STO team will receive information on its specific area of deployment, including:
- a list of the polling stations, identifying those that may be visited on election day;
- data on the number of registered voters at each polling station;
- a list of any specific polling stations or areas that the STOs are directed to visit (e.g., special polling stations or problematic areas);
- a list of the location of regional/local EMB offices and/or tabulation centres; and
- suggested routes between locations in the AoR, including estimated times of travel.

Familiarisation
Following their regional briefing, STO teams will familiarise themselves with their area of deployment. This includes preliminary visits before election day to polling stations and tabulation centres and a meeting with election officials. This will allow the STO team to gain a useful insight into the election day preparations, identify any potential concerns and plan a route and a schedule of visits on election day. STOs should select which polling station they will attend the opening of polling and the polling station/counting centre where they will observe the counting. The STO team may choose to modify their schedule on election day, for example if they believe it would be useful to return to a polling station a second time, or if

they decide it would be beneficial to observe the count at a different location form the one which they initially intended to observe. The STOs will only share their anticipated route and schedule with their designated LTOs and the security expert if required. Otherwise, it should remain confidential.

Post-Election Debriefing

STOs will be debriefed by their designated LTO team in order to discuss their observations on election day and clarify any issues that arise from their reports. This will take place at various times on election day and at the end of their observation. A group debriefing with other STO teams in the AoR will take place a day or two after election day, so that STOs can review and compare their collective findings.

Post-Election Observations

During their remaining period in their area of deployment, STOs observe key aspects of the post-election period. This will can include observing any on-going counting of votes or tabulation of results, visiting polling stations to collect published results data, and surveying the general post-election environment.

End of Mission Debriefing

STOs take part in a joint debriefing at the end of their mission. The debriefing is led by the DCO and provides an opportunity for the core team and all STOs to share and discuss their findings on the election process and political situation. STOs will be asked to identify possible recommendations for the mission's final report and improvements for future EU EOMs.

Appraisal

STO performance is appraised by the observer coordinator in consultation with the designated LTO team. The appraisal process is based on criteria established by the Commission which are provided to STOs and LTOs by the core team. In addition, STOs are provided with an opportunity to evaluate the role of their LTO team.

6.7.4 STO National Support Staff

Each STO team has a driver and usually has an interpreter/assistant (see Section *6.2 National Support Staff*). Each support staff member is managed jointly by the STO team members, in coordination with the LTO team. The STOs should brief their team on the work of the EU EOM, and the roles and responsibilities of STOs and the support staff. All contractual matters in relation to support staff should be referred to the core team and the IP. STOs should make every reasonable effort to enable their national staff to vote on election day.

6.7.5 Security for STOs

STOs receive a comprehensive security briefing and/or training upon arrival, which will include a thorough explanation of the security operating procedures, and security instructions applying to the mission as a whole and to specific areas of deployment. The security expert will establish a warden structure within the EU EOM, which usually involves designating one STO in each AoR as a contact point. In addition, one member of each STO team will be made the contact point for that particular team. The designated STO is responsible for ensuring compliance with security requirements, such as providing location reports. For security purposes, STO team members should undertake all activities together. For further information, see Section *5.4 Mission Security*.

6.7.6 Indicative Timeframe for STO Deployment

Day One	
Arrival	Overnight in capital city
Day Two	
Observer briefing (Welcome by CO, briefings on EU election observation methology, security, logistics, dealing with media, code of conduct, cultural background)	Overnight in capital city
Day Three	
Observer briefing continues (Background information on political context etc; voting, counting and tabulation procedures; observer report forms)	Overnight in capital city
Day Four	
Deployment and regional briefing	Overnight in deployment location
Day Five	
Familiarisation	Overnight in deployment location
Day Six	
ELECTION DAY	Overnight in deployment location
Day Seven	
Observation of counting / tabulation	Overnight in deployment location
Day Eight	
Observation of tabulation / regional debriefing by LTOs	Overnight in deployment location
Day Nine	
Return to capital city	Overnight in capital city
Day Ten	
Debriefing by the core team	Overnight in capital city
Day Eleven	
Departure	

SECTION SEVEN

7. Election Day

7.1 Overview of EU Observation of Election Day

The aim of election day observation is to assess whether voting, counting and tabulation are implemented in accordance with election legislation and international standards for elections. In this regard, EU observer teams are deployed to locations across the host country to assess whether:

- all eligible voters are provided with the opportunity to exercise their right to vote, and there are no restrictions on their freedom of movement;
- the right to a secret ballot is enjoyed;
- election officials perform their duties effectively, impartially, without interference and in a transparent way;
- voting, counting and tabulation is conducted in a peaceful and orderly atmosphere, so that voters are freely able to make their choice, and there are no incidents of violence or intimidation;
- election observers, including party/candidate representatives, domestic non-partisan observers, international observers and the media, are able to carry out their duties without interference;
- detailed results at all levels are published clearly, accurately and promptly after the votes are counted, and broken down to the lowest possible level; and
- the aggregation and tabulation of results by higher EMBs takes place accurately, transparently and promptly.

EU EOM coverage of election day is principally provided by STO teams. Coverage is often strengthened by the inclusion of locally-recruited observers from EU embassies in the host country, as well as by visits to polling stations by LTOs and the core team. The EU EOM will often be joined over the election day period by an observer delegation from the European Parliament. All observer teams will be coordinated in their area of deployment by a designated LTO team under the management of the observer coordinator and the DCO.

An EU observer team should arrive at the first polling station in time to observe the opening procedures. Following the opening, observers will travel to different polling stations to observe voting. An observer team will usually visit around eight to 15 polling stations on election day. A minimum of 30 minutes in each polling station is required, although the observer team may stay longer in a polling station, or return later to the same polling station. The observer team will attend the closing of a polling station, and stay to observe the counting of votes (in some countries observers will move to counting centres), a process that may take many hours. Throughout this work, the observer team will provide regular reports to their designated LTO team, who will themsesleves report to the core team. Each observer team will be required to provide frequent information on its location and next scheduled movement, in case of a security alert.

Each EU observer team will have different experiences of election day: some will be based in busy urban areas, others may cover rural areas of outstanding natural beauty; some may have to operate in tough conditions; some may see many problems with polling, while others may see no problems. EU election observation methodology means that the mission's assessment is not dependent on the observations of one team; instead there is a collective assessment based on information from a large number of independent and impartial observers working across the country.

7.2   Guidelines for EU observers on Election Day

☑   Each observer and each team's personal safety and security override all other considerations. Observers should not take undue risks. In the event of violence or serious threats of violence, observers should leave the area immediately. Particular care should be taken during road travel. Confrontations, especially with security personnel, should be avoided.

☑   Observers should report any violent incident or serious irregularity immediately to their designated LTO team or the core team.

☑   Observers are mandated only to *observe*. In accordance with the EU code of conduct for Election Observers, they should never provide advice or assistance to the election authorities. Nor should they instruct, disrupt, interfere

Waiting to vote, Nigeria, 2007.

or countermand the decisions of an election official. Observers should not attempt to resolve election-related disputes. However, observers may bring problems to the attention of election officials.

☑ Observers should not engage in any activity that creates a conflict of interest with their observation duties, such as participating in any campaign event, or accepting gifts or favours from political actors. Observers should be aware at all times of how their actions may be perceived by local counterparts. When meeting with election officials or party/candidate representatives, observers should try to meet with people from across the political spectrum.

☑ EU election observation methodology demands a high quality of reporting by observers. An assessment should be made of the environment inside and outside polling stations, as well as the implementation of voting and counting procedures. Observers should take notes of their observations, especially when meeting with polling officials, party/candidate representatives and other interlocutors.

☑ Observers should make a clear distinction between incidents observed directly and those reported by others. Observers should identify where incidents are reported by multiple and/or credible sources. Similarly, observers should highlight where incidents are reported by a single partisan source, or without supporting evidence.

☑ When informed of complaints, observers should try to take as many supporting details as possible from interlocutors. These should include: what happened; who was involved; when it happened; etc. Observers should clarify to interlocutors that the EU EOM does not adjudicate on election complaints, that a formal complaint should be made using the appropriate complaints procedures, and that the EU EOM observe the process by which complaints are addressed.

☑ Observers should treat sensitive or personal information/data with care and respect confidentiality.

☑ Observers should never compromise the voters' right to a secret ballot. They should never enter a polling booth when a voter is inside, or look at a voter's marked ballot. Observers should never ask a person how they have voted or how they intend to vote.

☑ Observers should not touch any item of sensitive election material, such as ballot papers. Should observers wish to scrutinise official documents, they should always do so in the presence of an authorised person, having first asked permission. Observers should not sign official documents unless required to do so by electoral regulations (e.g., to register their presence in the polling stations).

☑ Any refusal to allow observers into a polling station should be reported immediately to the designated LTO.

☑ Observers are required to make realistic and objective assessments. Observers should recognise where mistakes may be made by election officials because of inexperience or unfamiliarity with the law, rather than because of any deliberate intention to compromise the integrity of the process. Observers should be prepared to justify and explain their findings.

☑ An observer team should complete an observer report form for each polling station visited. If a team returns to a polling station for a second (or third) visit, a new form should be completed each time.

☑ Observers should not distribute any written material or publish any text that has not been specifically approved by the CO/DCO or the mission's press and public outreach officer.

7.3 Observer Report Forms

Each observer receives a series of report forms which contain a 'checklist' of questions on key aspects of the election day process. The forms ensure that observer teams from across the country use consistent criteria for observing and reporting. The information from these forms enables the core team to produce a quantitative statistical analysis, from which it can make its conclusions on the conduct of election day.

Observers will be provided with a comprehensive briefing and guidelines on how to use the forms. Each observer team will complete one form per team for each visit to a polling station. Separate 'comments' sections (or separate forms) allow observers to make written comments on their observations, or to record any significant event or irregularity which they observed or have had reported to them. Where further detail is needed, observers may prepare a 'flash report' on the event that is submitted immediately to the EU EOM headquarters.

It is extremely important that forms are completed in full and clearly. Comments should be written using block letters. 'Checklist' questions should be marked with a tick (✓) or a cross (**x**).

7.3.1 Types of Forms

Observers will be provided with a report form for each of the different stages of their election day observation, for example:

- *Opening*: includes a checklist of questions on the procedures for opening a polling station;
- *Voting*: includes a checklist of questions on the environment around a polling station, the voting procedures, the atmosphere inside a polling station, and an overall assessment of voting and the work of polling station staff;
- *Closing*: includes a checklist of questions on the closing procedures;
- *Counting*: includes a checklist of questions on the procedures for counting votes and publishing results, and an overall assessment of closing and counting; and
- *Tabulation*: includes questions on the transfer of polling materials and the procedures for tabulating results.

Example forms for observation of voting and counting are shown in Annex 2. Forms will vary depending on the voting procedures and issues arising in each country.

7.2.2 Returning Observer Report Forms

Completed forms are returned to the EU EOM headquarters at regular intervals during the day. In most cases, the forms are returned directly to the EU EOM headquarters by the observer team, either by fax or by courier. Observers will be briefed on the procedures for returning forms to the EU EOM headquarters by their designated LTO team.

To enable proper processing by the core team, the observer team should ensure that each form includes the team's unique number (the first two digits indicate in which AoR the team is working, and the following two digits identify the number of the observer team) and data that allows the specific polling station to be identified (e.g., its administrative number/name and the district in which it is based). In addition, the observer team should record the timing of its arrival at and departure from the polling station. This information should be completed before the form is returned, otherwise it will be of no statistical use.

7.3.3 *Analysis of Forms*

Upon their arrival at the EU EOM headquarters, the forms will be processed by the statistical analyst. The 'checklist' questions will be entered into a database to enable the preparation of a statistical analysis. Based on the data produced, the core team will be able to develop a reliable insight into the conduct of election day and, in particular, to identify whether irregularities have taken place and, if so, whether they were isolated or systematic, regional or national. The core team will also review all forms that contain additional comments, and, if necessary, follow-up directly with the teams concerned. The conclusions produced by the statistical analysis of the forms provide an important basis for the debriefing of observers.

7.4 Dealings with the Media on Election Day

The EU EOM will issue guidelines for observers on dealing with the media over election day. These guidelines will address occasions where observers are asked by the media for interviews or comments on their work. Such opportunities for transparency in the work of the EU EOM are important public outreach activities. (see Section *5.6.3 Dealing with the Media*).

In order to ensure a consistent message with the media, STOs should provide information on the following topics only:
- the role and mandate of the EU EOM;
- the long-term and countrywide coverage of the EU EOM and the number of EU observers;
- the commitment of the EU EOM to impartiality and non-interference;
- the backgrounds and experience of the members of the observer team; and
- the number of polling stations being visited by the observer team.

They should further inform the media that:
- the preliminary findings of the EU EOM will be made in a statement which will be issued at a press conference that all media outlets can attend;
- the EU EOM will publish a comprehensive final report within two months of the completion of the election process; and
- the CO and DCO may be contacted for further details via the EU EOM press and public outreach officer.

EU observers *should not*:
- offer any kind of assessment of the electoral process or any aspect of it, even if the assessment is characterised as a preliminary or personal view;
- express their personal opinion on any aspects of the electoral process;

- speculate on any aspect of the electoral process, such as the conduct of election day or the results; and
- compare the electoral process of the country being observed with any other country (including their own country, or other countries where they may have observed).

7.5 Observation of Voting[89]

7.5.1 Observations Outside Polling Stations

When approaching and entering a polling station, observers should assess the general situation and atmosphere outside and around its location. Possible issues to be aware of include:

- Is the polling station easily accessible, including for disabled people?
- Are there crowds around the polling station? If so, are people waiting to cast their ballot or are they there for another purpose? Are the crowds being kept in order?
- Are security personnel present, and, if so, are they behaving in an appropriate manner (e.g., not harassing voters or using excessive force)?
- Is there any evidence of tension, intimidation or other disturbance outside the polling station?
- Is there any campaigning near the polling station? Does it breach regulations on campaign exclusion zones?
- Are there signs of any irregularities, such as voters being offered inducements to vote for a particular candidate or party?
- Are voters being transported to the polling stations by buses? If so, who is providing the buses and from where are the voters travelling?
- Is there a significant discrepancy in the proportion of men and women voting or waiting to vote?

7.5.2 Meeting with Polling Staff

Upon entering the polling station, observers should introduce themselves and their assistant to the official in charge and show their accreditation. Observers should explain their role, explaining that they will have questions to ask but will not interfere in the voting process. Out of courtesy, observers should ask for agreement to observe in the polling station.

In the exceptional circumstances that a polling official refuses the observer team permission to observe, objects to their presence or gives instructions that prevent effective observation from taking place, the observer team should explain that they are accredited observers and have been invited to observe on election day by the EMB and the government or the authorities. If permission is still refused, the observer team should leave the polling station. Once outside, the observers should inform their designated LTO team. The incident should also be recorded in a 'flash report'.

At all times, observers should be courteous, and should ensure that their conduct outside and inside a polling station is beyond reproach. Interpreters/assistants should act in a similar manner. Observers should exercise restraint, where food and alcoholic drink is offered at polling stations. When leaving a polling station, observers should offer their thanks to the official in charge for their assistance.

7.5.3 Observations Inside Polling Stations

Observers should position themselves for a good view of voting procedures and should also move around the polling station to gain different perspectives. Whenever possible, observers should speak with a number of different polling station officials, particularly when

Voting in West Bank and Gaza, 2006.

the polling committee includes representatives of different political parties. EU observers should also try to speak with others who may be present, including candidate agents, political party representatives, and non-partisan observers. These people, who are often in the same polling station all day, may provide helpful information on the environment at the polling station and whether problems have occurred.

Issues to Consider Raising with Polling Officials

Polling Station Information

- What is the official name and registration number of the polling station?
- How many voters are registered at the polling station?
- Is the voter list for the polling station available for public inspection?
- Are there any supplementary voter lists in use?
- How many people have voted so far at the polling station?

Organisation and Structure of the Polling Committee

- Are all polling officials present?
- How were the polling officials selected? What is their usual employment?
- Do the polling officials represent political parties? Are all parties entitled to representation included in the polling committee? Have any parties been prevented from serving on the committee?
- Did the polling officials receive formal training? What was covered in the training? Did they regard the training as effective? What other training would they like?
- How are the tasks of the polling committee divided among its members?

Essential Materials

- Are there sufficient ballots and other polling materials?
- When were the ballots and other polling materials received? Have they been kept secure at all times?
- How many ballots were received by the polling station?

Others Present

- Are candidate agents or party representatives present? Are they accredited?
- Are domestic non-partisan election observers present? Are they accredited?
- Are observers and agents/representatives restricted in carrying out their activities in any way?
- Are unauthorised people present? Are they directing or interfering in the work of the polling committee?

Problems and Complaints

- Has the polling committee experienced any problems? If so, what?
- Has the polling committee received any complaints? If so, from whom and how were they addressed?
- Have any voters been turned away? If so, on what basis?

Overall Assessments by the Observer Team

- Do the polling officials appear well-trained and familiar with their responsibilities?
- Are the polling officials performing their duties impartially?
- Do the polling officials appear to be free to talk about their duties?
- Are observers and agents/representatives being active and effective in their role?

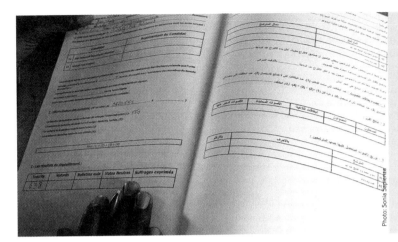

Preparing the polling station paperwork, Mauritania, 2007.

Photo: Sonia Sapiente

7.5.4 Observing the Opening of a Polling Station

The STO team should arrive at their first polling station at least 30 minutes ahead of opening in order to observe opening procedures. The EU observer report form will detail the key procedures to be followed. For the opening process, observers should generally note whether:

- opening procedures are complied with;
- all polling officialls are present;
- all essential materials are present;
- the ballot box was empty at the time of its sealing; and
- the polling station opened on time.

7.5.5 Observing Voting Procedures

Using their observer report forms as guides, STOs should carefully observe all procedures at the polling station. Polling procedures can differ among countries, however, there are some general issues of which to be aware.

- Compliance with the law:
  - Are polling officials conducting polling in accordance with the procedures established by electoral regulations?

- Impartiality of polling officials:
  - Is there evidence that the polling officials are acting in a partisan manner?
  - Are there any campaign materials present inside the polling station?

- Polling station atmosphere:
  - Is the polling station operating in an orderly manner? Is there any over-crowding inside the polling station?

- Are there any delays in the processing of voters?
- Is there evidence inside the polling station that pressure is being placed upon voters or inducements are being offered?
- Is there an atmosphere of intimidation or tension inside the polling station?

- Persons present inside the polling station:
  - Are there police, security forces or government officials present inside the polling station? Is their presence justified? Were they invited in by election officials and if so for what reason? Is their conduct appropriate?
  - Is any person present in polling station whose presence is unauthorised?
  - Is any person other than a polling official directing the work of the polling staff?

- Where voters are required to show identification:
  - Are all voters being required to produce the correct ID documents?

- Where voter lists are used:
  - Are polling officials checking if the voter is included in the voter list before allowing him/her to vote?
  - What measures are being taken to prevent multiple voting (e.g., marking the voter list, using indelible ink)?
  - Are people being turned away because they are not on the voter list?
  - Are people being allowed to vote even if they are not on the voter list?
  - Is there a supplementary list of any sort?

- Where voters are required to sign the voter list:
  - Are voters consistently being asked to sign the voter list?
  - Do there appear to be any identical signatures?

- Ballot papers:
  - Are unmarked ballots being kept securely?
  - Where ballots must be stamped or signed by polling station officials, are they being stamped or signed according to instructions?
  - Are voters being given the correct number of ballots?

- Ballot box:
  - Is the ballot box properly sealed?
  - Is the ballot box in use in full view of all polling officials, agents, observers and voters?
  - Are any full ballot boxes stored securely?

- Right to a secret vote:
  - Are voters provided with the opportunity to vote in secrecy using polling booths or similar arrangements? Does the layout of the polling station or structure of the polling booth breach secrecy?
  - Are polling officials ensuring that voters do not enter a polling booth together or mark their ballots outside of the polling booth?

- Assisted voting:
  - Are voters requiring assistance able to receive it? Is the number of persons requiring assistance unusually high?
  - Is the assistance being provided in accordance with the law?
  - Are the same people assisting many voters?

- Understanding of procedures:
  - Do polling officials appear to understand the procedures?
  - Do voters appear to understand the procedures? Is there any confusion (e.g., over complex ballot papers, use of new voting machines, materials in another language)?

- Participation of women:
  - Are women voters able to vote freely and in secret?
  - Are there female polling officials, observers and party/candidate representatives?
  - Is there a good turnout of women coming to vote? If not, what reasons are given for this?

- Participation of minorities:
  - Are voters from minorities able to vote freely and in secret?
  - Are there polling officials, observers and representatives from minorities?
  - Is there a good turnout of people from minotiries coming to vote? If not, what reasons are given for this?

- Problems:
  - Is there any evidence of disturbance?
  - Is there any evidence of any procedural and/or criminal irregularity? Examples can include:
    - 'multiple voting', where persons are voting more than once;
    - 'stuffed ballots', where the ballot box is unusually full or where ballots can be seen to have been placed in the ballot box in an unusual manner, e.g., without being folded or several ballots folded together;

167

- 'carousel voting', where voters are using pre-marked ballot papers given to them outside of the polling station;
- 'proxy voting', where voters cast ballots for others without formal permission;
- 'voter impersonation', where the person voting is not the person registered as a voter;
- 'under-age voting', where persons voting are clearly too young to be eligible to vote;
- 'group voting', where more than one person votes in a booth at the same time;
- 'family voting', where one family member votes on behalf of other members of the family;
- 'open voting', where voters mark their ballots outside of the polling booth.

Assisted voting, West Bank and Gaza, 2006.

7.5.6 Observing Special Polling Procedures

Some observer teams may be asked to follow special voting procedures, such as early voting, mobile voting, military voting etc. Such work may involve variations on the standard methodology for observation of election day, but will still focus on whether the special procedures are implemented in accordance with the law and international standards so that the electoral rights of citizens are protected. The core team will provide specific guidelines on the observation of special voting procedures.

7.5.7 Observing the Closing of a Polling Station

The observer team should arrive at their last polling station at least 30 minutes ahead of the scheduled closing time. The observer report form will detail the key procedures to be followed, which will include looking at whether:
- closing procedures are complied with;
- the polling station closed on time, unless polling hours have been extended in accordance with the law;
- nobody voted after closing time, except voters waiting in line at closing time;
- the ballot box is closed and sealed as soon as voting ends;
- the number of people who voted at the polling station is counted;

- the number of unused ballot papers is counted; and
- unused ballots are immediately rendered invalid and secured.

7.6 Observation of Counting

After the polling station is closed, the observer team will look at how the votes cast in that polling station are counted. In some countries, the ballot box(es) may be transferred from the polling station to a counting centre, in which case, the STO team should follow the transfer of the ballot box(es) from the polling station to the counting centre.

- In cases of counting at polling stations:
  - Does the counting of ballots take place immediately after the closing of polls (i.e., without a break for food or other purposes)?
  - Have there been any opportunities for interference with the ballot box(es) which may breach their integrity?

- In cases of counting at counting centres:
  - Are there any opportunities for interference in the security of the ballot box(es) during the transfer (e.g., the ballot box was not taken directly to the counting centre)?
  - Are the procedures for handing over the ballot box and other materials to the counting centre followed?
  - Is there any delay between the receipt of the ballot box(es) and the start of counting?
  - Is the ballot box(es) secure at all times after transfer?

- Compliance with the law:
  - Are counting officials conducting the count in accordance with the established procedures?

- Impartiality of counting officials:
  - Is there evidence that the counting officials are acting in a partisan manner?

- Atmosphere during the count:
  - Is the count being conducted in an orderly manner? Is there any overcrowding?
  - Is there a delay in the counting of votes?
  - Is there evidence of pressure being placed upon counting officials or others who are present?
  - Is there an atmosphere of intimidation or tension at the count?

- Persons present at the count:
  - Are there police or security forces present at the count? Is their presence justified? Is their conduct appropriate?
  - Are non-partisan domestic observers and party/candidate representatives present and, if so, are they able to observe the full counting process? If party/candidate agents are present, who do they represent?
  - Is any person present at the count whose presence is unauthorised?
  - Is any person other than a counting official directing the count?

- Reconciliation and counting of votes:
  - Was the ballot box opened and votes counted in the presence of all counting officials, party/candidate representatives and observers?
  - Is the total number of ballots inside the ballot box counted before votes for individual parties/candidates are counted?
  - Does the number of ballot papers inside the ballot box reconcile with the number of persons who are recorded as having voted?
  - Are all counting officials, party/candidate representatives and observers able to inspect ballots to see how they have been marked?
  - Are all ballots that indicate the clear choice of the voter considered valid?
  - Is the decision to determine the validity of a ballot being taken in accordance with the law?
  - Is the decision to determine the validity of a ballot being taken in in a consistent and consultative manner?
  - Are there any ballots that are marked in a manner that could identify the voter and thereby violate the secrecy of the vote (e.g., include the name of the voter or other unusual markings that could be used for identification)?

- Discrepancies:
  - Is there evidence of discrepancies in the results?

- Results:
  - Does the number of ballots inside the ballot box correspond with the number of ballots cast at the polling station?
  - Do the results accurately reflect the votes counted? Are the results recorded accurately onto official protocols?

- Understanding of procedures:
  - Do counting officials appear to understand the procedures?
  - Do observers and agents/representatives appear to understand the procedures and their role?

- Problems and complaints:
  - Is there any evidence of any procedural and/or criminal irregularity, such as 'stuffed ballots'?
  - Have there been any formal complaints relating to the counting process?
  - Does any counting official, candidate agent or party representative dispute the accuracy of the results?
  - If there is a dispute over the validity of a particular ballot or ballots, how is this resolved?

Results Protocols

The results from the counting of votes will be recorded in official results protocols, which will require all significant data, such as the number of people who voted, the total number of ballots cast, the number of votes for each candidate and the number of invalid votes. The protocol may also be used to identify discrepancies

Recording results, Mauritania, 2007.

in the results. Counting officials and persons present at the count may be required to sign the results protocol. Key issues in relation to the results protocol are:

- Was the results protocol completed by competent counting officials without confusion?
- Was the results protocol completed accurately and in detail?
- Did anyone refuse to sign the protocol or attach an objection or complaint?
- Are official copies of the results made available to candidate agents, party representatives and observers? and
- Is an official copy of the results immediately posted for public inspection?

Each observer team should record the results of the polling station, where it observed the counting of votes, and obtain a copy of the results protocol, if possible. The information contained within it can be used by the EU EOM in its cross-checking of the results of the election.

7.7   Observation of the Tabulation Process

Observing the tabulation is particularly important, since errors or irregularities can have a far greater effect on the election results than problems at individual polling stations. After the votes at polling stations have been counted, the results will need to be transmitted to a higher level EMB or tabulation centre, where they will be aggregated to determine which parties/candidates are successful. There may be several stages in a tabulation process, all of which should be undertaken in a prompt and fully transparent manner. Observer teams may be required to undertake the following tasks:

- accompany the physical transfer of electoral material, including the results protocol, from the counting location to a tabulation centre and observe the handover of electoral material at the tabulation centre;
- observe the process of tabulating results, in particular, to see whether results of the vote count are honestly and accurately included in the tabulation;
- assess whether the tabulation process is undertaken in a transparent and consistent manner;
- note whether detailed polling station results are published at every level of the election administration as soon as they are available, including the number of votes for each candidate or political party, and the number of invalid votes; and
- obtain copies of the tabulated data for cross-checking purposes.

The tabulation of results may be undertaken electronically, including sometimes via a computer network to a centralised tabulation centre, which may create access difficulties for observers. The observer team should seek permission from the election official in charge to see the procedural steps for the electronic tabulation of results, including receipt and inputting of data.

The EU EOM will often assign dedicated STO teams to tabulation or counting centres, or several STO teams may be assigned to work in shifts, in order to observe the full tabulation process after election day. In such cases, the core team will issue specific guidelines.

7.8   Post-Election Day Observation

As part of its assessment of the immediate post-election day period, the EU EOM will direct LTOs and STOs to undertake a range of tasks including:

- checking whether detailed results are posted at polling stations/counting centres and broken down to the possible lowest level, and are published at all levels of the EMB in the AoR;
- cross-checking the accuracy of published results to the results posted at polling stations;
- observing the work of counting or results tabulation centres, where this is ongoing;
- meeting with interlocutors and seeking their opinions on election day and the post-election day period and improvements that can be made to the framework and conditions for elections;
- following complaints or appeals have been submitted; and
- observing the general post-election day environment, including problems such as violence, intimidation and harassment.

89. See 'General Guidelines for Observers when visiting Polling Stations' (Council Decision 9262/98 at Annex III of the 2000 Communication on Election Assistance and Observation).

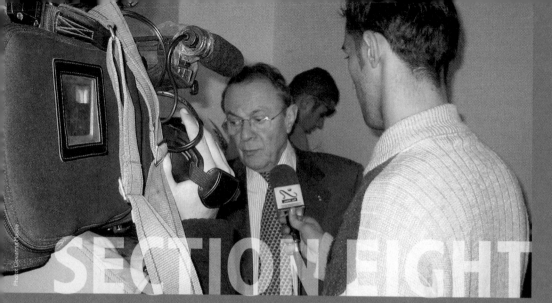

8. Reporting

8.1 Guidelines for Reporting by EU EOMs

The production of reports is a crucial element of the work of the mission. All reports produced by the EU EOM should be of the highest possible standards. Attention should be paid to ensuring that all information is accurate and objective and based on credible sources which can be substantiated with concrete examples. All mission reports should make clear what has been directly observed by EU observers, and what has been reported to them by interlocutors. While an EU EOM may refer to information from interlocutors that comes from credible or multiple sources, information that has no supporting evidence, or comes from a single partisan source, should be clearly indicated as such. Some information from interlocutors may be sensitive and need to be treated in confidence, with anonymity protected.

Mission reports should be concise, within the specified length, and written in clear language. They should follow a consistent structure, using the guidelines and templates that are provided by the European Commission.[90] When making reference to international standards for elections, a report should source the reference, detailing the relevant universal and/or regional instruments, to show that these are being used as the basis of the EU EOM assessment.

8.2   Interim Reports

The EU EOM core team produces interim reports that will provide a regular update and analysis of electoral developments. The reports are usually produced every week over the course of the deployment of the EU EOM. They are internal EU documents, distributed only to EU institutions.[91]

8.2.1 Purpose of Interim Reports

Interim reports provide an overview of all aspects of the electoral process assessed by the EU EOM during the reporting period. This includes political developments, administrative preparations for the elections, voter registration, candidate registration, party/candidate backgrounds, campaigning, the media environment, election-related complaints, human rights issues and the participation of women and minorities. Interim reports also provide key information on the elections (e.g., maps of the country, tables of data on candidates, and number of voters) and refer to key mission events, such as the deployment of LTOs and STOs to the field.

The information and analysis contained in interim reports should provide a basis for the findings and conclusions outlined by the EU EOM in its preliminary statement and final report. However, an interim report offers only preliminary analysis that is based on information available at the time and, thus, cannot be distributed publicly or to any persons or organisations outside the EU structures.

8.2.2 Preparation of Interim Reports

Interim reports are drafted by the DCO, on behalf of the chief observer, and are based on contributions from core team members and the summary of LTO weekly reports. The timing of the interim reports is incorporated in to the EU EOM calendar and corresponds with the reporting schedule for LTOs. Interim reports are written in English or French and should not exceed five pages, including a one page executive summary. A draft of the interim report is shared with the DG External Relations election desk for comments to ensure consistency in observation and reporting methodology. The chief observer has the final decision on the final text of the interim report.

8.2.3 Other Internal Reports

Where appropriate, the EU EOM may produce spot reports on events or developments that happen outside of the reporting schedule and need to be brought to the urgent attention of the EU structures. These reports supplement interim reports, but do not replace them. The EU EOM will also produce operational reports that cover logistical issues and the work of the IP during the course of the mission.

8.3 Preliminary Statement

The preliminary statement is the first post-election assessment by the EU EOM and is usually issued at a press conference within 48 hours of the close of polling. It is usually the highest profile output of the mission, attracting significant levels of political, diplomatic and media interest. The preliminary statement is a public document and should be written to be read by election stakeholders in the host country (candidates, political parties, domestic observers, journalists, voters etc.) as well as an international audience. Working towards a credible preliminary statement should be a primary focus for all core team members and observers during their work on the mission. When issued, the chief observer stresses the *preliminary* nature of the statement and underlines that the EU EOM will issue its overall assessment later, in its final report.

8.3.1 Purpose of the Preliminary Statement

The preliminary statement outlines the EU EOM's preliminary findings and conclusions on the stages of the electoral process that have taken place, and the extent to which the mission considers the election has so far been conducted in line with international standards for elections. As such, the preliminary statement establishes an important indicator for electoral stakeholders of the credibility of the election process. It is important that the mission highlights that it will continue to observe the completion of the counting an tabulation of votes (where ongoing), publication of results, the resolution of any complaints or appeals, and the wider post-election environment.

If there are significant problems with the post-election period, the EU EOM may choose to release a second preliminary statement ahead of the final report, to outline further preliminary findings and conclusions on such issues as the results process, complaints and appeals processes or the post-election political environment.

8.3.2 Preparation of the Preliminary Statement

The preliminary statement is drafted by the DCO, on behalf of the CO, based on contributions from the core team. It should follow the guidelines and template provided by the European Commission. Given the tight and immovable deadlines in place over an election day period, preparing a preliminary statement is a challenging task that requires a structured process of drafting, review and finalisation that should start well ahead of election day. An initial draft of the preliminary statement is shared with the DG External Relations election desk at least 48 hours before release for comments, to ensure consistency in reporting methodology. Shortly before release, the findings of EU observers on election day will be added. The CO has the final decision on the final text in the preliminary statement.

The preliminary statement is written in English or French and should be translated into the official languages of the host country. As far as possible, it should not exceed seven pages, including a bullet point summary at the beginning. The preliminary statement should provide a clear overall conclusion, outlined in a 'headline conclusion' and the first bullet point. The statement will be accompanied by a press release that provides an overview of the mission's findings, along with quotes from the CO, and the leader of the European Parliament observer delegation.

8.3.3 Sharing the Preliminary Statement

The preliminary statement is the independent assessment of an EU EOM. The CO will consult with the Head of the European Parliament (MEP) delegation, if one is present, with a view to the delegation's endorsement of the preliminary statement. There may also be circumstances where the mission will liaise closely with other observer delegations, before issuing the preliminary statement. It is also common practice for observer groups who are signatories of the *Declaration of Principles for International Election Observation* to share their findings prior to the release of the preliminary statement.

One hour ahead of the press conference, a copy of the preliminary statement should be provided to the state and electoral authorities (usually the head of the EMB and the Ministry of Foreign Affairs) with whom memorandums of understanding have been signed. It should be made clear, however, that the preliminary statement is being provided as a courtesy only, and that under no circumstances will the EU EOM change or negotiate the contents.

The preliminary statement should be finalised in sufficient time to ensure it is translated and photocopied for the press conference. Immediately upon its release, the statement (in languages in which it is produced) should be placed on the mission website. Copies should be distributed to the national and international media, and local interlocutors. The statement should also be distributed to LTOs for their information and, in appropriate languages, for distibution to interlcutors in their AoRs.

8.4   The Final Report

The final report contains the EU EOM's overall assessment of the election and is normally issued within two months of the completion of the electoral process. The report plays a highly important political and technical function in providing a comprehensive and independent assessment of the election process. As with the preliminary statement, the final report is a public document. This means that it should be written to be read by all election stakeholders in the host country, as well as by an international audience.

8.4.1 Purpose of the Final Report

The final report details the EU EOM's overall findings and conclusions on all aspects of the election process, and its assessment of the degree to which the election was conducted in accordance with international standards. A key feature of the final report is the detailed and constructive recommendations it offers to improve the framework and conduct of future elections and strengthen democratic institutions. In this context, it will also serve to identify possible areas for EU-supported technical advice and assistance.

8.4.2 Preparation of the Final Report

Drafting of the final report is undertaken by the DCO, under the direction of the CO, based on contributions from the core team. The final report will be prepared in accordance with the guidelines and template provided by the European Commission. A draft of the final report is shared with the DG External Relations election desk to ensure consistency in reporting methodology. However, ultimate responsibility for its content rests with the CO. In contrast to the brevity of the preliminary statement, the final report can provide detailed analysis and descriptions of technical issues which should be clearly explained. Whenever possible, in order to ensure accessibility for all stakeholders, the final report should avoid highly technical language or jargon. Whenever relevant, the final report should refer to and quote specific international and regional standards.

The final report builds upon the conclusions made by the mission in its preliminary statement. If the overall assessment of the mission has changed in any way from the preliminary assessments – for example if a generally 'positive' preliminary statement has become a 'negative' final report because of post-election problems with results or violence – the final report should clearly explain the reasons for this change.

The final report is usually prepared during the closing period of the mission, and, where possible, a first draft should be prepared before the departure of the core team. If there are on-going political and electoral developments (such as delays in the results process, the resolution of complaints or any post-election instability), it may be necessary for the draft to be updated after the return of the core team to Europe. The final report will be produced in English or French and translated into the official languages of the host country to make it as broadly available as possible. It will be placed on the EU EOM website and the website of the European Commission.

8.4.3 Recommendations

Recommendations to improve the electoral process are a crucial part of the EU EOM's final report. They are likely to be used in the assessment of future elections and the wider democratisation process in the host country observed. The European Commission will seek to follow-up on the implementation of the re-commendations, and often designs its electoral advice and technical assistance programmes drawing on the EU EOM's recommendations. An EU EOM is well-placed to provide important insight as to where electoral assistance is necessary, feasible, and useful.

In its final report, an EU EOM will make recommendations for improvements to the electoral process. Each recommendation will be constructive, and where appropia-

Launching the EU EOM in Lebanon, 2005.

te, based on concrete examples of problems referred to in the body of the final report, where the EU EOM identifies concerns over a failure for the election process to meet international standards or best practice for elections. The recommendations will highlight where action is needed to address issues (e.g., inconsistency, lack of transparency, lack of resources, or lack of public confidence) that have led to problems during the election process. Recommendations can also be offered where action should be taken to improve the efficiency, effectiveness, and institutional capacity of electoral stakeholders (e.g., the election administration, political parties, civil society, media).

Each recommendation should be realistically achievable, assuming there is political will to improve the electoral process ahead of future elections. The final report should attempt to distinguish between priority recommendations and others of lesser priority.

8.4.4 Release of the Final Report

The CO and the DCO return to the country to deliver the final report. In the course of this visit, they will present the report to the state and electoral authorities, political parties and CSOs. At these meetings, the CO should be prepared to explain the basis of the assessment contained in the report and, in particular, to discuss practical steps for the implementation of the recommendations. After sharing the final report with key interlocutors, the chief observer should hold a press conference to officially release the final report to the media and the wider public. A press release may also be issued to accompany the final report that includes quotes by the CO.

Preparation of the return visit, which will also include a briefing for the resident diplomatic community and organisation of roundtable for election stakeholders where the findings, conclusions and recommendations can be discussed, is organised by the European Commission Delegation.

8.5   Final Internal Report

The core team will produce a final internal report on the implementation of the EU EOM that provides an overview of logistical, administrative and security aspects of the mission, as well as reporting on public outreach activities. The final internal report will be prepared in accordance whith the mission terms of reference and will include a review of the work of the IP. A specific focus of the final internal report is identification of any lessons learned for improvements to EU EOM programming and methodology. The final internal report is drafted by the DCO, on behalf of the CO, and will be based on contributions from the core team. It will be submitted to the European Commission ahead of the core team final debriefing in Brussels.

8.6   Mission Follow-Up Report

An EU EOM is well-placed to identify where electoral assistance (to public bodies, observer groups, and other civil society organisations) is necessary, feasible and useful. Therefore, as part of its work, an EU EOM will consider the possible areas where technical advice and assistance can be provided to encourage the implementation of its recommendations. To this end, an EU EOM should prepare a brief follow-up report that outlines practical recommendations for possible areas of assistance on election-related matters. The follow-up report is internal and is submitted to the European Commission by the CO. It is drafted by the DCO in consultation with the core team.

---

90. Guidelines and templates examples for EU EOM reporting can be found on http://ec.europa.eu/external_relations/human_rights/eu_election_ass_observ/index.htm and on the NEEDS website (www.needs-network.org).

91. Within the European Commission, the interim reports will be distributed to: DG External Relations, DG EuropeAid, DG Development, the Cabinets of the Commissioner for External Relations and the Commissioner for Development, and the Delegation of the European Commission to the host country. The interim reports will also be distributed to the EU Presidency, the Ministries of Foreign Affairs of all EU Member States, including election teams, and the Election Coordination Group of the European Parliament.

Annex 1. Declaration of Principles for International Election Observation

October 27, 2005

Genuine democratic elections are an expression of sovereignty, which belongs to the people of a country, the free expression of whose will provides the basis for the authority and legitimacy of government. The rights of citizens to vote and to be elected at periodic, genuine democratic elections are internationally recognized human rights. Genuine democratic elections serve to resolve peacefully the competition for political power within a country and thus are central to the maintenance of peace and stability. Where governments are legitimized through genuine democratic elections, the scope for non-democratic challenges to power is reduced.

Genuine democratic elections are a requisite condition for democratic governance, because they are the vehicle through which the people of a country freely express their will, on a basis established by law, as to who shall have the legitimacy to govern in their name and in their interests. Achieving genuine democratic elections is a part of establishing broader processes and institutions of democratic governance. Therefore, while all election processes should reflect universal principles for genuine democratic elections, no election can be separated from the political, cultural and historical context in which it takes place.

Genuine democratic elections cannot be achieved unless a wide range of other human rights and fundamental freedoms can be exercised on an ongoing basis without discrimination based on race, colour, sex, language, religion, political or other opinion, national or social origin, property, birth or other status, including among others disabilities, and without arbitrary and unreasonable restrictions. They, like other human rights and democracy more broadly, cannot be achieved without the protections of the rule of law. These precepts are recognized by human rights and other international instruments and by the documents of numerous intergovernmental organizations. Achieving genuine democratic elections therefore has become a matter of concern for international organizations, just as it is the concern of national institutions, political competitors, citizens and their civic organizations.

International election observation expresses the interest of the international community in the achievement of democratic elections, as part of democratic development, including respect for human rights and the rule of law. International election observation, which focuses on civil and political rights, is part of international human rights monitoring and must be conducted on the basis of the highest standards for impartiality concerning national political competitors and must be free from any bilateral or multilateral considerations that could conflict with impartiality. It assesses election processes in accordance with international principles for genuine democratic elections and domestic law, while recognizing that it is the people of a country who ultimately determine credibility and legitimacy of an election process.

International election observation has the potential to enhance the integrity of election processes, by deterring and exposing irregularities and fraud and by providing recommendations for improving electoral processes. It can promote public confidence, as warranted, promote electoral participation and mitigate the potential for election-related conflict. It also serves to enhance international understanding through the sharing of experiences and information about democratic development.

International election observation has become widely accepted around the world and plays an important role in providing accurate and impartial assessments about the nature of electoral processes. Accurate and impartial international election observation requires credible methodologies and cooperation with national authorities, the national political competitors (political parties, candidates and supporters of positions on referenda), domestic election monitoring organizations and other credible international election observer organizations, among others.

The intergovernmental and international nongovernmental organizations endorsing this Declaration and the accompanying Code of Conduct for International Election Observers therefore have joined to declare:

1) Genuine democratic elections are an expression of sovereignty, which belongs to the people of a country, the free expression of whose will provides the basis for the authority and legitimacy of government. The rights of citizens to vote and to be elected at periodic, genuine democratic elections are internationally recognized human rights. Genuine democratic elections are central for maintaining peace and stability, and they provide the mandate for democratic governance.

2) In accordance with the Universal Declaration of Human Rights, the International Covenant for Civil and Political Rights and other international instruments, everyone has the right and must be provided with the opportunity to participate in the government and public affairs of his or her country, without any discrimination prohibited by international human rights principles and without any unreasonable restrictions. This right can be exercised directly, by participating in referenda, standing for elected office and by other means, or can be exercised through freely chosen representatives.

3) The will of the people of a country is the basis for the authority of government, and that will must be determined through genuine periodic elections, which guarantee the right and opportunity to vote freely and to be elected fairly through universal and equal suffrage by secret balloting or equivalent free voting procedures, the results of which

are accurately counted, announced and respected. A significant number of rights and freedoms, processes, laws and institutions are therefore involved in achieving genuine democratic elections.

4) International election observation is: the systematic, comprehensive and accurate gathering of information concerning the laws, processes and institutions related to the conduct of elections and other factors concerning the overall electoral environment; the impartial and professional analysis of such information; and the drawing of conclusions about the character of electoral processes based on the highest standards for accuracy of information and impartiality of analysis. International election observation should, when possible, offer recommendations for improving the integrity and effectiveness of electoral and related processes, while not interfering in and thus hindering such processes. International election observation missions are: organized efforts of intergovernmental and international nongovernmental organizations and associations to conduct international election observation.

5) International election observation evaluates pre-election, election-day and post-election periods through comprehensive, long-term observation, employing a variety of techniques. As part of these efforts, specialized observation missions may examine limited pre-election or post-election issues and specific processes (such as, delimitation of election districts, voter registration, use of electronic technologies and functioning of electoral complaint mechanisms). Stand-alone, specialized observation missions may also be employed, as long as such missions make clear public statements that their activities and conclusions are limited in scope and that they draw no conclusions about the overall election process based on such limited activities. All observer missions must make concerted efforts to place the election day into its context and not to over-emphasize the importance of election day observations. International election observation examines conditions relating to the right to vote and to be elected, including, among other things, discrimination or other obstacles that hinder participation in electoral processes based on political or other opinion, gender, race, colour, ethnicity, language, religion, national or social origin, property, birth or other status, such as physical disabilities. The findings of international election observation missions provide a factual common point of reference for all persons interested in the elections, including the political competitors. This can be particularly valuable in the context of disputed elections, where impartial and accurate findings can help to mit-igate the potential for conflicts.

6) International election observation is conducted for the benefit of the people of the country holding the elections and for the benefit of the international community. It is process oriented, not concerned with any particular electoral result, and is concerned with results only to the degree that they are reported honestly and accurately in a transparent and timely manner. No one should be allowed to be a member of an international election observer mission unless that person is free from any political, economic or other conflicts of interest that would interfere with conducting observations accurately and impartially and/or drawing conclusions about the character of the election process

accurately and impartially. These criteria must be met effectively over extended periods by long-term observers, as well as during the more limited periods of election day observation, each of which periods present specific challenges for independent and impartial analysis. International election observation missions should not accept funding or infrastructural support from the government whose elections are being observed, as it may raise a significant conflict of interest and undermine confidence in the integrity of the mission's findings. International election observation delegations should be prepared to disclose the sources of their funding upon appropriate and reasonable requests.

7) International election observation missions are expected to issue timely, accurate and impartial statements to the public (including providing copies to electoral authorities and other appropriate national entities), presenting their findings, conclusions and any appropriate recommendations they determine could help improve election related processes. Missions should announce publicly their presence in a country, including the mission's mandate, composition and duration, make periodic reports as warranted and issue a preliminary post-election statement of findings and a final report upon the conclusion of the election process. International election observation missions may conduct private meetings with those concerned with organizing genuine democratic elections in a country to discuss the mission's findings, conclusions and recommendations. International election observation missions may also report to their respective intergovernmental or international nongovernmental organizations.

8) The organizations that endorse this Declaration and the accompanying Code of Conduct for International Election Observers pledge to cooperate with each other in conducting international election observation missions. International election observation can be conducted, for example, by: individual international election observer missions; ad hoc joint international election observation missions; or coordinated international election observation missions. In all circumstances, the endorsing organizations pledge to work together to maximize the contribution of their international election observation missions.

9) International election observation must be conducted with respect for the sovereignty of the country holding elections and with respect for the human rights of the people of the country. International election observation missions must respect the laws of the host country, as well as national authorities, including electoral bodies, and act in a manner that is consistent with respecting and promoting human rights and fundamental freedoms.

10) International election observation missions must actively seek cooperation with host country electoral authorities and must not obstruct the election process.

11) A decision by any organization to organize an international election observation mission or to explore the possibility of organizing an observation mission does not imply that the organization necessarily deems the election process in the country holding the elec-

tions to be credible. An organization should not send an international election observation mission to a country under conditions that make it likely that its presence will be interpreted as giving legitimacy to a clearly undemocratic electoral process, and international election observation missions in any such circumstance should make public statements to ensure that their presence does not imply such legitimacy.

12) In order for an international election observation mission to effectively and credibly conduct its work basic conditions must be met. An international election observation mission therefore should not be organized unless the country holding the election takes the following actions:

(a) Issues an invitation or otherwise indicates its willingness to accept international election observation missions in accordance with each organization's requirements sufficiently in advance of elections to allow analysis of all of the processes that are important to organizing genuine democratic elections;

(b) Guarantees unimpeded access of the international election observer mission to all stages of the election process and all election technologies, including electronic technologies and the certification processes for electronic voting and other technologies, without requiring election observation missions to enter into confidentiality or other nondisclosure agreements concerning technologies or election processes, and recognizes that international election observation missions may not certify technologies as acceptable;

(c) Guarantees unimpeded access to all persons concerned with election processes, including: (i) electoral officials at all levels, upon reasonable requests, (ii) members of legislative bodies and government and security officials whose functions are relevant to organizing genuine democratic elections, (iii) all of the political parties, organizations and persons that have sought to compete in the elections (including those that qualified, those that were disqualified and those that withdrew from participating) and those that abstained from participating, (iv) news media personnel, and (v) all organizations and persons that are interested in achieving genuine democratic elections in the country;

(d) Guarantees freedom of movement around the country for all members of the international election observer mission;

(e) Guarantees the international election observer mission's freedom to issue without interference public statements and reports concerning its findings and recommendations about election related processes and developments;

(f) Guarantees that no governmental, security or electoral authority will interfere in the selection of individual observers or other members of the international election observation mission or attempt to limit its numbers;

(g) Guarantees full, country-wide accreditation (that is, the issuing of any identification or document required to conduct election observation) for all persons selected to be observers or other participants by the international election observation mission as long as the mission complies with clearly defined, reasonable and non-discriminatory requirements for accreditation;

(h) Guarantees that no governmental, security or electoral authority will interfere in the activities of the international election observation mission; and

(i) Guarantees that no governmental authority will pressure, threaten action against or take any reprisal against any national or foreign citizen who works for, assists or provides information to the international election observation mission in accordance with international principles for election observation.

As a prerequisite to organizing an international election observation mission, intergovernmental and international nongovernmental organizations may require that such guarantees are set forth in a memorandum of understanding or similar document agreed upon by governmental and/or electoral authorities. Election observation is a civilian activity, and its utility is questionable in circumstances that present severe security risks, limit safe deployments of observers or otherwise would negate employing credible election observation methodologies.

13) International election observation missions should seek and may require acceptance of their presence by all major political competitors.

14) Political contestants (parties, candidates and supporters of positions on referenda) have vested interests in the electoral process through their rights to be elected and to participate directly in government. They therefore should be allowed to monitor all processes related to elections and observe procedures, including among other things the functioning of electronic and other electoral technologies inside polling stations, counting centers and other electoral facilities, as well as the transport of ballots and other sensitive materials.

15) International election observation missions should: (i) establish communications with all political competitors in the election process, including representatives of political parties and candidates who may have information concerning the integrity of the election process; (ii) welcome information provided by them concerning the nature of the process; (iii) independently and impartially evaluate such information; and (iv) should evaluate as an important aspect of international election observation whether the political contestants are, on a nondiscriminatory basis, afforded access to verify the integrity of all elements and stages of the election process. International election observation missions should in their recommendations, which may be issued in writing or otherwise be presented at various stages of the election process, advocate for removing any undue restrictions or interference against activities by the political competitors to safeguard the integrity of electoral processes.

16) Citizens have an internationally recognized right to associate and a right to participate in governmental and public affairs in their country. These rights may be exercised through nongovernmental organizations monitoring all processes related to elections and observing procedures, including among other things the functioning of electronic and other electoral technologies inside polling stations, counting centers and other electoral facilities, as well as the transport of ballots and other sensitive materials. International election observation missions should evaluate and report on whether domestic nonpartisan election monitoring and observation organizations are able, on a

nondiscriminatory basis, to conduct their activities without undue restrictions or interference. International election observation missions should advocate for the right of citizens to conduct domestic nonpartisan election observation without any undue restrictions or interference and should in their recommendations address removing any such undue restrictions or interference.

17) International election observation missions should identify, establish regular communications with and cooperate as appropriate with credible domestic nonpartisan election monitoring organizations. International election observation missions should welcome information provided by such organizations concerning the nature of the election process. Upon independent evaluation of information provided by such organizations, their findings can provide an important complement to the findings of international election observation missions, although international election observation missions must remain independent. International election observation missions therefore should make every reasonable effort to consult with such organizations before issuing any statements.

18) The intergovernmental and international nongovernmental organizations endorsing this Declaration recognize that substantial progress has been made in establishing standards, principles and commitments concerning genuine democratic elections and commit themselves to use a statement of such principles in making observations, judgments and conclusions about the character of election processes and pledge to be transparent about the principles and observation methodologies they employ.

19) The intergovernmental and nongovernmental organizations endorsing this Declaration recognize that there are a variety of credible methodologies for observing election processes and commit to sharing approaches and harmonizing methodologies as appropriate. They also recognize that international election observation missions must be of sufficient size to determine independently and impartially the character of election processes in a country and must be of sufficient duration to determine the character of all of the critical elements of the election process in the pre-election, election-day and post-election periods — unless an observation activity is focused on and therefore only comments on one or a limited number of elements of the election process. They further recognize that it is necessary not to isolate or over-emphasize election day observations, and that such observations must be placed into the context of the overall electoral process.

20) The intergovernmental and international nongovernmental organizations endorsing this Declaration recognize that international election observation missions should include persons of sufficiently diverse political and professional skills, standing and proven integrity to observe and judge processes in light of: expertise in electoral processes and established electoral principles; international human rights; comparative election law and administration practices (including use of computer and other election technology); comparative political processes and country specific considerations. The endorsing organizations also recognize the importance of balanced gender

diversity in the composition of participants and leadership of international election observation missions, as well as diversity of citizenship in such missions.

21) The intergovernmental and international nongovernmental organizations endorsing this Declaration commit to: (i) familiarize all participants in their international election observation missions concerning the principles of accuracy of information and political impartiality in making judgments and conclusions; (ii) provide a terms of reference or similar document, explaining the purposes of the mission; (iii) provide information concerning relevant national laws and regulations, the general political environment and other matters, including those that relate to the security and well being of observers; (iv) instruct all participants in the election observation mission concerning the methodologies to be employed; and (v) require all participants in the election observation mission to read and pledge to abide by the Code of Conduct for International Election Observers, which accompanies this Declaration and which may be modified without changing its substance to fit requirements of the organization, or pledge to abide by a pre-existing code of conduct of the organization that is substantially the same as the accompanying Code of Conduct.

22) The intergovernmental and international nongovernmental organizations endorsing this Declaration commit to use every effort to comply with the terms of the Declaration and the accompanying Code of Conduct for International Election Observers. Any time that an endorsing organization deems it necessary to depart from any of terms of the Declaration or the Accompanying Code of Conduct in order to conduct election observation in keeping with the spirit of the Declaration, the organization will explain in its public statements and will be prepared to answer appropriate questions from other endorsing organizations concerning why it was necessary to do so.

23) The endorsing organizations recognize that governments send observer delegations to elections in other countries and that others also observe elections. The endorsing organizations welcome any such observers agreeing on an ad hoc basis to this declaration and abiding by the accompanying Code of Conduct for International Election Observers.

24) This Declaration and the accompanying Code of Conduct for International Election Observers are intended to be technical documents that do not require action by the political bodies of endorsing organizations (such as assemblies, councils or boards of directors), though such actions are welcome. This Declaration and the accompanying Code of Conduct for International Election Observers remain open for endorsement by other intergovernmental and international nongovernmental organizations. Endorsements should be recorded with the United Nations Electoral Assistance Division.

[The Code of Conduct follows on the next page.]

Code of Conduct for International Election Observers

International election observation is widely accepted around the world. It is conducted by inter-governmental and international nongovernmental organizations and associations in order to provide an impartial and accurate assessment of the nature of election processes for the benefit of the population of the country where the election is held and for the benefit of the international community. Much therefore depends on ensuring the integrity of international election observation, and all who are part of this international election observation mission, including long-term and short-term observers, members of assessment delegations, specialized observation teams and leaders of the mission, must subscribe to and follow this Code of Conduct.

Respect Sovereignty and International Human Rights

Elections are an expression of sovereignty, which belongs to the people of a country, the free expression of whose will provides the basis for the authority and legitimacy of government. The rights of citizens to vote and to be elected at periodic, genuine elections are internationally recognized human rights, and they require the exercise of a number of fundamental rights and freedoms. Election observers must respect the sovereignty of the host country, as well as the human rights and fundamental freedoms of its people.

Respect the Laws of the Country and the Authority of Electoral Bodies

Observers must respect the laws of the host country and the authority of the bodies charged with administering the electoral process. Observers must follow any lawful instruction from the country's governmental, security and electoral authorities. Observers also must maintain a respectful attitude toward electoral officials and other national authorities. Observers must note if laws, regulations or the actions of state and/or electoral officials unduly burden or obstruct the exercise of election-related rights guaranteed by law, constitution or applicable international instruments.

Respect the Integrity of the International Election Observation Mission

Observers must respect and protect the integrity of the international election observation mission. This includes following this Code of Conduct, any written instructions (such as a terms of reference, directives and guidelines) and any verbal instructions from the observation mission's leadership. Observers must: attend all of the observation mission's required briefings, trainings and debriefings; become familiar with the election law, regulations and other relevant laws as directed by the observation mission; and carefully adhere to the methodologies employed by the observation mission. Observers also must report to the leadership of the observation mission any conflicts of interest they may have and any improper behavior they see conducted by other observers that are part of the mission.

Maintain Strict Political Impartiality at All Times

Observers must maintain strict political impartiality at all times, including leisure time in the host country. They must not express or exhibit any bias or preference in relation to national authorities, political parties, candidates, referenda issues or in relation to any contentious issues in the election process. Observers also must not conduct any activity that could be reasonably perceived as favoring or providing partisan gain for any political competitor in the host country, such as wearing or displaying any partisan symbols, colors, banners or accepting anything of value from political competitors.

Do Not Obstruct Election Processes

Observers must not obstruct any element of the election process, including pre-election processes, voting, counting and tabulation of results and processes transpiring after election day. Observers may bring irregularities, fraud or significant problems to the attention of election officials on the spot, unless this is prohibited by law, and must do so in a non-obstructive manner. Observers may ask questions of election officials, political party representatives and other observers inside polling stations and may answer questions about their own activities, as long as observers do not obstruct the election process. In answering questions observers should not seek to direct the election process. Observers may ask and answer questions of voters but may not ask them to tell for whom or what party or referendum position they voted.

Provide Appropriate Identification

Observers must display identification provided by the election observation mission, as well as identification required by national authorities, and must present it to electoral officials and other interested national authorities when requested.

Maintain Accuracy of Observations and Professionalism in Drawing Conclusions

Observers must ensure that all of their observations are accurate. Observations must be comprehensive, noting positive as well as negative factors, distinguishing between significant and insignificant factors and identifying patterns that could have an important impact on the integrity of the election process. Observers' judgments must be based on the highest standards for accuracy of information and impartiality of analysis, distinguishing subjective factors from objective evidence. Observers must base all conclusions on factual and verifiable evidence and not draw conclusions prematurely. Observers also must keep a well documented record of where they observed, the observations made and other relevant information as required by the election observation mission and must turn in such documentation to the mission.

Refrain from Making Comments to the Public or the Media before the Mission Speaks

Observers must refrain from making any personal comments about their observations or conclusions to the news media or members of the public before the election observation mission makes a statement, unless specifically instructed otherwise by the observation mission's leadership. Observers may explain the nature of the observation mission, its activities and other matters deemed appropriate by the observation mission and should refer the media or other interested persons to the those individuals designated by the observation mission.

Cooperate with Other Election Observers

Observers must be aware of other election observation missions, both international and domestic, and cooperate with them as instructed by the leadership of the election observation mission.

Maintain Proper Personal Behavior

Observers must maintain proper personal behavior and respect others, including exhibiting sensitivity for host-country cultures and customs, exercise sound judgment in personal inter-actions and observe the highest level of professional conduct at all times, including leisure time.

Violations of This Code of Conduct

In a case of concern about the violation of this Code of Conduct, the election observation mission shall conduct an inquiry into the matter. If a serious violation is found to have occurred, the observer concerned may have their observer accreditation withdrawn or be dismissed from the election observation mission. The authority for such determinations rests solely with the leadership of the election observation mission.

Pledge to Follow This Code of Conduct

Every person who participates in this election observation mission must read and understand this Code of Conduct and must sign a pledge to follow it.

Original Endorsing Organizations as of October 24, 2005:

African Union

Asian Network for Free Elections (ANFREL)

The Carter Center

Center for Electoral Promotion and Assistance (CAPEL)

Commonwealth Secretariat

Council of Europe European Commission for Democracy through Law (Venice Commission)

Council of Europe – Parliamentary Assembly

Electoral Institute of Southern Africa (EISA)

European Commission

European Network of Election Monitoring Organizations (ENEMO)

Electoral Reform International Services (ERIS)

IFES

International IDEA

Inter-Parliamentary Union

International Republican Institute (IRI)

National Democratic Institute (NDI)

Organization of American States (OAS)

Organization for Security and Cooperation in Europe, Office of Democratic Institutions and Human Rights, (OSCE/ODIHR)

Pacific Islands, Australia and New Zealand Electoral Administrators' Association (PIANZEA)

Pacific Island Forum

United Nations

Annex 2. Example Voting and Counting Observation Forms

Example 1.   Voting Observation Form

Example 2.   Counting Observation Form

European Union Election Observation Mission
Country, Type of Election
Date

Observation Report Form
The Voting Process
2 pages

Team number:

Form number:
(leave blank)

A Polling Station (PS) identification

Constituency   District   PS #

The PS is: a. ☐ Rural   ☐ Urban
              b. ☐ Regular   ☐ Prison   ☐ Military   ☐ IDP   ☐ Other

The PS Chairperson is: ☐ Male   ☐ Female

B. Observer time in the Polling Station (24hr clock)

Arrival time (hh:mm):   Departure time (hh:mm):

C. Outside the Polling Station

	Y	N	N/K
1. Were **campaign materials** present/visible within XX meters of the PS?	☐	☐	☐
2. Were **campaign activities** taking place within XX meters of the PS?	☐	☐	☐
3. Were there any signs of **intimidation** taking place outside of the PS?	☐	☐	☐
4. Were there any **other problems** in the vicinity of the polling station?	☐	☐	☐
5. Was the PS **accessible** for persons with disabilities?	☐	☐	☐

D. Voter list

1. **How many** people are on the voter list for this PS?

2. How many people had **voted so far at this PS at the time of your departure**?

E. The Polling Station – environment and atmosphere

	Y	N	N/K
1. Were **campaign materials** visible inside the PS?	☐	☐	☐
2. Did you directly observe any **intimidation** inside the PS?	☐	☐	☐
3. Did you directly observe any attempts in the PS to **influence** electors on how to vote?	☐	☐	☐
4. Was there **tension** inside the PS?	☐	☐	☐
5. Were you in any way restricted in your **access** to observing the work of the PS?	☐	☐	☐
6. Were there any problems with PS officials giving you **information** you asked for ?	☐	☐	☐
7. Were there any **other problems** observed?	☐	☐	☐

F. Unauthorised persons

1. Were unauthorised persons present?   ☐ ☐ ☐

2. If, *YES*, to question F1, who?
   ☐ Police   ☐ Military   ☐ Security   ☐ Local authorities   ☐ Other

3. If *YES*, to question F1: Were they directing/interfering in the work of the polling officials?   ☐ ☐ ☐

G. Authorised persons

1. Were representatives from **parties/candidates** present?   ☐ ☐ ☐

2. If, *YES*, to question G1, from which parties/candidates?
   ☐ Party 1   ☐ Party 2   ☐ Party 3   ☐ Party 4   ☐ Other

3. Were **domestic observers** present?   ☐ ☐ ☐

4. If, *YES*, to question G3, from which organisations?
   ☐ Org 1   ☐ Org 2   ☐ Org 3   ☐ Org 4   ☐ Other

H. Election material

1. Were all necessary election materials present?   ☐ ☐ ☐

2. If, *NO*, to question H1, what was missing?
   ☐ Voter list/s   ☐ Ballot box/es   ☐ Polling booths   ☐ Ballot papers   ☐ Protocols
   ☐ Ink   ☐ Envelopes   ☐ Other

I: Voting procedures   (3: Always; 2: Mostly; 1: Sometimes; 0: Never)

	3	2	1	0	N/K
1. Did voters show the **required identification** before being allowed to vote?	☐	☐	☐	☐	☐
2. Were voters' **names crossed out** in the voter list?	☐	☐	☐	☐	☐
3. Were ballot papers **stamped** before being issued to voters?	☐	☐	☐	☐	☐
4. Did voters **sign** the voter list upon receipt of their ballot paper?	☐	☐	☐	☐	☐
5. Did voters have **ink** applied to the finger upon receipt of their ballot paper?	☐	☐	☐	☐	☐
6. Did PS officials **explain the voting process** to voters?	☐	☐	☐	☐	☐
7. Were voters marking their ballot in **secret**?	☐	☐	☐	☐	☐
8. Were **voters individually placing** their completed ballot paper in the ballot box?	☐	☐	☐	☐	☐

European Union Election Observation Mission to ....

European Union Election Observation Mission
Country, Type of Election
Date

Observation Report Form
The Voting Process
2 pages

Team number:

PS #:

J. Possible irregularities

	Y	N	N/K
1. Did you observe any problems with the ballot box **seals**?	☐	☐	☐
2. Did you observe voters being handed **more than one ballot** *(multiple voting)*?	☐	☐	☐
3. Did you observe voters receiving **ballots for other persons** *(proxy voting)*?	☐	☐	☐
4. Did you observe electors **voting in groups** *(family or group voting)*?	☐	☐	☐
5. Did you observe voters using **pre-marked ballots** *(carousel voting)*?	☐	☐	☐
6. Did you observe the same person **"assisting"** numerous voters?	☐	☐	☐
7. Did you observe anyone being **denied the right to vote** for inappropriate reasons?	☐	☐	☐
8. Was the process seriously hampered by **overcrowding** or **disorganisation**?	☐	☐	☐
9. Was the **secrecy** of the vote breached?	☐	☐	☐
10. Were there a series of **identical signatures** on the voter list?	☐	☐	☐
11. Were there **other procedural problems**?	☐	☐	☐

K: Refused electors

1. During your visit, was any person refused from voting **for legitimate reasons** (as stipulated in the law and regulations)?   ☐ ☐ ☐
2. If *YES* to K1, for what reason?

☐ Failing ink test ☐ Voter's name not in the list ☐ No ID / wrong ID
☐ Refusing ink test ☐ Registered at another PS ☐ Other

L. Official complaints submitted

1. Have any **official complaints** been submitted at the PS?   ☐ ☐ ☐
   If *YES*, please record the details in the Comments section below.

M. Number of voters during your visit

1. Approximately **how many voters** cast their ballots while you were observing at this PS?
   ☐ Fewer than 5   ☐ 5-10   ☐ 11-50   ☐ More than 50

N. Overall assessment   (4=very good, 3=good, 2=bad, 1=very bad)*

	4	3	2	1
1. How do you rate the conduct of polling at this PS?	☐	☐	☐	☐

O. Evaluation   (5=very good, 4=good, 3=not good/not bad, 2=bad, 1=bad)

	5	4	3	2	1	N/K
1. How do you rate the general **environment/circumstances**?	☐	☐	☐	☐	☐	☐
2. How well do you think **procedures** were followed?	☐	☐	☐	☐	☐	☐
3. How do you rate most **voters' understanding** of the voting procedures?	☐	☐	☐	☐	☐	☐
4. How do you rate the **PS officials' understanding** of the voting procedures?	☐	☐	☐	☐	☐	☐
5. How do you assess the **performance** of the PS officials?	☐	☐	☐	☐	☐	☐
6. How do you assess the **transparency** of the voting process?	☐	☐	☐	☐	☐	☐
7. How would you rate the performance of the **party/candidate representatives**?	☐	☐	☐	☐	☐	☐
8. How would you rate the performance of the **domestic observers**?	☐	☐	☐	☐	☐	☐

P. Comments

* **Overall assessment options**

4 – Very Good	Generally professional and smooth process, no real problems observed, procedures assessed positively.
3 – Good	All procedures followed or some minor breaches, all problems overcome, a positive observation.
2 – Bad	Some procedures not followed, problems caused difficulties but with no or minor impact on the quality of the election, a negative observation.
1 – Very Bad	Problems likely to have impact on the quality of the election, some or all observations assessed negatively

European Union Election Observation Mission
Country, Type of Election
Date

| Observation Report Form C |
| **The Counting Process** |
| 2 pages |

Team number: [ ][ ][ ][ ]

Form number: [ ][ ][ ][ ]
(leave blank)

A. Polling Station(PS) identification:

Constituency [ ]   District [ ][ ][ ]   PS # [ ][ ][ ]

The PS is: a.   ☐ Rural   ☐ Urban
                 b.   ☐ Regular   ☐ Prison   ☐ Military   ☐ IDP   ☐ Other

The PS Chairperson is: ☐ Male   ☐ Female

B. Time in Polling Station

Arrival time (hh:mm): [ ][ ] : [ ][ ]   Departure time (hh:mm): [ ][ ] : [ ][ ]

	Y	N	N/K
C. Closing of the Polling Station			
1. At closing time, were there voters **inside** the PS/polling centre **waiting to vote**?	☐	☐	☐
2. If *YES* to C1, were they allowed to vote?	☐	☐	☐
3. Was anybody who was **not** already waiting inside the PS/polling centre at closing time allowed to vote?	☐	☐	☐
3. Did the PS **close on time**?	☐	☐	☐
4. If *NO* to C3, at what time did the PS close? [ ][ ] : [ ][ ]			
D. Steps to be completed before the ballot box/es are opened			
Observers should record reconciliation and results figures on a separate form			
1. Was the **number of voters** on the voter list established?	☐	☐	☐
2. Were the **signatures** on the voter list counted?	☐	☐	☐
3. Were the **unused ballot papers** counted?	☐	☐	☐
4. Were the number of **spoiled ballot papers** counted?	☐	☐	☐
E. Opening of the ballot box/es			
1. Were the **seals** of the ballot box/es intact and undamaged before opening?	☐	☐	☐
2. Were the ballot box/es **opened transparently** in front of all present?	☐	☐	☐
3. Were the **total numbers** of ballots in each ballot box counted separately and recorded?	☐	☐	☐
4. Were all ballot papers handled in a **secure and transparent manner**?	☐	☐	☐
F. Counting of the votes			
1. Were the **valid/invalid** ballots determined in a reasonable and consistent manner? If *NO*, please comment.	☐	☐	☐
2. Were ballots always **allocated** to the correct party/candidate? If *NO*, please comment.	☐	☐	☐
3. Were all PS officials **able to examine** the ballot papers?	☐	☐	☐
4. Were any **recounts** conducted?	☐	☐	☐
5 Did the polling officials separately **pack and seal** the ballots for each party / candidate?	☐	☐	☐
6. Was the prescribed **sequence of steps** in the counting process strictly followed?	☐	☐	☐
G. Completion of the protocol			
2. Did all the **polling officials agree** on the figures entered in the protocol?	☐	☐	☐
3. Did any PS official **refuse to sign** the protocol?	☐	☐	☐
4. Was any **dissenting opinion** attached to the protocol?	☐	☐	☐
5. Did all requesting **entitled persons receive** a copy of the protocol?	☐	☐	☐
6. Did Hannah Roberts **receive** a copy of the protocol?	☐	☐	☐
H. Possible irregularities			
1. Was the PS **overcrowded and/or unruly?**	☐	☐	☐
2. Did you **observe** any falsification of **voter list** entries?	☐	☐	☐
3. Did you **observe** any **falsification of the ballots**?	☐	☐	☐
4. Did you **observe** any **falsification of the protocols**?	☐	☐	☐
5. Did you **observe** any significant **procedural errors or omissions**?	☐	☐	☐
I. Unauthorised persons			
1. Were unauthorised person/s present?	☐	☐	☐

2. If, *YES*, to question I1, who?
   ☐ Police   ☐ Military   ☐ Security   ☐ Local authorities   ☐ Other

	Y	N	N/K
3. If *YES*, to question I1: Were they directing/interfering in the work of the polling officials?	☐	☐	☐

European Union Election Observation Mission to ....

195

European Union Election Observation Mission
Country, Type of Election
Date

Observation Report Form C
The Counting Process
2 pages

Team number: ☐ ☐ ☐ ☐   **PS #:** ☐ ☐ ☐ ☐

J. Authorised persons

1. Were representatives from **political parties/candidates** present?   ☐ ☐ ☐

2. If, *YES*, to question J1, from which party/candidate/?
   ☐ Party 1   ☐ Party 2   ☐ Party 3   ☐ Party 4   ☐ Other

3. Were **domestic observers** present?   ☐ ☐ ☐

4. If, *YES*, to question J3, from which organisation?
   ☐ Org 1   ☐ Org 2   ☐ Org 3   ☐ Org 4   ☐ Other

K. Transparency

1. Did all persons present have a **clear view** of the counting procedures?   ☐ ☐ ☐
2. Were you in any way **restricted in your observation** of the counting procedures?   ☐ ☐ ☐
3. Were all party/candidate representatives and observers **free to examine** the ballot papers?   ☐ ☐ ☐
4. Was a copy of the **protocol immediately posted** for public inspection?   ☐ ☐ ☐
6. Did any observers or party/candidate representatives **inform you about problems** at this PS during the count?   ☐ ☐ ☐

L. Official complaints submitted

1. Have any **official complaints** been submitted at the PS in relation to the count?
   If *YES*, please record the details in the Comments section below.   ☐ ☐ ☐

M. When did the count and protocol completion finish (hh:mm) ☐☐ : ☐☐   N/K ☐

N. Overall assessment (4=very good, 3=good, 2=bad, 1=very bad)*

	4	3	2	1	N/K
1. How do you rate the conduct of the count at this PS?	☐	☐	☐	☐	☐

O. Evaluation (5=very good, 4=good, 3=not good/not bad, 2=bad, 1=bad)

	5	4	3	2	1	N/K
1. How do you rate the general **environment/circumstances**?	☐	☐	☐	☐	☐	☐
2. How well do you think the **counting procedures** were followed?	☐	☐	☐	☐	☐	☐
3. How do you rate the **PS officials' understanding** of the counting procedures?	☐	☐	☐	☐	☐	☐
4. How do you assess the **performance** of the PS officials?	☐	☐	☐	☐	☐	☐
5. How do you assess the **transparency** of the counting process?	☐	☐	☐	☐	☐	☐
6. How **accurate** would you say the results are?	☐	☐	☐	☐	☐	☐
7. How would you rate the performance of the **party/candidate representatives**?	☐	☐	☐	☐	☐	☐
8. How would you rate the performance of the **domestic observers**?	☐	☐	☐	☐	☐	☐

P. Comments

* Overall assessment options

4 – Very Good	Generally professional and smooth process, no real problems observed, procedures assessed positively.
3 – Good	All procedures followed or some minor breaches, all problems overcome, a positive observation.
2 – Bad	Some procedures not followed, problems caused difficulties but with no or minor impact on the quality of the election, a negative observation.
1 – Very Bad	Problems likely to have impact on the quality of the election, some or all observations assessed negatively

Annex 3. List of Useful Websites

ACE Electoral Knowledge Network	http://www.aceproject.org
Acuerdo de Lima (Lima Accord)	http://www.acuerdodelima.org
African Union (AU)	http://www.africa-union.org
Asian Network for Free Elections (ANFREL)	http://www.anfrel.org
Carnegie Endowment for International Peace	http://www.ceip.org
Carter Center	http://www.cartercenter.org/peace/democracy/index.html
Commonwealth Secretariat	http://www.thecommonwealth.org
Council of Europe, European Committee for the Prevention of Torture and Inhuman or Degrading Treatment or Punishment	http://www.cpt.coe.int/en
Council of Europe, European Court of Human Rights	http://www.echr.coe.int
Council of Europe, Parliamentary Assembly (PACE)	http://www.assembly.coe.int/default.asp
Council of Europe, Venice Commission	http://www.venice.coe.int/site/main/presentation_E.asp?MenuL=E
Democracy Reporting International (DRI)	http://www.democracy-reporting.org
Domestic election observer website for Europe and Central Asia	http://www.electiondog.net

Economic Community of West African States (ECOWAS)	www.ecowas.int
Elections and electoral systems around the world	http://www.psr.keele.ac.uk/election.htm
Electoral Institute of Southern Africa (EISA)	http://www.eisa.org.za
European Commission: Election Assistance and Observation	http://ec.europa.eu/comm/external_ relations/ human_rights/eu_election_ ass_observ/index.htm
European Commission: EuropeAid Cooperation office, how to become an EU election observer, request for candidates, training, national focal points	http://ec.europa.eu/europeaid/ observer/index_en.htm
European Commission: Handbook for EU Election Observation, Compendium of International Standards for Elections and reporting materials (guidelines, templates and examples)	http://ec.europa.eu/external_relations/ human_rights/eu_election_ass_observ/ index.htm
European Network of Election Monitoring Organisations (ENEMO)	http://www.enemo.eu
European Parliament Election Observation Services	http://www.europarl.eu.int/intcoop/ election_observation/default_en.htm
IFES	http://www.ifes.org
Institute for War and Peace Reporting	http://www.iwpr.net
International Crisis Group (ICG)	http://www.crisisweb.org
International Institute for Democracy and Electoral Assistance (International IDEA)	http://www.idea.int
International Knowledge Network of Women in Politics (iKNOW)	http://www.iknowpolitics.org
International Organisation for Migration (IOM)	http://www.iom.int/jahia/jsp/index.jsp
International Republican Institute (IRI)	http://www.iri.org
Inter-Parliamentary Union (IPU)	http://www.ipu.org/english/home.htm
Journal of Democracy Election Watch	http://muse.jhu.edu/journals/journal_ of_democracy/election_watch
League of Arab States (LAS)	http://www.arableagueonline.org/ las/index_en.jsp
Liphart´s Archive, Elections Archive	http://dodgson.ucsd.edu/lij

National Democratic Institute for International Affairs (NDI)	http://www.ndi.org
National Endowment for Democracy (NED)	http://www.ned.org
NEEDS	http://www.needs-network.org
Norwegian Centre for Human Rights http://www.humanrights.uio.no/english	
Norwegian Refugee Council	http://www.nrc.no
Organization of American States (OAS)	http://www.oas.org
Organization for Security and Cooperation in Europe (OSCE)	http://www.osce.org
OSCE, Office of the High Commissioner on National Minorities	http://www.osce.org/hcnm
OSCE, Office for Democratic Institutions and Human Rights (OSCE/ODIHR)	http://www.osce.org/odihr-elections
Political Resources on the Net	http://www.politicalresources.net
United Nations (UN)	http://www.un.org
UN Development Programme (UNDP)	http://www.undp.org
UN Electoral Assistance Division (UN EAD)	http://www.un.org/depts/dpa/ead/eadhome.htm
UN Human Rights Committee (UNHRC)	http://www.unhchr.ch/html/menu2/6/hrc.htm
UN Human Rights	http://www.un.org/rights/index.html
UN Office of the High Commissioner for Human Rights (OHCHR)	http://www.ohchr.org/english/about/index.htm
UN Treaty Collection Database	http://untreaty.un.org

Annex 4. Glossary of Terms

Accreditation	Document(s) providing authorisation for presence in an electoral site (polling station, tabulation centre etc.).
Agent (for a party or candidate)	A person who represents a political party or candidate during different aspects of an electoral process, e.g., as an observer of the voting or counting processes in polling stations. An agent may have authority to act and take decisions on behalf of the party or candidate.
Aggregation and tabulation of results	Aggregation is the process of collecting and adding the totals of election results following the counting of votes. Tabulation is the process of putting the results data into a table format so that each sub-total of the aggregated results can be shown (e.g., by party/candidate, by polling station, by district etc.).
Appeal	A legal submission to a higher authority that seeks to challenge or overturn the decision of a lower body.
Ballot box	A container into which a voter places his or her marked ballot paper. The ballot box is usually sealed closed while polling is taking place.
Ballot paper	A sheet of paper or card upon which a voter can mark his/her choice.
Booth (polling)	An area where ballot papers can be marked in secret and alone.

Bribery	An offering of money, gift or favour that allows a person to gain unfair and/or illegal advantage.
By-election*	An election to fill a vacant seat in an elected assembly held at any time other than at a general election.
Campaign*	Political activity, including meetings, speeches, rallies, parades, broadcasts, debates and other media events designed to inform the electorate and gather support for the platform of a particular candidate or political party in an election or to promote a choice available to voters in a referendum, a citizens' initiative or a recall vote.
Canvassing	Activity undertaken by a candidate to ascertain the views of voters and to solicit their votes.
Chief observer	Holds overall responsibility for an EU EOM, usually a Member of the European Parliament (MEP).
Civic education	Methods by which citizens can acquire knowledge, skills and awareness on democratic issues. This normally takes place via information or education programmes, workshops, seminars, information campaigns and other outreach activities.
Code of conduct	A set of principles and/or expectations that are considered binding on any person who is a member of a group such as an election management body, political party, or an election observation mission.
Complaint	An expression of dissatisfaction, for example with the actions of an electoral management body, which may be made informally or formally through an official complaints procedure.
Constituency	The body of voters who elect a representative/s for their area. Also the area itself.
Constitution	Law determining the fundamental political principles, nature, function and limits of a government.
Core team	A group of independent specialists recruited specifically for an EOM who provide the main analytical and logistical frameworks and substance of the mission.
Council of Ministers	The Council is the main decision-making body of the European Union usually legislating jointly with the European Parliament. The Member States meet within the Council of Ministers where the Commission also participates.
Counterfoil	Complementary part of a voting paper (a ballot) retained by the issuer which shows the details of a transaction.

Debriefing	Meeting for two-way exchange of information, analytical discussion, feedback and lessons learned.
Delimitation	Demarcation of the boundaries of electoral units, a process also sometimes referred to as 'districting'.
Deputy chief observer	The principal political and technical advisor to the chief observer who deputises for the chief observer in his/her absence. Has management responsibility for the political, analytical, methodological, operational and security aspects of the EU EOM and for the coordination of the activities of all mission members and the implementing partner.
Disenfranchise	To deprive a citizen of a right of citizenship; in particular, the right to vote.
Domestic (or national) observer	An election observer who is based in the country in which elections are taking place.
Early voting	Polling, usually for special categories of voters that takes place before election day. May also include postal voting.
Election day	The day on which voting in an election takes place.
Election Management Body (EMB)*	An organisation which has been founded for the sole purpose of, and is legally responsible for, managing some or all of the essential elements for the conduct of elections, including determining who is eligible to vote, receiving and validating nominations, conducting balloting, counting votes, and tabulation of results.
Election Management Body (EMB) commissioners	Election administrators, persons comprising the highest level of the EMB who are responsible for directing the electoral process in line with electoral laws and regulations.
Election Management Body (EMB) secretariat	An administrative unit responsible for the planning and administration of the election under direction from EMB commissioners.
Election offence	Breach of any law or regulation governing the conduct of elections.
Election regulations*	Rules subsidiary to legislation, often made by the EMB, under powers contained in the electoral law which govern aspects of the organisation and administration of an election.
Electoral district, zone, ward, etc*	One of the geographic areas into which a country or region may be divided for electoral purposes.

Electoral law*	One or more pieces of legislation governing all aspects of the process for electing the political institutions defined in a country's constitution or institutional framework.
Electorate	Those entitled to vote, the body of enfranchised citizens.
Enumerator	A person who collects voter data to establish or maintain the voter register.
European Commission	The executive body of the European Union, responsible for proposing legislation, implementing decisions, upholding the Union's treaties and the general day-to-day running of the Union.
European Parliament	Directly-elected body of the European Union with 785 (November 2007) members elected once every five years by voters in the Member States.
EuropeAid (also known as AIDCO)	The Directorate-General of the European Commission responsible for implementing most aid programmes and projects in countries outside the European Union.
EU Presidency	The Presidency of the Council of Ministers is held for six months by each Member State on a rotational basis. It is responsible for presiding over all aspects of the Council of the European Union.
Exit poll	An informal poll taken as people leave the voting station used to predict the outcome of the election before voting ends.
Exploratory mission	A team of European Commission officials and external and Member States' experts who visit the host country four to six months ahead of an anticipated election to assess the usefulness, feasibility and advisability of sending an EU EOM to that country.
Franchise	The right to be able to vote in an election.
Fraud	Intentional deception to gain unjust advantage.
Gerrymandering	Changing the physical boundaries of a voting district in order to increase one candidate or political party's chances of winning an election.
Host country	A country where elections or a referendum is taking place, which issues an invitation for an EOM to observe.
Human rights	The rights and freedoms to which all human beings are entitled and without which it is impossible to live in dignity.
Impartial	Not biased or prejudiced towards any side in a contest or dispute.

203

Indelible ink	Ink which cannot be removed, erased or washed away.
Independent candidate*	A candidate for an elected position who is not nominated by a political party.
Internally Displaced Person(s) (IDP)	Persons who have been forced or obliged to flee or to leave their homes or places of habitual residence, who have not crossed an internationally recognised state border. In particular as a result of or in order to avoid the effects of armed conflict, situations of generalised violence, violations of human rights, or natural or human-made disasters.
International standards	International standards for elections stem from political rights and fundamental freedoms which are enshrined in universal and regional instruments. These instruments establish legal and political commitments to meet specific standards in relation to elections.
Invalid ballot*	Ballots which cannot be counted in favour of any entity in an election due to accidental or deliberate errors of marking by the voter or incorrect issuing by the polling officials.
Long-term observer	Member of an EOM, with a partner observer, is deployed to a region of the host country for a period of six to eight weeks to assess and report to the core team on election-related activities and events.
Media monitoring	Qualitative and quantitative analysis of media coverage of the election including: time and space allocated to each political contestant, the tone of coverage, compliance of media with relevant legislation and analysis of the legislation itself and the degree to which it allows for compliance with international standards.
Memorandum of understanding (MoU)	The written agreement between the host country and the European Commission which defines the roles and responsibilities of both parties during deployment of an EU EOM. This is not legally binding.
Military voting	Where members of the armed forces vote at designated local civilian polling stations or in their barracks. Military voting may take place on a different day from civilian voting.
Mobile ballot box	A ballot box transported by polling officials to immobile voters (e.g., the elderly or ill) on election day, in order that they may enjoy their right to vote.
Nomination*	Putting forward name(s) for candidacy, selection or appointment to another body or to a position.

Non-governmental organisation	A private organisation, independent from the government. Generally refers to non-profit-making social and/or cultural groups and includes charities.
Null (and void)	No longer valid or enforceable.
Observation (election)*	Witnessing and assessing, but not intervening in, the proceedings of an electoral process.
Parallel Vote Tabulation (PVT)	Observers record the results from a scientific sample of polling stations and independently tabulate these results in parallel to, and for comparison with, the official results of the election authorities.
Partisan	Biased in support of a particular political party, candidate or position
Party (political)	An organised group of people with at least roughly similar political aims and opinions that seeks to influence public policy by getting its candidates elected to public office.
Petition	A formal written request that is submitted to an authority.
Poll	An enquiry into public opinion, e.g., by voting at an election.
Polling official*	A member of staff who participates in the administration of a polling station. Polling officials can be appointed only for the purpose of working on election day and may or may not be staff of the EMB.
Protocol	Standardised documentation format containing results data. Or a diplomatic document, often terms of a treaty.
Reconciliation (of results)	Checking that the number of ballot papers issued to a polling station corresponds with the combined numbers of used, unused and spoilt ballot papers recorded for that polling station, and checking these figures against the voter list record of the number of people who have voted.
Referendum*	A vote of the electorate on an issue of public policy such as a constitutional amendment or a bill. The results of the vote may be either binding or consultative.
Registration (of political parties and candidates)	Acceptance of applications by political parties and candidates that meet defined criteria, to participate and stand in an election.
Registration (of voters)	The act of entering the names of eligible voters, and other relevant information, in a register or list of electors.

RELEX (DG External Relations)	The Directorate-General of the European Commission responsible for formulating the external relations policy of the European community.
Results	Partial results may be announced during the course of the tabulation process. If released, they must always be clearly referred to as representing only a proportion of the votes cast. Preliminary results should be announced as soon as the tabulation of results is completed at a regional or countrywide level. Final results should be declared after the deadline for the submission of any challenges to the preliminary results has passed.
Seal	The wax or plastic fastening over a ballot box opening or other senstive materials.
Sensitive material	Election materials that are critical to a secure and accurate voting process, e.g., ballot papers (marked and unmarked) and a voter list that has been signed by voters when casting their ballots.
Short-term observer	Member of an EOM who remains, with a partner observer, in a particular region of the host country for a period of 5–10 days.
Spoiled ballot*	A spoiled ballot is generally one that a voter has inadvertently spoiled by marking it incorrectly. It is handed back to the polling officials in exchange for a new blank ballot paper that is then marked by the voter and placed in the ballot box.
Tabulation	See aggregation.
Tally	The results count.
Tamper-proof	Designed to prevent, or provide evidence of interference.
Transparency	Openness, visibility of process or event to the public. Improves accountability and trust.
Treaty	A written contract or agreement between states or between an international organisation and its states. Treaties are legally binding instruments in the context of international law.
Treaty bodies	Expert groups which monitor implementation of UN human rights treaties. Each treaty has its own treaty body which receives and comments on implementation reports submitted by countries which are bound by the treaty.
Turnout	The proportion of registered voters who voted.

Valid (ballot)	An official ballot paper that clearly shows the intention of the voter and does not reveal the identity of the voter.
Voter education*	A process by which people are made aware of the electoral process and the particulars and procedures for voter registration, polling, and other elements of the electoral process.
Voter register/list*	The list of persons registered as qualified to vote. Sometimes known as the electoral roll.
Voting	Casting a ballot paper.

---

* Directly quoted or substantially based on definitions first published by the International Institute for Democracy and Electoral Assistance, International IDEA. For more information, see http://www.idea.int

Annex 5. List of Acronyms

ACP	Africa, the Caribbean and Pacific (countries)
AIDCO	AIDCO is not an official acronym, see EuropeAid
AoR	Area of Responsibility
AU	African Union
AV	Alternative Vote
BV	Block Vote
CFSP	Common Foreign and Security Policy
CO	Chief Observer
CoC	Code of Conduct
CoE	Council of Europe
CSO	Civil Society Organisation
CT	Core Team
DCO	Deputy Chief Observer
DEV	European Commission DG Development
DOG	Domestic Observer Group
EC	European Commission
ECOWAS	Economic Community of West African States
E-day	Election Day
EIDHR	European Instrument for Democracy and Human Rights
EMB	Election Management Body
EOM	Election Observation Mission
EU	European Union
EU EOM	European Union Election Observation Mission
EuropeAid	European Commission DG EuropeAid Co-operation Office
E-voting	Electronic Voting
ExM	Exploratory Mission

FPTP	First Past the Post
IDEA	(International) Institute for Democracy and Electoral Assistance
IDP	Internally Displaced Person
INGO	International Non-Governmental Organisation
IOM	International Organisation for Migration
IP	Implementing Partner
LAS	League of Arab States
LTO	Long-Term Observer
MEP	Member of European Parliament
MMP	Mixed Member Proportional
MoI	Ministry of Interior
MoJ	Ministry of Justice
MOSS	Minimum Operational Security Standards
MoU	Memorandum of Understanding
NEEDS	Network of Europeans for Electoral and Democracy Support
NGO	Non-Governmental Organisation
OAS	Organization of American States
ODIHR	OSCE Office for Democratic Institutions and Human Rights
OIC	Organization of the Islamic Conference
OSCE	Organization for Security and Cooperation in Europe
PBV	Party Block Vote
PC	Polling Centre
PR	Proportional Representation
PS	Polling Station
PVT	Parallel Vote Tabulation
RELEX	European Commission DG External Relations
SADC	Southern African Development Community
SITREP	Situation Report
SNTV	Single Not Transferable Vote
SP	Service Provider
STO	Short-Term Observer
STV	Single Transferable Vote
TA	Technical Assistance
ToR	Terms of Reference
TRS	Two-Round System
UDHR	Universal Declaration of Human Rights
UN	United Nations
UNDP	United Nations Development Programme
UNDSS	UN Department of Safety and Security
UNHRC	UN Human Rights Committee
VL	Voter List
VR	Voter Register

Acknowledgements

Recognition and thanks must be given to all those who have contributed to the preparation of this handbook. Initially, the first edition of the handbook was prepared by Mark Stevens, Gerald Mitchell and Anders Eriksson. Content and methodology were inspired by OSCE/ODIHR experience and practice. Hereafter, the European Commission further developed this methodology to include greater focus on international standards, as reflected in this second edition. A first re-working of the handbook was undertaken by Michael Meyer. Richard Chambers has been the principal author of the second edition. Details were provided and text was written for some sections by Rebecca Cox, Victor Perez, Giovanna Maiola, Cathryn Upshon, Lucy Young and Paul Hardy. In addition, Delphine Blanchet, Carlo Accame, Anders Eriksson and Sarah Fradgley contributed to the development of various sections. Substantial reviewing and editing was undertaken by Peter Eicher, Cathryn Upshon and Jessie Pilgrim. Additional reviewing was provided by Derek MacLeod, David Ward and Hans Schmeets. Specialist comments were provided by the Norwegian Refugee Council and Markku Suksi of Abo Acadamy. Hannah Roberts (NEEDS), Andrew Bruce (DG External Relations, European Commission) and Isabel Mohedano-Sohm (DG EuropeAid, European Commission) were the project managers and overall editors. Additional comments were provided by members of the DG External Relations and DG EuropeAid Election Teams. Glossary explanations were, in part, based on definitions first published by International IDEA. Graphics and design work was done by Micael Fröjdlund and general proof-reading was undertaken by Mia Melin. Executive oversight of production was provided by Anders Eriksson. Recognition and thanks also goes to the various people who contributed photographs to the handbook.

The Network of Europeans for Electoral and Democracy Support

 **The Network of Europeans for Electoral and Democracy Support (NEEDS)** brings together some of the leading European organisations and individuals involved in the field of democratisation and election observation. The aim of NEEDS is to increase the capacity of both the European Union and civil society organisations to conduct credible and effective election observation missions. NEEDS is funded by the European Commission and draws on expertise from around the world. The NEEDS website is a resource for all organisations and individuals interested in election observation (see www.needs-network.org).

During the current project cycle, NEEDS has trained several hundred people for EU Election Observation Missions (EOMs). This has included training for core team positions and for long term observers. NEEDS has also produced a number of resources to maximise the quality and efficiency of EU EOMs. These include an updated Handbook for EU Election Observation, an updated Compendium of International Standards for Elections, and various guidelines and templates. These resources are fully available on the NEEDS website and may be used by other observer groups and interested persons. Additionally, NEEDS works with domestic observers in holding regional forums for skills and knowledge development and networking. NEEDS has also produced a handbook on domestic observer work around the world, and conducts some technical assistance with domestic observers. NEEDS aims to promote election observation being conducted systematically and comprehensively with accuracy and impartiality. Through such professional activities, observation missions can substantially contribute to positive electoral environments and developments.

Electoral Reform International Services (ERIS) – Specialises in the provision of expertise on democracy and good governance, notably in the fields of election assistance, election observation missions and training of domestic and international observers. *www.eris.org.uk*

Abo Akademi University – A specialist department in human rights law and a key institution in the specialist courses on civilian crisis management, the European human rights masters programme and NEEDS election expert training. *www.abo.fi*

Austrian Study Centre for Peace and Conflict Resolution (ASPR) – A leading institution in training across a wide range of disciplines for UN, EU, OSCE and NGO activities, including civilian crisis management, conflict resolution, election observation and public information campaigns. The Centre also has extensive experience of training in peace building and work in conflict zones. *www.aspr.ac.at*

MEMO 98 – A specialist media institution, with extensive experience of delivery media monitoring on behalf of international institutions as well as technical assistance to civil society groups. *www.memo98.sk*

Osservatorio di Pavia – Another specialist media institution, also highly experienced in media monitoring within international election observation missions as well as more wide ranging media and communication activities including work on media standards and freedom of expression and development of civil society capacity building projects. *www.osservatorio.it*

Scuola Superiore Sant'Anna – A highly renowned learning establishment with a long track record in training in the fields of conflict resolution, human rights and election observation. The Scuola brings substantial expertise to the network, notably in the field of development of training curriculum and evaluation techniques but also in the design and delivery of training programmes. *www.itpcm.sssup.it*